The Complete
Illustrated Guide to
Runes

★ ★ ★ ★ ★

The Complete
Illustrated Guide to
Runes

★★★★★

NIGEL PENNICK

ELEMENT

Shaftesbury, Dorset • Boston, Massachusetts • Melbourne, Victoria

First published in Great Britain in 1999 by
ELEMENT BOOKS LIMITED
Shaftesbury, Dorset SP7 8BP

Published in the USA in 1999 by
ELEMENT BOOKS INC.
160 North Washington Street, Boston MA 02114

Published in Australia in 1999 by
ELEMENT BOOKS
and distributed by Penguin Australia Ltd.
487 Maroondah Highway, Ringwood, Victoria 3134

Reprinted October 1999

Designed and created for Element Books with
The Bridgewater Book Company Limited

ELEMENT BOOKS LIMITED
Editorial Director SUE HOOK
Senior Commissioning Editor CARO NESS
Editor DIANA FERGUSON
Production Manager SUSAN SUTTERBY
Production Controller FIONA HARRISON

THE BRIDGEWATER BOOK COMPANY
Art Director SARAH HOWERD
Design/Page Production PAUL MESSAM
Editorial Director FIONA BIGGS
Managing Editor ANNE TOWNLEY
Project Editor CAROLINE EARLE
Picture Research LIZ MOORE

Printed and bound in Italy
by Graphicom S.r.l.

Library of Congress Cataloging in Publication
data available

British Library Cataloging in Publication
data available

ISBN 1 86204 100 8

ACKNOWLEDGMENTS

THE PUBLISHER WISHES TO THANK
THE FOLLOWING

Illustrations: Linda Baker-Smith, Andy Farmer,
Lorraine Harrison
Model makers: David Donkin, Mark Jamieson
Calligraphy: Stephen Raw
Wood carver: Alan Bridgewater
Photography: Ian Parsons
Project Manager: Stephen Adamson

Special thanks go to
Alain Allard, Lisa Beresford, Rosie Perks, Emma Scott
for help with photography

PICTURE LIBRARIES
AKG London Ltd: 2,11t,13b, 17t, 19b, 21b, 41r, 42b, 43cl,
43r, 62, 96br, 117t,150b
Bridgeman Art Library: 9t,b, 18t, 26l, 36l, 39t, 43b, 69t, 90t,
100l, 100b, 101tl, 101tr, 111t, 112t, 113b, 118b, 120t, 121t;
/Chris Beetles 84bl.
British Museum, London: 28-9, 29c.
CM Dixon Photo Resources: 7, 8b, 15b, 25, 26t, 26-7, 28b,
29t, 31t, 33t, 33b, 35b, 37b, 47, 49b, 50bl, 53cr, 59br, 88t,
91b, 97t, 101b, 108b, 110b, 120b, 122b, 139c, 172t, 178t.
ET Archive: 30r, 66tr, 89tr.
Mary Evans Picture Library: 18b, 21t, 23, 42t, 65l, 87, 90b,
92b, 95t, 96t,117b, 141b, 154t.
Werner Forman Archive Ltd: 12, 22t, 26l, 27tl, br, 34, 54bl,
58cl, 64r, 65r, 67l, 67r, 83, 86, 115, 116b, 119c, 119b, 122t,
152b, 171r, 174l.
Fortean Picture Library: 36r, 63c, 63b, 85tr, 89b, 98b, 104t,
116b, 152t.
Garden Matters and Wildlife Matters
Photographic Library: 134t.
Groninger Museum, Netherlands: 92l.
Hermann Haindl: 158bl.
Sonia Halliday Photographs: 45tr, 102t, 130b.
Robert Harding Picture Library: 16t, 61cr, 118t.
HarperCollins Publishers Ltd: 45tl.
Images Colour Library: 13t, 27tr, 32-3, 40t, 40c, 40b, 43t,
44, 48b, 50c, 57cl, 59cl, 60bl, 68, 85b, 88b, 134b,
139b, 160t.
Lunds Universitet Historiska Museet, Lund, Sweden: 35t.
Jeff Moore courtesy Mr & Mrs D Hutchinson: 60cr.
Nationalmuseet, Copenhagen: 32c.
Nigel Pennick: 8l,14l, 41t, 69b, 78, 89tl, 94l, 94b, 102b, 103t,
103b, 104l, 105t,105b, 107b, 112b, 138, 155t, 159br, 183b.
Runestone Museum, Minnesota, USA: 38r.
Stock Market/Zefa: 19t.
Trip:/J. Braund 15t; /J Ellard 55bl; /G Gunnarrsson 97b; /GV
Press 84t, 119t; /Mender 150t; /H Rogers 8t, 17b, 73b; /TH-
Foto Werbung 106.
Universitetet I Oslo: 109t.
Susanne Walther, Böttcherstrasse GmbH: 107tl.

CONTENTS

* * * * * * * * * * * * * * * * * *

Signs, Symbols, and Alphabets

★ ★ ★ ★ ★

Other species have many ways of communicating, but only human beings have created meaningful signs with which to communicate. Human-made signs have their origins in the natural world but have developed far beyond these, acquiring meanings that only humans can understand. They represent ideas or sounds and can be combined in what we call writing.

The invention of writing was an act of true creativity. In traditional society, writing was viewed as otherworldly in origin. Because it originated in the conceptual world of the mind, it was said to come from the gods, and was the means of preserving and transmitting human knowledge. Before writing was invented, information could only be transmitted by word of mouth, but once writing came into being, the limitations of time and distance no longer mattered. Now human knowledge no longer relied upon individual memories, and even the words of the dead could survive. Creating the alphabet was the next step forward.

ABOVE Runic writing is a method of communicating that has been used for centuries. This Viking slab inscribed with runes comes from Maughold, Isle of Man.

THE ORIGIN OF THE ALPHABET

* * * * * * * * * * * * * * * *

Humans have used signs for thousands of years. Archaic ideomorphs – signs that stand directly for an object, rather than its name or its sound – that date from the Magdalenian period (17,000–12,000 years ago) have been found in many caves in Europe. Although we do not know what they mean, some of them look like the characters of later alphabets. A fine example is painted on a mammoth skull dating from around 14,000 years ago that was found at Mezhirich in the Ukraine. A series of lines is painted in red ocher on the front of the skull. Although these signs are so ancient that we cannot interpret them, they do show that our remote ancestors were very like us.

Over 7,000 years ago, a high culture called "Old Europe" flourished in much of Central and Eastern Europe. It was a sophisticated, Stone Age culture, building timber-frame houses up to 100 feet (30 meters) long. Old Europe produced many artifacts, including pottery with recognizable signs and symbols. Many of these signs survived into later days in the rock-carvings that still exist in many parts of Europe. The rock-carvings in Val Camonica, northern Italy, for example, follow in continuous sequence from 5000 B.C.E. until the Middle Ages. In Scandinavia, especially Sweden, where such carvings are called *hällristningar*, they are most plentiful in the Bronze Age, around 1300 B.C.E. They include signs called "prerunic symbols" that later became runes. Prerunic symbols may even have had the same meaning as the later runes of the same shape. Other rock-signs are probably magical and religious symbols. They include the cross, the sunwheel, and the swastika.

Unlike these rock-signs, the simple symbols in an alphabet are not used to express magical or runic meanings but to represent the sounds of a language. The Phoenician or West Semitic alphabet was the first in history to do this. It developed in what is now the Lebanon and was the origin of all of the later European alphabets, including the runes. The Hebrew, Samaritan, Arabic, Ethiopian, Cyrillic (attributed to St. Cyril), Bengali, Tibetan, and Javanese alphabets are also derived from the Phoenician alphabet.

The Phoenician alphabet came into use around 1200 B.C.E. It had 22 characters, and the letters read from right to left. The alphabet came into being because the Egyptians in the Sinai were finding their writing inadequate. Being a form of picture-writing, the Egyptian hieroglyphs were ambiguous. A hieroglyph could mean not only the actual object it depicted but also a corresponding sound or a magical concept.

RIGHT Examples of the Phoenician script, the first true alphabet, have survived on stone tablets.

BELOW This inscribed lignite (brown coal) disk from southwestern Scotland dates to the early Iron Age, around 500 B.C.E.

RIGHT This reconstruction shows a mammoth hunter's house in the Ukraine as it would have been at the time of mammoth-bone carvings of the Magdalenian period. These bone carvings may have been an early form of alphabet.

Since it was not obvious which of these a hieroglyph meant, other characters were added for clarification. Usually, it was necessary to show the sound as well, and eventually a system of 24 consonants was standardized. Gradually, as more foreign words and names crept into the Egyptian language and there were no hieroglyphs for them, they had to be written in the newer consonantal system. This was the origin of two forerunners of the Phoenician alphabet: the "Sinaitic" script known from the Egyptian mines at Serabit el-Khedem in Sinai; and the "proto-Canaanite" writing known from Gebal.

Once it had been established, the standard Phoenician alphabet of King Ahiram proved very useful. It was spread widely by traders and colonists. It was taken along the coast of North Africa, where, in Carthage, it became the Punic script. Further west, in Spain, it gave rise to the Tartessian alphabet. A Phoenician inscription is also known from a tomb at Knossos in Crete. Phoenician certainly laid the foundations for the ancient Greek alphabet that arose during the middle of the eighth century B.C.E. In ancient Greece, the word *phoenikeia* ("Phoenician things") was used to denote writing. Cadmos, the Phoenician founder of the city of Thebes, was celebrated as the alphabet's inventor. In Italy, either Phoenician or early Greek may have been the starting point for the Etruscan alphabet, whose late version, called North Italic, was the forerunner of the runes.

Egyptian and Phoenician Writing

Ancient Egyptian hieroglyphs were a form of picture-writing that only referred to Egyptian words and names. So when Egyptian merchants abroad needed to deal with foreign colleagues and workers, hieroglyphs could not be used to write their names. A new form of writing was developed to deal with the problem. From this came the letters that the Phoenicians (in modern Lebanon) formed into their alphabet in around 1100 B.C.E. All of the Western alphabets, including Greek, Roman, Etruscan, Runic, Cyrillic, Hebrew, and Arabic, were developed from the Phoenician alphabet.

ABOVE A gold plate dating to the fifth century B.C.E. inscribed with Phoenician writing.

WHAT ARE RUNES?

* * * * * * * * * * * * * * * *

HISTORICALLY, THE OLDEST-KNOWN full rune-row, or collection of runes, is the Elder Futhark. It is sometimes called the Common Germanic Futhark or the Longer Rune-row (a misleading title since later rows are, in fact, longer). Like the Greek alphabet, it contains 24 runic characters in a specific order.

Technically, Runic should not be called an "alphabet" at all. The word "alphabet" or lesser-known "abecedary" really means a row of characters beginning, as do the Greek,

F U Þ A R K

f u th a r k

ABOVE The runic "alphabet" is known by the sounds of its first six letters: futhark.

Hebrew, Roman, and Gaelic, with the characters *alpha* and *beta* or their equivalents – A, B, and so on. Letter-rows that have a different order are called by other appropriate names. Runic begins with the letters F, U, Th, A, R, K, so runic "alphabets" are always known as futharks.

But whether we call their array an alphabet or a futhark, the runes are far more than mere phonetic signs designed for information interchange. Each is a precise concept in its own right, encapsulating symbolic meaning. Linguistically, the word "rune" has connotations of mystery. The word is believed to come originally from the Indo-European root *ru*, which meant "a mysterious or secret thing." The word itself has associations with the carefully guarded inner secrets of spirituality and magic. The Old German word *runa*, which meant a whisperer, is believed to have referred to "one who knows," a "wise woman," or "cunning man." In the early Anglo-Saxon poem *Beowulf*, the king's counselor is called a *runwita*, which means a wise man who knows (and keeps) secrets.

Words like "rune" exist in other old languages of northern Europe, where they are connected with words meaning "to whisper." Thus the Old Norse word *run* means a secret or mystery. Similar words with the same meaning – *rhin* and *rún* – exist in Middle Welsh and Old Irish. In modern German, the word *raunen* also has connections with secrecy and mystery. The Scots dialect word *roun* means "to whisper" or "to speak much and often about one thing." The administrators of Anglo-Saxon England called their discussions *runes*, and it is likely that actual runes were used to make difficult decisions.

Particular sites where runes were consulted were also considered to have special powers. In the year 1215, the enactment of the Magna Carta, the "Great Charter" that

10

guaranteed citizens of England certain civil rights, was held at a location traditionally used for royal meetings called Runnymede, or the "Meadow of the Runes."

One might think that the idea of mystery present in the runes could be no more than the awe that illiterate people had for the secret of writing. But ancient writings show us a recurring connection with actual magic. In Great Britain, the "tree of runes," the rown-tree or rowan, is one of the most important in magical protection. In Scotland, its red berries are called "rowns," and the old Scottish adage "Rowan tree and red threid gar the witches tyne their speed" ("Rowan tree and red thread make the witches lose their speed") emphasizes the magic power of the runic tree against black magic and bad luck.

A rune is literally a mystery containing the secrets of the inner structure of existence. Every character that we call a rune is a storehouse of knowledge and meaning. But we can access this wisdom only after diligent study of runecraft in all its aspects. To the runemaster, each rune expresses an eternal reality that we experience in the specific objects or processes that it characterizes. When we use the runes symbolically, they are analogs of reality, in which each individual runic character represents and describes a specific set of events.

Unlike the types of symbols used in many other spiritual traditions, the runic system is dynamic, flexible, creative, and capable of further development. The runes can be understood at different levels. At the most superficial level, their archetypal meanings are fixed. Reality, however, is essentially fluid, and so each time the runes are used they react in a new way toward this fundamental reality. Each new day brings new experiences and new relationships. No time and no place can ever be exactly like any other, before or afterward and, accordingly, the action of the runic archetypes is continually being expressed in fresh ways.

At the deepest level, all of these new experiences nevertheless still conform to the broad patterns that govern existence and control the way that things happen. The runes reflect this profound reality, too, since they are visible representations of these underlying patterns. The usefulness of the runes therefore lies not only in their individual meanings, but also in their ability to be combined in a vast number of ways to give composite meanings that reflect underlying realities.

ABOVE A page from the eighth-century English epic poem *Beowulf*, which refers to a wise man as a *runwita*. The word "rune" is thought to be connected to the Old German word *runa*, meaning "whisperer" or "wise man."

LEFT The rowan tree, or mountain ash, was thought to have magical powers and was known in Great Britain as the "tree of runes."

ODIN'S INNER VISIONS

★ ★ ★ ★ ★ ★ ★ ★ ★ ★ ★ ★ ★ ★ ★ ★ ★

SINCE THE EARLIEST times, it seems, people have tried to gain visions of the future. The belief that it is possible to foresee what is to come may have its origins in the world of dreams. In dreams, people are able to visit places long since destroyed, or places that do not exist in the material world. They can talk with the dead, meet beings who have no material existence, or sometimes even see events that come to pass later in the real world. Similarly, the delirious visions experienced by the drugged, sick, and dying often involve visions of the world to come.

In the same way, carefully employed techniques of envisioning and meditation can produce experiences beyond everyday consciousness, allowing us to journey into the inner space of the mind and thus gain valuable knowledge. Such techniques have been used by soothsayers and seers in order to enter this dangerous and uncharted inner landscape. They may climb alone onto almost airless mountaintops. They may enter deep trances that mimic death itself. They may eat and drink dangerous and sometimes toxic substances. They may fast and perform ceremonial rites of self-injury, willingly undergoing ordeals at the edge of death. As a result of these dangerous practices, they experience dreams, hallucinations, or visions. Those returning to some level of sanity after such experiences (for some are destroyed by them) are believed to have brought back with them information about other worlds, including that of the future.

In legend, the runes were discovered by the god Odin through a self-inflicted ordeal. Some of the signs in the ancient rock-carvings are identical to the characters of the alphabet that gave rise to the runes, so it is probable that a gifted individual joined the two systems together, bringing the runes into being. This act of creative insight is symbolized in the Norse poem *Hávamál*, written as the words of Odin. It tells us:

I know that I hung on the windswept tree
For nine days and nine nights.
Stuck with a spear,
Bloodied for Odin,
Myself an offering to myself,
Bound to that tree
Whose roots no one knows where they go.

No one gave me bread.
No one gave me drink.
Down into the depths I looked
To take up the runes.
Screaming, I fell back from that place.

In the Norse pantheon, Odin is the god of magic, poetry, divination, and inspiration, qualities that, in ancient societies, were possessed by shamans. The word "shaman" comes from the Tungus of Siberia, and means "exalted" or "excited." A shaman,

BELOW Odin, the chief of the gods, taken from a twelfth-century Viking tapestry. One of the major features in the myths surrounding Odin was that he hung upside down in a tree for nine days and nights in order to discover the first runes.

therefore, is a person who combines the functions of diviner, medicine-person, and mediator between the worlds of humans and transcendental powers – spirits, demons, or gods. Shamans were important people in ancient tribal societies before established priesthoods came into being. The remnants of Northern European shamanry exist to this day in the surviving guising and mumming traditions of midwinter.

Shamanry gives direct access to otherworldly states of being that cannot be reached in normal consciousness. To gain access to this otherworld, shamans undergo self-destructive processes. They experience the psychic trauma of being dismembered, scattered through the worlds, and finally re-assembled. Anyone who survives this ordeal overcomes the horror, becoming

reintegrated as a person with special powers. Sometimes this happens spontaneously, as the result of an injury or illness. But more often it is done knowingly. Odin's ordeal is a good description of just such a shamanic initiation. His torment was concluded by a flash of insight that allowed him to release the full potential of the runes for human use. Such moments, when the two sides of the brain, analytical and intuitive, are linked by a unified response, are rare in human experience.

ABOVE A young woman blowing on a modern shaman's trumpet. Shamans use such instruments in the rituals that lead to their mystic insights and soul journeys.

Such visions as Odin's have a basis in neurological fact. Neurophysiologists have discovered what they call "phosphenes," geometrical shapes and images in the brain's visual cortex and neural system. Phosphenes are present in everyone. We can see them with shut eyes. They also appear to us when our consciousness is altered, such as in a trance or during meditation, when geometric shapes resembling alphabetic letters often appear in the early stages of the trance state.

The legend of Odin seems to recall a conscious realization and classification of the inner phosphene patterns of the brain. If this is true, the runes relate to the "nerve circuitry" of each human being.

LEFT Central Asian shamans of around 1900. Shamanism is still widespread in Siberia.

THE GENESIS OF THE RUNES

* * * * * * * * * * * * * * * *

SCHOLARS ARGUED FOR many years over the origin of the futhark, or runic "alphabet." At one time the runes seemed to have no obvious precursors. There was no record of their origins, except for a few archeological remains from the period when they were first used. However, the relative shortage of material has not prevented researchers from coming up with many alternative theories. During the 1870s, the Danish scholar L.F.A. Wimmer suggested that the runes had their origins in the Roman alphabet. They were, he believed, created by a single individual as a cryptic code. Wimmer's ideas were expanded upon later by Sigurd Agrell in 1938, who claimed, not very convincingly, that the runes were derived from late Latin handwriting.

The Roman-alphabet theory was clearly wrong, and other ideas were put forward instead. In 1904, O. von Friesen suggested that the runes were derived from the Greek alphabet. He believed that the Goths were the first to use them, but he had no real evidence to support this idea.

The most likely theory, backed up by evidence from archeological remains, was suggested by C.J.S. Marstrander and M. Hammarström in 1928 and 1930 respectively. They contended that the runes were derived from North Italic, a form of the Etruscan alphabet used by the people of Etruria in central Italy. Before the rise of the Romans, literate Etruscan merchants journeyed along the

ABOVE A stone with an inscription carved in Etruscan letters from the Etruscan settlement at Fiesole, near Florence, Italy. The runes are thought to have been derived from the Etruscan alphabet.

amber-trading routes from Italy through the heartlands of Europe to the shores of the Baltic Sea, and Etruscan culture was very influential in Central Europe. This can be seen from the motifs found on Celtic and Germanic artifacts dating from as early as 600 B.C.E. that are clearly Etruscan in style.

ABOVE The Etruscans occupied a large area in northeastern Italy and traded widely around the Mediterranean and as far away as the Baltic.

A hoard of 26 bronze helmets discovered in 1812 at Negau (near the Austria-Croatia border) provides evidence for the Etruscan theory. The helmets dated from around the second century B.C.E. Engraved into them were inscriptions in honor of Germanic gods, written from right to left in the North Italic script. One was a votive formula, *harigasti teiva*, "to the god, Harigast" (a warrior-deity). It is likely that the individual letters of the Etruscan alphabet did have meanings, as do Greek and Hebrew. What these meanings were is unknown today, but they may have been incorporated in rune lore.

If a date can be placed on an Etruscan origin for the runes, it would probably have occurred some time in the years between 250 and 150 B.C.E., when a brilliant individual took the North Italic alphabet and restructured it as Runic. It would most likely have happened in the Tyrolean Alps, since early runestaffs carved with North Italic characters have been discovered at Kitzbühel in the Tyrol.

The reasonable suggestion that, as a form of writing, the runes were a modification of an earlier Italian alphabet was accepted by most Runic scholars. But this idea was rejected violently by the German and Austrian historical revisionists of the National Socialist (Nazi) era, whose political objectives played a stronger role than a desire for proper scholarship. It was part of the Nazi political agenda to pretend that the runes were exclusively "Nordic Aryan" in origin, having originated in a fictional lost land in the north called Thule. They turned history on its head and insisted that the runes were the oldest writing on earth. Furthermore, they asserted that the Roman and Greek alphabets were derived from the runes. Of course, this idea is completely untrue, being nothing more than crude propaganda designed to further political ambitions. However, these false teachings are still believed by some people today.

The truth is that the runes probably have no one, single origin, because many of the characters that later became runes already existed as individual signs. During the late Bronze and early Iron Ages (1300–800 B.C.E.) pictographic rock-carvings were made in various parts of Europe, including the Alps and Scandinavia. (It is likely that these pictorial carvings also appeared on perishable material, such as wood, leather, and textiles.) Among these surviving rock-carvings are various "prerunic symbols" that also appear in the earliest rune-row.

LEFT Horned Viking helmets, contrary to popular belief, were not for normal use but were reserved for rituals, as with this bronze example from Denmark. Helmets dating from the second century B.C.E. were engraved with North Italic script, which shows that Germanic cultures adopted the Etruscan script to form runes.

LEFT A Bronze Age Danish rock-carving. Pictorial rock-carvings from this period are common in Scandinavia.

THE MYSTERY OF THE RUNES

* * * * * * * * * * * * * * * * *

TRADITIONAL teachings about Western alphabets tell us that they were invented in order to describe reality in a magical way. In the Bible, the Gospel of St. John tells us: "In the beginning was the Word, and the Word was with God, and the Word was God. The same was in the beginning with God." In one Greek legend it was Hermes, the god of travelers, commerce, and writing, who had the idea of the alphabet when he saw a flock of cranes flying through the sky. The different shapes they made showed him that shapes could be arranged to represent sounds.

Because the word has such power, many ancient Western alphabets have strong symbolic associations. Among them are Hebrew, Greek, Gothic, Glagolitic, Westphalian, Coelbren (Welsh bardic), Ogham (ancient Irish and British), Gaelic, and, of course, Runic. In each of these alphabets every character has a name that reflects its sound, which, in turn, has a series of related meanings. It is through these meanings that we can gain a greater understanding of the world.

The earliest-known reference to divination in ancient Northern Europe describes signs that were probably letters. In his book *Germania*, written in the year 98 C.E., the Roman author Tacitus gives a description of the Germanic peoples and tells of slivers of fruit-tree wood that were inscribed with divinatory signs. "Beyond any other people, they take note of divination and casting lots," he wrote. "Their technique of casting lots is simple: they cut a branch from a fruit-bearing tree and cut it into small portions. They mark these with certain signs and scatter them at random without order over a white cloth. Then, having invoked the gods and with eyes toward the heavens, the community's priest, if the divination is public, or if in private the father of the family, picks up three pieces, one at a time, then interprets them according to the signs previously written upon them."

Although Tacitus does not use the word "rune," this is a good description of the traditional three-rune divination. Later, the Roman writer Venantius Fortunatus describes the same process, using the word *runa*. These early witnesses show that the runes have been used since early times for drawing lots and for divination in general.

As well as its connection with secret things, the word "rune" also means a "lot," as used in divination. This is the meaning it had in Scotland in former times. Here, the land around each village was held in common and villagers traditionally farmed a number of strips of this land in different parts of the surrounding fields. Each year, these strips

were allotted by means of "runrig," a custom in which lots called "runs" were drawn to determine who should farm each strip, or "rig." This process prevented one family from having productive land to farm all the time and prospering, while their neighbors were left with bad, unproductive land. In an area where land was variable in quality, drawing lots gave all the villagers a fair chance. Since they came from the gods, the runes sanctified the proceedings, giving divine authorization to the land allocation.

At the most basic level, the word "rune" refers to some aspect or other of the mysterious inner structure of existence. These are the specific objects, qualities, and processes described by each rune's name. The names of the runes are derived from everyday objects that existed at the time when the runes came into being, such as ox, horse, bow, tree, or flaming torch. But the concept present in each rune's name goes far beyond this mundane level. Each name also encompasses all of the ideas and correspondences that surround it. In this way, every runic letter is a storehouse of knowledge and meaning that can only be fully understood by those who study runecraft.

Runrig

In Scotland, in former times, strips of common land, called "rigs," belonging to a village were allotted by a form of lottery. Each family had a runic house-mark that was carved on a stick (see *right*). The sticks were drawn to see which family should farm a certain "rig" for the coming year. Because, according to legend, the runes came from Odin, the allocation of land by runes was seen as the will of the gods. Runrig was an effective way of allocating both good and bad land without favoritism.

BELOW An aerial view of Scottish peat land divided up in a similar way to runrig.

KENNINGS, RIDDLES, AND ORACLES

* * * * * * * * * * * * * * * * * *

EVERYTHING IN EXISTENCE can be viewed in several different ways. No one way is more correct than any other, nor more incorrect: it is just that the viewer has his or her own interpretation. Only by understanding and comparing all view-points can we come to the most complete under-standing possible. This pluralistic way of seeing the world is fundamental to the art of runecraft, a view that was understood and valued by the poets of ancient Northern Europe – the bards of England, the *ollamhs* of Ireland, and the *skalds* of Scandinavia. These poets made great use of allusions or poetic descrip-tions called kennings, a term that comes from the verb "to ken," meaning "to know."

Kennings can take various forms. They may, for example, be drawn from incidents in history or myth. In the Norse sagas, kennings described gold as "the Seed of Kraki," "the Plains of Fyris," "the Otter's Ransom," or "Sif's Hair." Each of these kennings refers to some famous mytho-logical or historical episode related to gold. More general kennings, such as "the Glory of Elves," describing the sun, were also used. Yet another sort of kenning is

the direct poetic description. A ship becomes "the Sea-plow," sailing on "the Fishes' Bath."

In the *Edda*, collections of early Icelandic literature, the twelfth-century poem, *Alvismal*, or "The Lay of Alvis," tells the story of the dwarf Alvis, whose name means "The All-Wise," who went to the home of the gods, Asgard, to marry Thrud, one of the daughters of the god Thor. Thor, knowing that dwarfs were wise and enjoyed displaying their learning, asked Alvis to describe the 13 most significant things in exis-tence, according to the four viewpoints of humans, gods, giants, and the dwarfish-elven folk. Humans give things literal names, the gods describe how things function, the giants see the world in terms of material resources, while the dwarfs and elves use poetic kennings. Accordingly, said Alvis, trees are just "wood" to humans. To the gods, they are "the shelter of the fields." The brutal giants view them as "fuel," while the poetic dwarfs and elves view trees as the "fair limbs, adorners of the hills." Similarly, Alvis's kennings for the moon are "mock sun," "night traveler," and "month-shower, the whirling wheel." The wind is "noise-maker," "wailer," and "the roaring traveler," while the clouds are "shower-bringers," "wind-floes," and "the helmets of darkness."

Like kennings, the runes emphasize the correspondences and resemblances that exist

RIGHT Dwarfs were renowned for their cunning, none more so than Alberick in Wagner's *Ring*, illustrated here by Arthur Rackham in 1910.

BELOW Mime, a dwarf in an illustration by Arthur Rackham, 1910. According to the Icelandic *Edda*, dwarfs used poetic kennings to describe worldly objects.

between different things. In this way, they bring us fresh ways of looking at the world. They are alternative descriptions of simple things that contain much deeper meanings. As well as recording and entertaining, ancient runic writings make connections between things in the unconscious mind.

Like a kenning, a riddle is an alternative description of an action or object. Riddles present reality in unfamiliar or oblique ways that baffle the hearer, inviting us to uncover a hidden meaning. A well-thought-out riddle can provide a valid and exciting metaphorical description of anything. In his work *On Poetry*, the ancient Greek philosopher Aristotle wrote: "The very nature indeed of a riddle is this, to describe a fact in an impossible combination of words (which cannot be done with the real names for things, but can be with their metaphorical substitutes)."

Because they were dealing with alternative realities, the ancient oracles answered questions in riddles. Frequently, their answers were ambiguous and were, as a result, often criticized for not giving clear information. But the ancient critics were expecting too much. No oracle or divination can give a direct answer. Their function is not to tell what is inevitable but to provide new insights into the matter in question at present.

Modern thinking dismisses these alternative and ambiguous ways of describing the world. Instead, we invent new technical terms or jargon in an attempt to define indescribable realities. But the traditional ways have not been superseded. There is still a need for the poetic worldview – a view that is typified by the runes.

In runic, oracular, and other forms of divination, kennings and riddles play an essential role. They are the only way that language can provide new associations to think about. They give voice to areas of consciousness and viewpoints that cannot be expressed in any other way, and offer a means to deal with difficult problems that otherwise might go unresolved.

ABOVE Kennings describe our perceptions of objects. Trees can be viewed either poetically as "fair limbs, adorners of the hills" or just as plain "wood."

ABOVE Aristotle (384–322 B.C.E.) gave an analysis of the nature of riddles that serves equally well for the Norse riddles that emerged centuries later.

CHARACTERS OF CREATION

★ ★ ★ ★ ★ ★ ★ ★ ★ ★ ★ ★ ★ ★ ★ ★ ★

LETTERS IN AN alphabet are metaphors for reality. Although they are ultimately derived from picture-writing, most individual characters or shape-forms have lost these original associations, and their meaning is now only in the minds of those who use them. However, myths and legends from all over the world tell how ancient symbols once had a magical and religious significance, being given by the gods to human beings.

creation. The Greek word *stoicheia* – "the alphabet" – encompasses the idea of these universal elements, a concept that is most developed in the Hebrew alphabet and the runes. According to the Cabalistic (mystical Jewish) text called the *Sepher Yetzirah*, the 22 letters of the Hebrew alphabet are expressions of the fundamental structure of creation. Three of these characters are called the "mothers." They are the letters *Aleph*

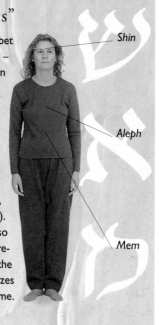

The Three "Mothers"

The letters of the Hebrew alphabet express the structure of creation – three of these characters are known as the "mothers": *Aleph*, *Mem*, and *Shin*. According to Jewish mysticism, the human body's structure reflects that of the cosmos. Parts of the human body are therefore connected to these three Hebrew letters. *Aleph* rules the chest (the breath), *Mem* the stomach (water), and *Shin* the head (fire, the intellect).

The "mothers" are also connected with time. *Aleph* represents the seasons of spring and fall, the time of the equinoxes. *Shin* symbolizes the summer, while *Mem* is wintertime.

Shin

Aleph

Mem

ABOVE Fehu, Hagalaz, and Teiwaz, the three "mother runes" that correspond to the mystic Hebrew Cabala.

Generally, alphabets explore the presence of the infinite within the finite. The letters of an alphabet are a finite set of elements from which an infinite number of combinations can be made. According to religious ideas, they represent divine power within the world, showing the infinite possibilities that can come into being.

Ancient alphabets were believed to express the fundamental elements of everything in

(A), *Mem* (M), and *Shin* (Sh). They represent three elements: air, water, and fire respectively. To the Jewish Cabalists, all creation emanated from these three elements. The heavens are composed of fire, and the earth of water, while between them the air symbolizes the mediating spirit. The three "mothers" are also associated with parts of the body and time (*see box left*).

The Welsh bardic tradition also teaches that the universe emanates from three "mother" letters of the alphabet, called *Coelbren Y Beirdd*. The Elder Futhark similarly has three "mother" runes: *Fehu* (F), *Hagalaz* (H), and *Teiwaz* (T). They are the primary runes of the three groups known as *aettir*, into which rune-rows are divided.

THE RUNIC COSMOS

The runes belong to the Northern Tradition – a system of beliefs and culture shared by the Germanic, Norse, and Celtic peoples – which has its own way to describe existence. The tradition sees the cosmos in a ninefold way. Nine is the most potent of numbers, being, as an old English spell says, "the power of three times three." Nine appears frequently in ancient writings. There are nine worlds in the cosmos, and the ninefold grid is the most powerful pattern in Northern European magic.

According to the Norse sages, there are nine distinct aspects in every human being. They are the physical body, the *Lík* or *Lich*, and *Hamr*, one's personal shape or body image. The body also possesses *Odhr*, the faculty of inspiration, *Hugr*, the power of cognition and perception, and *Minni*, the mind, the reflective capability. These are empowered by *Önd*, the vital breath of the cosmos, of which we each have a share, and the *Hamingja*, our "luck" or "guardian angel" that brings protection and good fortune. Connected with the body-aspects but external to them are the *Sál*, an after-death image, a shade or ghost. Lastly, there is the *Fylgja* (the Old Norse equivalent of the Old English *Fetch*), a partly separate aspect of ourselves that sometimes appears in animal form as a power-beast.

The number nine is found in the legend of Odin, who hung on the "windswept tree" for nine days and nights to obtain the runes. This tree was, in fact, the world tree, known in ancient Germany as *Irminsul* and in Norse myth as *Yggdrasil* (commemorated in the maypoles set up every May Day). Symbolically, this World Tree is the cosmic axis that links the three levels of the universe containing the nine worlds of creation. In the upper level is the heavenly Asgard, home of the gods; in the middle is Midgard, or Middle Earth, the world of humans; and below is the underworld of Utgard.

The runes operate on all three of these levels. Fundamental, of course, is the earthly, Midgard, level, which deals with everyday interpretations. But we must not forget the spiritual, Asgard, level above it, and the unconscious, Utgard, level, below. When we use the runes, we must interpret them in the light of all. Every rune can relate to one or other of the nine parts of the human being, giving us an enormous range of possibilities.

ABOVE This print is an 1847 interpretation of Yggdrasil, the World Tree on which Odin hung.

LEFT The Norse World Tree, or Yggdrasil, is commemorated each year in the Northern and Central European maypole. Drawing by Hans Sebald Beham (1500–1550).

WISE WOMEN AND THE RUNES

TECHNIQUES TO DISCOVER the will of the goddesses and gods played an important role in ancient Northern Europe, and methods of divination are well attested. In his book *Germania*, the Roman author Tacitus gives a description of German diviners making lots using twigs that were marked with "different signs." These signs were probably runes. Even if Tacitus was not referring to runes, they were certainly used in later centuries by Germanic and Norse diviners. Women who worked as *sybille* (sybils or seeresses) were important in Germanic paganism, so much so that we know some of their names. The sybil Weleda, who was captured and taken to Rome in 78 C.E., is described by Tacitus as "long honored by many of the Germans as divine: even earlier they bore a similar veneration for Aurinia …"

Another famous early Germanic sybil was the Alamannic-Frankish wise woman named Thiota. The seeress of the Semnonii tribe who went to Rome with King Masyas in 91 C.E. was known as Ganna, a name that comes from the Old German word for magic, *gandno*. The wise woman Waluburg, named for her *walus*, or magic staff, was in Egypt with Germanic troops during the second century. Wise women called *haliarunos* were expelled from the lands of the Goths by their king, Filimer. It is likely that these ancient Germanic wise women were runemistresses; the oldest name known

to be written in runic script, found on a weaving stay, is the woman's name Blithgund.

Scandinavian sybils were called *spákonr* or *vólva*. In Iceland, a famous sybil called Thordis Spákona is mentioned in the *Biskupa*, *Heidhavíga*, and *Vatnsdoela* sagas. In Sweden, the wise women of the woods were known as *vargamors*, and they were said to have a special rapport with the wild wolves. These fearsome creatures served the *vargamors* as their familiars.

The respect given to sybils can be seen in the Icelandic text the *Voluspá* – the "Sybil's Vision" – which is thought to date from the tenth century. The poem teaches Northern Tradition cosmology and beliefs in the form of a question-and-answer session with a seeress. Women in Scandinavia and Iceland performed ceremonies of trance-seership that were known as *seidhr*. During such a ceremony, a sybil was sung into a state of ecstasy and she then answered questions that were put to her. In pagan times, seeresses would travel from settlement to settlement, performing at feasts. The Icelandic *Flateyjarbók*, a medieval historical book, tells us that: "At that time wise women used to travel the

RIGHT A Viking pendant showing Freyja, the goddess who taught magic to the wise women.

RIGHT The Germanic wise woman Waluburg was so called because of her *walus*, or magic staff. The staff or wand is the "badge of office" of the runemistress.

land. They were called 'spae-wives' and they foretold people's futures."

The traditional costume and trappings of a *vólva* of a thousand years ago are described in the Norse saga of Erik the Red. She wore a hooded blue cloak covered with magic stones and straps or hangings. On her hands were gloves made of wildcat skin, lined with white fur, and on her feet she wore calfskin boots with the fur out-

most, and glass beads. She carried a staff bound in brass with a knob at the end, and a skin bag for her magic charms, tied with drawstrings. Each part of her clothing had a symbolic meaning and a ceremonial purpose, reflecting the dress of the goddess Freyja. Indeed, the practice of seidhr was believed to have come from this goddess, and the *Ynglinga* saga tells us how Freyja taught the magical art of seidhr to the gods of Asgard.

An important element of seidhr was *utiseta*, "sitting out," in which the sybil sat outdoors on a raised seat or platform and there went into trance. Often, she was accompanied by helpers and had a large congregation around her. The Norse *Orvar Odds* saga tells us that a sybil was accompanied by a choir of 15 maidens and 15 youths. Seidhr was considered so useful that it continued after the Christian religion was introduced. The saga of Erik the Red tells how seances were conducted in the Christian Westviking community of Greenland. But the Norse Christian Gulathing Law decreed the death penalty for those "who do seers' journeys and sittings-out in order to raise trolls thereby performing heathen deeds." Sitting out continued in secret and in remote districts far from the enforcement of national laws. The practice of sitting out continued with the Dutch *witta wijven*, or wise women, of Drenthe Province in western Frisia until well into the seventeenth century.

PART ONE

The Runes in History

★ ★ ★ ★ ★

Around 200 B.C.E., probably in the eastern Alpine region of Europe, a new alphabet was devised. Someone with the time and ability created a system of runic characters that has endured for more than two millennia. In those 2,200 years, the runes have spread all over the world and have had varied fortunes. Pagan in origin, they were first used for magic and divination, then as everyday writing in business and for record-keeping. Later, in some places, the Church used them for inscriptions on crosses and fonts – but in seventeenth-century Iceland a person could be executed for owning runes.

Knowledge of the runes has never been forgotten. In Sweden, they were in everyday use until the 1700s, and in the 1800s new studies were made by academics and students of the esoteric. In the first half of the twentieth century, the runes were misused by political fanatics before flowering again as an important element of the spiritual movement looking toward the Age of Aquarius. Today, they are better known and more widespread than at any time in their history.

ABOVE Runic inscriptions can be found all over Europe. This sixth-century C.E. funerary urn with runic markings was found in Lincolnshire, England.

HISTORIC RUNIC RECORDS

* * * * * * * * * * * * * * *

THE VARIOUS DIFFERENT versions of the runic futhark are known from a number of historical sources. There are whole futharks that have been carved on stone, or cut into wooden or into metal artifacts. There are also numerous magical and dedicatory inscriptions that have provided further information on variant forms and additional runes. Early runic inscriptions come from a remarkably wide area of Europe, from the Baltic to the Balkans. The oldest-known complete rune-row is carved on an early fifth-century stone from Kylver, on the Baltic island of Gotland. It was erected by the Goths. Another early and almost complete row was also discovered in Sweden, at Vadstena in Östergotland. The runes are inscribed on a stamped gold talisman known as a bracteate that dates from the middle of the sixth century. Another bracteate of the same period, from Grumpan in the province of Scaraborgs Län, also in Sweden, has most of the runes visible, though they are damaged.

Almost contemporary with the Scandinavian rune inscriptions is a runic stone pillar that was discovered at Breza, near Sarajevo in Bosnia-Herzegovina. Dated to

RIGHT A German gold bracteate from around 500 C.E. combining Roman-style drawing with runic lettering.

BELOW A seventh-century enamelwork brooch. Such objects often bear runic inscriptions.

the first half of the sixth century, it bears 19 Elder Futhark runes. The first 20 runes, in order, are inscribed on a late sixth-century silver brooch that was found at Charnay, in Burgundy, France. Another early example of the Elder Futhark is carved on a wooden magical sword that was discovered at Arum in Westfriesland in The Netherlands. this sword dates from around 600 C.E. and carries a runic inscription that means "return, messenger." There are also later runic objects that show the whole rune-row. A magnificent ninth-century English single-edged iron sword, which was discovered in the Thames River in London, has the entire Anglo-Saxon rune-row inlaid in brass and silver wire.

The two Swedish bracteates mentioned above have all 24 Elder Futhark runes divided by dots into groups of eight. Each group of eight is called an *aett*, a Norse word that is also used for the eight directions of space, a division that has been used from the earliest times. In accordance with

Aettir

Each *aett*, or group of eight letters, in the Elder Futhark is ruled over jointly by a god and a goddess. The first aett, beginning with the letter Fehu (F), is ruled by the fertility deities Frey and Freyja. They are the chief deities of the older Nordic gods, the Vanir. Beginning with Hagalaz (H), the second aett is ruled by the guardian god and goddess Heimdall and Mordgud. The third begins with Teiwaz (T). It is the aett of Tîwaz and Zisa, god and goddess of law and justice. The runes in each aett have aspects of the qualities of their corresponding deities, and the third but last rune, Inguz, is the name of another god. These gods are of the Aesir, the younger deities, chief of whom was Odin.

LEFT AND RIGHT Two views of Freyja, the goddess of fertility who presides over the first aett. The first is from around 600 B.C.E. the other a twentieth-century drawing by Arthur Rackham.

the spiritual teachings of the Northern Tradition, which encompasses Germanic, Norse, and Celtic belief systems, each of the three groups, or *aettir* (the plural of *aett*), of the Elder Futhark is said to be ruled over by a god and goddess.

We know what the runes mean because their meanings were recorded in three ancient poems: the Anglo-Saxon or Old English rune poem, the Norwegian rune poem, and the Icelandic rune poem. The Anglo-Saxon rune poem is the oldest. It probably dates from the eleventh century, but it contains elements dating as far back as the eighth century.

The Norwegian rune poem dates from the thirteenth century, while the Icelandic rune poem is later, dating from the fifteenth century. However, it is evident that the information contained in all of the rune poems is much older than the surviving manuscripts. All of the manuscripts from which the poems come are copies of earlier versions that are now lost. It is also significant that the description of runes in all three rune poems do not differ greatly. This suggests that they may all be derived from a common ancestral rune poem that existed before the eighth century. The rune meanings recorded in the rune poems show that the characters have always had a magical, as well as a functional, use. However, no rune poem exists for the last historical runic alphabet, the Swedish Dotted Runes, which had few magical connections.

LEFT This sword was found in the Thames River, London, and has the whole Anglo-Saxon rune-row inscribed on it.

BELOW A Viking carving showing three ships' prows and a runic inscription.

FRISIAN AND ANGLO-SAXON RUNES

* * * * * * * * * * * * * * * * *

UNLIKE THE GREEK and Roman alphabets, the runes were never fixed. There was no pagan church, academy, or state institution to enforce standardization of runes. Because of this, new forms evolved continually as new requirements arose. The widely used 24 runes of the Elder Futhark proved to be insufficient in number for the people of Frisia, a region that today straddles the northeastern parts of The Netherlands and northwestern Germany. The rune-row was extended here because of changes in the language. The new Frisian Futhark of 28 staves, or runic characters, was developed between 550 and 650 B.C.E. The extra letters in this rune-row are Ac, the oak tree; Os, mouth or speech; Yr, a yew bow; and Aesc, the ash. The order of the runes was also changed. The fourth

Britain *Germany* *Netherlands* *Region of Frisia*

around 800 C.E., bears a runic spell that promised to give its possessor power over the ocean's waves and tides. Another, very fine example of the Frisian 28-character rune-row was dredged up from the bed of the Thames River in London in 1857. This was a short sword or ceremonial knife known as a *scramasax*, which was inlaid in brass and silver wire, probably dating from the ninth century. It is now in the British Museum.

The "Anglo-Saxon" Futhork of 29 runes was created when early Frisians and Anglians in Britain added a further rune, Ear, meaning "the earth-grave," to the Frisian rune-row. Later, this additional rune was re-imported by Frisians to their homeland and used there in magical inscriptions.

rune, Ansuz, now called Aesc, was placed twenty-sixth, and a new rune, Os, became the fourth rune.

This new futhork (so called because "O" not "A" is the fourth character in this row) was carried to England by settlers from Frisia, where it formed the basis of the even longer Anglo-Saxon one. Frisian runes were used frequently for magical purposes, and several magical runestaffs of this era have been discovered preserved in waterlogged ground. One, which has been dated to

By the sixth century, Runic was the major form of writing in these countries. Coins that were minted in the English kingdoms of East Anglia and Mercia for the kings Beonna, Ethilberht, Peada, and Aethelred had inscriptions in runes. Kingship and warrior cults in pre-Christian England all had runic connections. The second king of Kent (488–512 C.E.) was named Aesc, the "god rune" and the cosmic tree, and subsequent kings of the Kentish nation were known as the Aescings, meaning "becoming a god." Many other Saxon, Anglian, and Jutish kings in early England

had names redolent of runic power: Ethelbert, Ethelric, Ethelred, Kenric, Osred, Osric, Oswald, and Sigeric.

Around 800 C.E., in the north of England and what is now the south of Scotland, the Anglo-Saxon Futhork expanded again. Another four runes were added to this rune-row, creating the 33-character Northumbrian Futhork. This marked the end of Anglo-Saxon runic development. The Northumbrian rune-row is divided into four aettir, plus one more – the final rune, Gar. Some of the runes of the fourth aett have a Celtic influence, with names and meanings similar to their corresponding letters in the Ogham alphabet (the Irish "tree alphabet" in which letters have tree names). These extra runes are Cweorth, meaning swirling fire; Calc, a cup, calculating stone, or sandal; Stan, a stone; and Gar, a spear.

Some of the best runic objects in England are Northumbrian. The most remarkable is the "Franks Casket," most of which is preserved in the British Museum. This is a box carved from whale's bone and decorated with scenes from pagan and Christian mythology, described in Northumbrian runes.

With 33 runes, the Northumbrian Futhork was the longest rune-row. But when the king of Wessex, Alfred the Great, introduced Roman-style education to England, he taught with the Roman alphabet we use today, and the runes gradually faded from everyday use.

Although the Church had formerly used runes, they soon acquired an aura of paganism. The Danes who invaded England in the time of Alfred used the real "Viking Runes," a version of the Younger Futhark (*see page 68*). As well as the Elder Futhark, the Anglo-Saxon Futhork, and the Northumbrian Futhork, all the Younger Futhark systems were used in Britain and Ireland by Norwegian and Danish merchants, raiders, and settlers. After the Danes became Christian, the runes survived in monkish writings, several of which are still in existence. They also continued in folk magic, which included runic "ornament" on items such as tools, musical instruments, boats, and buildings. They are still used there today.

ABOVE The ninth-century British "Franks Casket" combines the pagan runes with Christian scenes, such as this depiction of the Adoration of the Magi.

LEFT Sixth-century English coins bearing runic inscriptions.

BELOW On ships such as these, the Vikings carried their culture widely throughout Northern Europe.

SCANDINAVIAN RUNES

* * * * * * * * * * * * * * * * *

LONG AFTER THE runes went underground in mainland Europe, rune use flourished in Scandinavia and the Scandinavian colonies, including Iceland, Greenland, and parts the British Isles. The main reason was the continued practice of Norse paganism in Scandinavia and the Baltic long after Christianity had taken over in Western

Europe. The pagan temples in Sweden were in use until 1100, in Pomerania (on the Baltic shores of modern Poland) until 1169, and in Finland until the 1680s.

In the Scandinavian realms, Runic was used for all types of writing, both sacred and secular. At the same time that the Elder Futhark was expanding in England, a new version of the runes was emerging in Scandinavia. There, during the eighth century, the 24 runes of the original Elder Futhark were reduced in number to make a new 16-rune futhark, with several sound-values for each rune. This new rune-row was known as the Younger Futhark.

The Younger Futhark was never fully standardized, and two closely related versions came into being. These are known as the Danish Futhark and Swedish-Norse Futhark. The Danish version is probably older. The Swedish-Norse runes follow the same order as the Danish but are slightly simpler in shape. The earliest complete row of the Swedish-Norse Futhark may be seen on a stone found at Rök in Östergötland, Sweden, dating from around 850 C.E., while a complete Danish row exists on the stone discovered at Gørlev in Zealand, Denmark, which dates from around 900 C.E.

The oldest record of the Younger Futhark's rune names is in the *Abecedarium*

ABOVE Viking settlers spread throughout the British Isles and Iceland and across the southern coast of Greenland.

RIGHT This stone from Rök in Sweden dating from *c*.850 C.E. is carved with the earliest extant full Swedish-Norse Futhark.

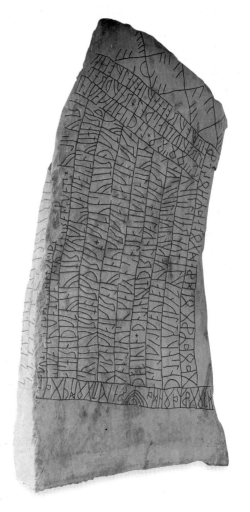

Nordmannicum, a manuscript dating from the ninth century. This text is a record of the studies made by German Christian monks, who included Hrabanus Maurus (780–876) and his student, Walahfrid Strabo, who was at the monastery of Fulda, in what is now central Germany, from 827 until 829. The *Abecedarium Nordmannicum* names the 16 characters of the Danish Futhark as follows: "Feu first; Ur thereafter; Thuris the third stave; Os thereabove; Rait at the end is written; Chaion connects with Hagal; Naut has Is, Ar and Sol; [Tyr], Bria and Man in middle; Lagu, the light-filled; Yr ends all."

These rune names are close to those in the Elder Futhark. The names of the Younger Futhark runes, and their meanings, were also recorded in the Norwegian and Icelandic rune poems of the twelfth and thirteenth centuries. Like the Elder Futhark, both versions of the Younger Futhark were divided into three aettir. The first aett has six runes, while the other two each have five. The aettir are named Frey, Hagal, and Tyr respectively.

Simplification of the Swedish-Norse Futhark continued further in Sweden, culminating in the twelfth century with the appearance of the Hälsinge Runes. As far as possible, the earlier upright stems were abolished, which made the Hälsinge Runes the most minimalist of all, and almost a form of shorthand. Like the other Scandinavian runes, the Hälsinge Runes are written inside two parallel lines. When they are written on stone, they sometimes snake and interlace across the surface. In Sweden, during the eleventh and twelfth centuries, the Danish Futhark, imported from Denmark, took over from the Swedish-Norse version.

In Norway, meanwhile, another version of the Younger Futhark, called the Mixed Runes, came into being. This used characters from both the Danish and Swedish-Norse rune-rows. All of these versions had the same 16 runes, but their forms varied.

But this was not the end of Scandinavian runic development. In Sweden, around 1200, a new, extended 25-rune row emerged. It was based on the Swedish-Norse version of the Younger Futhark, but had more characters. Known as the Pointed or

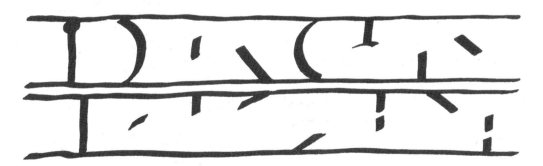

Dotted Runes, and arranged in the order of the Roman alphabet, this rune-row created new runes by adding points or dots to some of them. There were several variants, notably one used on the Baltic island of Gotland, but a standard form eventually emerged. The Dotted Runes have less of a mystical dimension than earlier rune-rows. The inner meanings of the earlier runes remained, but the new ones do not seem to have developed the level of meaning of the older runes.

which details the laws of the province of Skane using runic script.

In the 1540s, Mogens Gyldenstjerne, admiral of the Danish Royal Navy, used runes to write his private journal. In 1611, the Dotted Runes were still in such common use that the scholar Johannes Bureus attempted to get them adopted as the official alphabet of Sweden. He was unsuccessful. However, during the Thirty Years War (1618–48), the Swedish general Jacob de la Gardie, wrote his secret military orders in Dotted Runes. The Dotted Runes continued to be used in Sweden until the late eighteenth century, in manuscripts, church inscriptions, and private correspondence.

ABOVE A beautifully carved runic stone from Kingingtorussaq, Upernarvik, in Greenland.

Many of the 3,000 runestones in Sweden are carved with Dotted Runes, as are most church inscriptions. The tombstone of Bishop Gisike at Lösen, for example, dating from 1311, has a runic inscription. Another, dating from 1500, was carved by the master mason Adam van Düren in Lund cathedral. It says *Got help*, "May God help us."

By the thirteenth century, the runes (mainly the Dotted version) were being written in ink on parchment by scribes. The rune shapes then became more rounded. A number of Danish runic manuscripts dating from the fourteenth and fifteenth centuries still exist. The fourteenth-century manuscript *Codex Runicus*, preserved in Copenhagen, records the *Skaanse Lov*,

Outside Scandinavia, the runes had long been used wherever the Viking adventurers had settled, including various regions of the British Isles. As well as the Elder Futhark, the Anglo-Saxon Futhork, and the Northumbrian Futhork, the whole of the Scandinavian Younger Futhark systems were used in Britain and Ireland. Most Scandinavian runic inscriptions in Britain occur in the Orkneys and the Isle

RIGHT One of the most famous runestones of all, the Jelling Stone, was carved in about 985 C.E. on the order of King Harald Bluetooth, to mark the conversion of Denmark to Christianity.

of Man. Both were under Norwegian rule for many years, while the Orkneys came under Scottish rule only in 1468. The Orcadian runes are close to the Danish types, while those on the Isle of Man are a version of the Swedish-Norse type and are known as Man-Jaer Runes. On the Isle of Man, the runes date from the tenth to the twelfth centuries. Most were carved on standing stone crosses as memorials, and contain the names of the runemasters responsible for both the carvings and the runes themselves. Gaut Bjørnsson is the most famous.

Although Ireland had its own Ogham script, Scandinavian influence meant that several runic systems were used there as well. At one period, it seems that in Ireland Runic was the main form of writing. This is clear from the words related to writing in the modern Irish language, which all contain the letter-compound *rún*. Scandinavian settlement sites in Ireland have revealed objects with Danish and Swedish-Norse runes, including a Viking Age wooden sliver showing the Younger Futhark, found in excavations of Dublin. Later versions of the Younger Futhark, exist in medieval Irish manuscripts.

Ironically, the strongest reaction against the use of the runes emerged in Iceland, which was once the heartland of Nordic culture and tradition. Here, Church authorities condemned the runes as witchcraft and, in 1639, they were banned. After that, people found with runes in their possession were executed. But outside Iceland, in Scandinavia and the Baltic, the runes remained in use in both folk magic, family-marks (used to mark family property), and calendars. As late as 1755, calendars with runes denoting the cyclic numbers (used to calculate the date of Easter in any year) were printed in Sweden. As long as people continued to use the Julian Calendar (a calendar instituted by Julius Caesar in 46 C.E. but amended by Pope Gregory XIII in 1582), peasants and farmers continued to carve runes on the wooden calendars or almanacs known as *rimstocks* and *prime-staves*. Derivatives of these types of runes could still be found in use on wooden almanacs in Estonia until early in the twentieth century.

The Runes and Ogham Script

Even though Ireland had its own tree alphabet, known as Ogham, used by the Druids and early Celtic monks in which the letters were named after trees, Scandinavian settlers introduced runes as well. After Scandinavian rule was overthrown in 1014, versions survived in medieval monastic manuscripts, where they are called Gall Ogham and Lockland Ogham. These are developments of the Mixed and Dotted Runes, with some extra characters that were necessary for writing in the Irish language.

RIGHT Stone with Ogham script from Killalde in County Clare.

THE GOTHS AND THE RUNES

★ ★ ★ ★ ★ ★ ★ ★ ★ ★ ★ ★ ★ ★ ★ ★

THE ANCIENT GOTHIC nation played an important part in the history of the runes. The Goths were originally a tribe living in part of what is now Sweden and the Baltic island of Gotland. Here they worshiped their own gods and goddesses and adopted

Attila and the Huns, the Goths conquered Italy, southern France, and Spain.

When the pagan Goths arrived at the Black Sea, they still worshiped their national gods, and there was a struggle between them and various sects of Christians who tried to

Hagalaz, the sound "h"

Early form of Sowulo, giving the sound "s"

RIGHT This stone from Kylver has the oldest representation of the 24-rune alphabet in Sweden. It dates from the early fifth century C.E.

Early form of Inguz, giving the sound "ug"

the runes. Some of the oldest rune names come from the Old Gothic language. The oldest complete rune-row of all was carved by a Goth on the Kylver Stone on Gotland.

At a certain point in their history, the Goths left Scandinavia and migrated to the southern shores of the Baltic Sea and then through Prussia, Lithuania, Poland, and the Ukraine to the northern shores of the Black Sea. There they established a nation that grew greatly in numbers, power, and prosperity. At a later date, they migrated once more – this time to the west, where they challenged the power of the Roman Empire. As well as helping the Romans to defeat

convert them. Some Goths adopted the Arian version of the Christian religion, while others remained pagan. The struggle between the two religions went on for many years. But members of both religions used a version of the runes.

To write the Arian Christian scriptures and liturgy in the Gothic language, Bishop Ulfila, a Gothic cleric who tried to convert his fellows, created a new alphabet. He based it on the Elder Futhark runes familiar to the Goths. Taking some letters from the Greek, he kept and modified some Gothic runes. But the alterations were not great. Each character of the Gothic alphabet had a similar name and retained the meaning of its runic counterpart. Although the Gothic letters were created by a bishop, they were, like the runes, also used in magic and divination. Since the Goths did not all become Christians, they used both the new Roman alphabet and the runic alphabet in parallel for many years. Gradually, however, the runes went out of use.

In Spain and the south of France, the Visigoths (the western Goths) continued to use the Gothic alphabet for a long time. But in 589 C.E. a Church council convened at Toledo condemned the Gothic alphabet as heretical. Then, unfortunately, most of the books written in Gothic script were burned.

Just as the Goths had their own names for the runes, they used similar names for the letters of their alphabet. The Gothic alphabet has the same letter order as the runes, and it is divided into three *aettir*. The Gothic alphabet uses 11 Greek-style letters in place of the original runic shapes.

Since the Goths migrated all over mainland Europe, taking the runes with them, it is fitting that the customary runemaster's title, Erilaz, comes from a Gothic tribal name: it is a Scandinavian version of the name Herulian. Originally, "Herulian" described a member of a little-known tribe called the Heruli that was expelled from the north by the Danes and migrated across Europe with the Goths.

The Heruli tribe is remembered for the battles it fought. It successfully besieged Athens in 267 C.E., sacking the city. However, it was later defeated and destroyed as a tribe, and the survivors scattered and assimilated into other tribes and nations. The Heruli ceased to exist as an entity, but its name lived on as a description of "one skilled in the runes."

The earliest-known object that bears this Herulian runemaster's title is a sixth-century bone amulet found at Lindholm in Sweden. Inscribed on it is the runic formula "*ek erilaz sa wilagaz hateka*," which translates as "I, Erilaz, am the cunning one." Beginning with "ek" – "I" – followed by a personal name or title, this is a standard formula for a runemaster's declaration. This formula is known from over 20 inscriptions dating from between 200 and 600 C.E. Along with their title, it was customary for the runemasters to write their own names on inscriptions. There are many ancient Scandinavian runestones that are still in existence, and from them we know the actual names of several runemasters. Among the best represented are the Swedish Opir and the Manx Gaut Björnsson. Though they were not Goths, they still used the title Erilaz.

THE RUNAMO ENIGMA

★ ★ ★ ★ ★ ★ ★ ★ ★ ★ ★ ★ ★ ★ ★

ONE OF THE strangest episodes in runic history centers on Runamo, close to Brakne-Hoby, in Blekinge, Sweden. It tells us a lot about the nature of the runes. In former times, Runamo was revered as a sacred place. Here, what looked like a long line of runes could be seen running along veins of quartz that stood out from a granite rock-face. Alongside them ran a path. Writing in the thirteenth century, Saxo Grammaticus described the phenomenon: "Even though the path sometimes leads across the mountains and sometimes leads through the valleys, traces of runic writing can be seen along the whole pathway." Even in the twelfth century, when many people could read Runic, the Runamo runes were puzzling. Although they did not know what the inscription meant, people revered the ribbonlike quartz band as a *lindorm* – an earth dragon.

According to local legend, the runes recorded the Battle of Bravoll, fought between the armies of Sigurd Hring and Harald Hilditonn around 700 C.E. But nobody could be sure what they really meant. In the twelfth century, King Valdemar the Great of Denmark ordered a study of the Runamo runes. Danish scholars visited the site and copied the runes onto wooden tablets. But, recalls Saxo, "they could make no sense out of it." Later, other scholars tried to decipher the runes, also without success.

In 1833, the Royal Society of Denmark set up a committee of investigation. Led

RIGHT Part of the enigmatic stone at Runamo in Sweden. Shapes long believed to be runes appear as if cut in the rock over a length of 72 feet (22 meters). For centuries people speculated about their meaning.

ABOVE A Viking battle scene. Legend had it that the Runamo runes gave the account of a clash between two Scandinavian armies in the eighth century.

by Finnur Magnusson of Copenhagen University, a group of academics visited Runamo and recorded runes from 72 feet (22 meters) of rock-face. Then Magnusson spent ten months attempting to decipher the runes. He was almost at the point of giving up when he noticed what he thought was a wendrune (a rune written backward, from right to left). This triggered a sudden revelation. In what he described as an "ecstasy" or "trance," Magnusson wrote down a translation of the Runamo runes, revealing a fine metrical poem in the classical Old Norse form called *fornyrdislag*.

Magnusson's decipherment was hailed as a great breakthrough in ancient-rune studies – until geologists examined the quartz band. Shortly afterward they announced that the runes were not deliberate carvings at all, but only natural cracks in the quartz vein. However, Magnusson did not believe the geologists, so, in 1841, he went ahead and published his book, *Runamo og Runerne.*

Despite Magnusson's protests, the geologists were right. The Runamo runes are a natural phenomenon and were never carved by human hands. However, the mystery is not so easy to dismiss, for how could such a fine piece of Old Norse poetry come out of natural rock-patterns? Magnusson's ability and honesty were never in question – it was obvious even to his opponents that Magnusson was sincere, and that he had had some kind of revelation from the rocks.

Years passed, and the matter was left to rest, unresolved. Although geologists had proved that the signs were natural, this did not mean that they could not be read as runes. Local people had always believed that they could experience the runes at Rumano through spiritual exercises. When the Swedish geologist Berzelius visited Runamo in 1836, he was told that there was only one man in the district who could interpret the runes. He did so by standing on his head near the rock. Perhaps Magnusson had also come into contact with this same source.

From the Runamo experience, it is clear that natural runic patterns can tell us a lot. They have their own geomythic content, from which we can learn. How we recognize runic patterns in divination depends on the conditions present when we see the patterns. These conditions include the weather, time of day and year, light direction, and our own internal state. The runes we see at places such as Rumano tell us as much about our own state of consciousness as they do about themselves. Also, at such places, strange things can happen. If we return at another time, we may not see the same runes that we did on our first visit. This is puzzling, but it is the very essence of the otherworldly insight that lies at the core of the runic mysteries.

Magnusson's Poem

Professor Magnusson claimed that the Runamo inscription was an Old Norse poem that referred to the Battle of Bravoll:

Hildekind captured the kingdom
Gardar carved the runes
Ola took the oath
May Odin hallow the magic
May King Hring
Fall in dust
The Elves, the Love-gods
Must leave Ola
Odin and Frey
And the race of Aesir
Must destroy,
Destroy,
Our enemies
Give Harald
Great victory.

RUNES IN NORTH AMERICA

* * * * * * * * * * * * * * *

IN NORTH AMERICA there are a number of very controversial "Scandinavian runic remains." The possibility of runes having reached North America is very high: there were certainly European people there long before Columbus. Around the year 1000, brave Norse navigators, including Erik the Red, Leif Eiriksson, and Thorfinn Karlsefni, landed on the North American mainland.

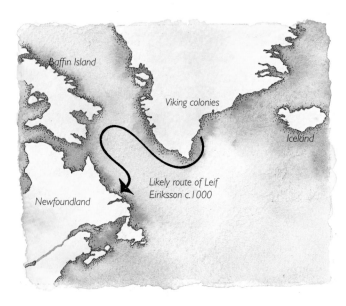

Baffin Island

Viking colonies

Iceland

Likely route of Leif Eiriksson c.1000

Newfoundland

ABOVE The Vikings certainly traveled to the coast of modern Canada; whether they went farther inland is far from certain.

RIGHT The Kensington Runestone, found in Minnesota, is held by some to be a genuine Viking artifact, though most scholars consider it a fake.

They called it Vinland, "the land of vines." They reached Vinland via the Westviking colony on Greenland. The Scandinavian settlement on Greenland lasted almost 500 years. It flourished in the years around 1100–1200, but by the middle 1300s, owing to a drop in average temperatures, the colony began to decline. But although the last Bishop of Greenland died in 1378, there was constant contact with Scandinavia until 1408. Occasionally, in later years, Northern European sailors visited Greenland. The last Westvikings died around the time Columbus reached the West Indies.

This long history makes regular Norse visits to Vinland during this period very likely. But because it died out, the settlement on Greenland has left little historical record. However, the discoveries of runic artifacts in North America give rise to questions about the extent and duration of Norse exploration and settlement there.

One of the most controversial runic artifacts in North America is the so-called Kensington Runestone. It was discovered in 1898 near Kensington, Minnesota. Pulling up a tree stump, a farmer named Olaf Ohman unearthed a slab of stone weighing about 200 pounds (100 kilograms). Ohman showed the stone to friends and neighbors, and soon academics got to hear of it. Almost to a person, they said it was a fake. In their

opinion, there were "anomalies" in the text, and, anyway, no Viking stone of this quality had ever been found in North America. All the same, the runestone was still put on show in the museum at Alexandria, Maine.

The Kensington Runestone has an inscription in late Scandinavian runes. The numerical figures are written in stave-numbers, the runic version of Roman numerals. Part of the text translates as: "eight Goths and twelve Norsemen on a voyage of exploration from Vinland of West. We had camp on two islands, one day's journey north from this stone … ten men red of blood and dead. *Ave Virgo Maria*. Save from ill."

The date of 1362 for a Norse expedition to Minnesota does not correspond with known historical records of visits from Europe, and so this, rather than other evidence, was taken as proof that it is a fake. Unfortunately, one piece of crucial evidence was destroyed when the stone was dug up. It was a tree root, which had grown in contact with the runes and contained their imprint. Tree-ring analysis of the root could have provided valuable evidence of dating. But it was burned as firewood.

When the Norse scholar Hjalmar Holand examined the text, he claimed that the anomalies in the text, which others had cited as evidence of fraud, were compatible with its fourteenth-century dating. Nevertheless, most academic Runic scholars still consider the Kensington Runestone to be a fake because it does not date from the 1300s, but is from the later European settlements after Columbus. Occasionally, other runestones have appeared in North America, but they too have been dismissed as fakes. These runestones include ones from Rushville, Ohio, from Spirit Pond, Maine, and from Poteau, Heavener, and Shawnee, all in Oklahoma.

Except for the Kensington Runestone, the most interesting runic object from North America is a horn found in 1952 by Ronald Mason near Winnetka, Illinois. Mason saw the horn in a freshly cut roadside bank. On one side, it has a carving of a man pointing to the Sun. He is standing amid vegetation next to a tree. On the other side is Vidar, Odin's son, fighting the Fenris-wolf on the last day, Ragnarök, the Twilight of the Gods. His magic boot is in the wolf's mouth, while he pulls at its upper jaw with his gloved hands. Beneath the carving is a two-winged panel with runes that describe the scene. As with the Kensington Runestone, the age and origin of the horn are still contested.

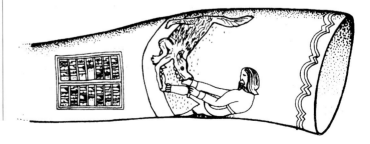

RUNES IN NATIONALIST GERMANY

* * * * * * * * * * * * * * * * * *

THE ARMANEN RUNES are different from all the previous rune-rows. These runes are a twentieth-century system that has its origins in the pan-Germanic movement that developed during the late nineteenth century. In German-speaking nations, the creation of the Second German Empire (the *Kaiserreich*) in 1871 led to a new awareness of, and search for, ethnic roots. This Germanic "back-to-the-roots" movement

was connected intimately with nationalist sentiments, which soon led to the development of extreme right-wing politics, together with their associated racist theories.

The Armanen Runes reflect this spirit, being the brainchild of a Viennese mystical nationalist, Guido List (1848–1919), or "Guido von List," as he became known after he had adopted the aristocratic "von," to which he was not entitled. These runes, which List claimed to have discovered through a spiritual revelation, are an essential part of his sociopolitical theories about the so-called "Aryo-Germanic" people. During convalescence after an eye operation, List maintained he had a vision of the most ancient of all runes, which he called the "world symbols of a prehistoric age." He said that this "Armanen Futhork" originated thousands of years earlier than the Elder Futhark and was therefore more authentic. In fact, what he had really done was to invent a new runic system. Many people believed him, and they felt that these "original" runes would empower them to go on to do great things.

List's teachings had much in common with then-current ideas about the legendary city of Atlantis. He appears to have been influenced by the Theosophical writers Madame Helena Blavatsky and Ignatius Donnelly, whose books about the ancient Aryans and Atlantis were bestsellers in

Madame Blavatsky and the Nazis

LEFT Theosophists were very interested in Atlantis, which they thought had been a continent in the Atlantic.

ABOVE Madame Blavatsky, cofounder of the highly influential Theosophical Society.

The Theosophical movement was founded in 1875 by Madame Helena Blavatsky, a Russian mystic, and an American colonel, Henry Olcott. Blavatsky promoted the myth of an ancient high civilization on the "lost continent" of Atlantis. In her influential book, *The Secret Doctrine*, Blavatsky claimed that throughout history enlightened mystics of a "universal brotherhood" had guided human evolution toward the production of a higher "super race," an idea taken up by Adolf Hitler. Blavatsky's teachings promoted dangerous racial theories that formed the core of Austrian and German anti-Semitism.

the late nineteenth century. In the same way as other Germanic occultists of his day, List felt that the Aryans must have originated in a sunken land somewhere in the region of

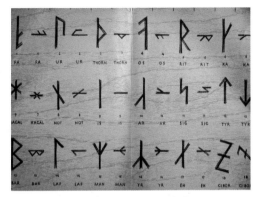

the present North Sea. Called variously Hyperborea, Atland, or Thule, this Atlantis-like island had been destroyed by a natural catastrophe. There, maybe 12,000 years ago, a golden age of high civilization was said to have flourished. As well as having a sophisticated material culture, the inhabitants enjoyed a highly developed spiritual life.

To List, the runes that he "rediscovered" were no less than the sacred writing of these lost Aryans. In 1908, he published this new "primeval script" in his book, *Das Geheimnis der Runen* (*The Secret of the Runes*). The name he gave the script – "Armanen" – was derived from an alleged Aryan priesthood of the same name, which, List claimed, had used the runes during the long-lost "golden age" of Aryan culture.

List's followers saw themselves as the new Armanen priesthood, dedicated to accelerating social evolution toward a renewal of the ancient "Aryo-Germanic" supremacy – a trend that became dominant a few years later in Nazi Germany, with horrendous results. By the time List published his book, the Guido von List Gesellschaft (Guido von List Society) had already been in existence for four years. The aim of the society was to promote List's runic, historical, and esoteric ideas. Through an inner elite "order" called the Armanen Orden, the society soon became a focus of pan-German chauvinism viewed from a mystic angle. Members of the order were enthusiastic supporters of war. A tribute to List published in 1917 shows him in his office on the thousandth day of what is described as the "Holy German War" – World War I.

List died shortly after the end of World War I, but his followers continued to develop his ideas. Some were prominent in the postwar mystical-nationalist circles that significantly influenced Adolf Hitler's ideology. This strand of propagandist rune-lore culminated in

the period of the Third Reich, when the runes were taken, along with other historical German signs, into the Nazi corporate image favored by Hitler. In this period, non-Nazi runemasters were persecuted, and several were done to death in Nazi concentration camps. The Armanen Orden itself disintegrated when Nazi Germany was destroyed by the war it had started.

LEFT A spread of the Armanen Runes. This example was used by Guido List in his teachings to promote his view of an "Aryo-Germanic" supremacy.

ABOVE Despite all the horrors and massive slaughter of World War I, List's followers regarded this war as a holy campaign.

THE NAZIS AND THE RUNES

★★★★★★★★★★★★★★★★

IN THE EARLY twentieth century, before the rise of the Nazis, German racial-nationalist ideas were linked with the runes by speculative writers. They included Rudolf Gorsleben, Karl Willigut, Rudolf von Sebottendorf, Bernhard Körner, Philipp Stauff, and Ernst Lauterer, who used the pseudonym "Tarnhari." Following Guido List's lead, they mixed then-popular myths of the ancient Aryan race with a nationalist reading of history that took in rune magic. Before these writers, the runes had been used for over 2,100 years without either nationalist or racist connotations. By using the runes along with political action, they argued, the German race could rise to world supremacy. Politicized esoteric organizations, including the Armanen Orden, the Germanen Orden, and Thule Gesellschaft, were set up to spread these ideas.

During their rise to power, the Nazis adopted the Armanen Runes. Simple, striking, and symbolic, they were useful propaganda tools, and the Nazis gave them meanings that suited their beliefs. The Armanen Sig rune was the most common. It was used because of the link that List had made with the German word for victory – *Sieg*. The Deutsche

ABOVE Heinrich Himmler, the leader of the S.S., instigated research into the runes, in the belief that this would further knowledge of a vigorous Germanic culture.

RIGHT The Nazis used the Sig rune, standing for *Sieg*, the German word for victory, almost as widely as the (nonrunic) swastika.

Jungvolk youth organization used a single Sig in white on a black background, while Hitler's bodyguard, the S.S., adopted two Sig runes as its emblem.

Sponsored by the S.S. leader Heinrich Himmler (1900–45), the Deutsches Ahnenerbe ("German Heritage") organization undertook rune research which it published in the magazine *Germanien* and a series of books. Its logo was a rounded Othil rune enclosing a sword. As part of this propaganda program, S.S. ideology classes indoctrinated new recruits with the meaning of Nazi runic signs. S.S. officers wore the runic S.S. ring. S.S. daggers and swords bore the runes as recreations of ancient Germanic weapons. It is believed that Himmler's inner circle, the "knights" of the Black Order, practiced List's rune meditation. In 1937, Himmler commissioned Professor Karl Diebitsch to design rune-based heraldic coats of arms for members of his inner circle. Nazi obituaries and tombstones were marked with the Armanen Man rune for the birth date and Yr for the date of death.

Under the Nazis, state youth organizations and the military used runes as badges of rank. These included the Armanen Sig

Nazi Symbols

The Nazis embraced Guido List's Armanen Runes. Seeing them as a product of the so-called "Aryan" culture to which they considered the German people belonged, they latched onto them as symbols of the qualities they wished to promote. Like much Nazi thinking, the "history" of these runes was a mixture of misunderstanding, wishful thinking, and invention.

The most widely seen of the runes in Nazi Germany was the Armanen Sig rune, which was repeated as the symbol of the Schutz-Staffel (S.S.), meaning "protective force." Originally Adolf Hitler's personal bodyguards, the members of this organization became a much-feared force of repression in occupied Europe. The double Sig was a badge worn as an armband and also appeared on weapons and wall slogans. The even more famous swastika symbol was not based on a rune, but was a revival of an Indo-European symbol of solar power that appears on ancient Scandinavian rock-carvings.

rune, Eh, Hagal, and Othil. They were used according to List's meanings. The Armanen Man rune was the badge of a medical officer in the German armed forces. The logo of the Nazi Aryan child-rearing program, called *Lebensborn,* was a Hagal rune. But the Nazis used runes only as symbols, not as actual inscriptions. When these were needed, they were made with traditional German blackletter script, or a special Roman script that resembled runes. Hitler Youth award badges for sports proficiency had this lettering in a circle around a swastika on top of a larger Tyr or Sig rune. In the same period in Britain, Sir Oswald Mosley's British Union of Fascists adopted a lightning-flash logo inspired by Nazi symbolism.

The S.S. runes, designed to intimidate their tortured victims, rightly became a symbol of tyranny after World War II. During the student uprising in Paris in 1968, posters appeared all over the city. Some showed the French state riot police, the C.R.S., carrying shields with the S.S. runes upon them. But many years after the Nazis' fall, many Germans still see the runes as politically suspect. Sometimes this is with reason. In early 1981, there was a scandal when a flag bearing the Othil rune appeared at the funeral of Grand Admiral Karl Dönitz (1891–1981), Hitler's successor. Neo-Nazi graffiti often contains this symbol today. In 1997, a stamp commemorating the writer Heinrich Heine (1797–1856) was withdrawn before issue because his birth and death dates were marked with runes, a cross for his death being unsuitable because he was Jewish.

ABOVE A portrait of Heinrich Heine. A German stamp commemorating the Jewish writer that featured runes was withdrawn in 1997 as runes are still associated with the Nazis.

LITERARY AND ARTISTIC RUNES

* * * * * * * * * * * * * * * * *

I N THE NINETEENTH century, there was an awareness of the runes outside German and Scandinavian circles. In his fantasy adventure *A Journey to the Center of the Earth* (1864), the French author Jules Verne (1828–1905) introduced Icelandic runes as an important element in the story. The Swiss-French illustrator Eugène Grasset (1841–1917) used the runes in his Wagnerian illustrations. In his poster for *La Valkyrie* at the Paris Opéra, about 1880, Wotan (Odin) holds a spear with a magical inscription beginning with the proper noun

BELOW Odin and Brünnhilde, from *Hero Tales and Legends of the Rhine* (1915). Helped by Wagner's *Ring,* literary interest in Norse mythology was high in the late nineteenth and early twentieth centuries.

"Ek" – "I." Brünnhilde's shield, and that of the Valkyrie Brünnhilde, also bear runes.

More than any other writer, J. R. R. Tolkien (1892–1973) popularized the runes in English-speaking countries. As professor of English at Oxford University, he was well qualified to use the runes. The book jacket for *The Hobbit* (1937), which he designed, has a border in Anglo-Saxon runes. They give the book's title, the publisher's name, and tell how the book was compiled from the memoirs of Bilbo Baggins by J. R. R. Tolkien. The binding of the hardback first edition also had a large Dagaz and two smaller Thurisaz runes on the spine. Inside, the "Moon Runes" revealed in Thror's map were also Anglo-Saxon.

But in his later Middle Earth trilogy, *The Lord of the Rings,* Tolkien did not use historical runes. He devised several new scripts, including the Tengwar Angerthas alphabets. Tolkien's Angerthas Moria and Angerthas Daeron scripts used characters from historical rune-rows. They were composed largely of Northumbrian characters, some Elder Futhark variants, and a few bindrunes (two or more runes joined together). But Tolkien gave them totally different meanings. The bestselling success of *The Hobbit* and, from the 1950s, *The Lord of the Rings,* brought an awareness of the runes to millions.

In the 1950s and 1960s, designers occasionally used runes as company logos. The logo of the British Campaign for Nuclear Disarmament (C.N.D.), designed by Gerald Holtom, is the most widespread. Derived from the semaphore letters "N" and "D," it is also the Younger Futhark "death rune," Yr.

Around the same time, the designer Hans Schleger produced a logo for Finmar Ltd., a company that imported furniture and glassware into Britain. It was a bindrune of the Younger Futhark runes Fé and Madhr. In Norway, the trademark of the Norsk Design-Centrum (Norwegian Design Center) was the result of a competition won by local designer, Odd Karlberg. It is a bindrune of the letters "N" and "D" from the Elder Futhark.

In the 1970s, the runes emerged as an element in heavy-metal music. The New York band Kiss used the S.S. runes as part of its written name, while the English band Black Sabbath included the Sowulo rune in its name on the covers of several early albums. Later, "rock-and-roll-rebel" Ozzy Osbourne's 1982 album *Talk of the Devil* used runes in the artwork. Designed by Steve "Krusher" Joule, they include a runic epitaph for Osbourne's colleague, the guitarist Randy Rhoades, who had just died. Black Sabbath's 1990 album *Tyr*, based on Norse myth, had images of a Swedish runestone and incorporated a logo designed by Satori with a prominent Teiwaz (Tyr) rune. From the same year, *I Took up the Runes* came from Jan Garbarek, with a cover of three runes scratched on stone.

In the early 1980s, the American author Ralph Blum's highly successful *The Book of Runes*, packaged with a set of ceramic rune-stones, brought the runes to a wide new audience. By the time the book appeared, there was already a sufficient amount of interest in the English-speaking countries for some esoteric rune-study groups to be functioning. The best known of these is the Rune Guild, founded by Edred Thorsson in 1980 in Austin, Texas.

ABOVE The C.N.D. symbol (used as a general antiwar symbol in the United States) incorporates Yr from the Younger Futhark.

Since the 1980s, the art of ancient Europe, including Celtic designs and runes, has reappeared in body art. Although we do not know whether people tattooed runes upon them-selves in ancient times, we do know that in ancient Europe tattooing of the body was carried out in honor of the gods, using motifs that were symbols or emblems of individual deities that were worshiped by the wearer of the tattoo. Tattooing was banned by early Christian missionaries for that reason. In the 1700s, the art of tattooing was revived in Western Europe by pilgrims to Jerusalem who had been given Christian tattoos there. Today, we can see tattoos used to decorate the body that include runes in their design.

BELOW In ancient Europe, people tattooed their bodies to honor the gods. In recent times, this ancient art has enjoyed a revival, and runic designs are popular as tattoos.

PART TWO

WHAT THE RUNES MEAN

★ ★ ★ ★ ★

The Elder Futhark is the basis for all the runes. It came first, and all other systems are derived from it. Later systems have modified some of the meanings, but the basic interpretations were not changed until the emergence of individualistic ideas in the twentieth century. Knowing the traditional rune meanings enables us to use the runes for meditation, magic, and divination.

The runes' meanings cover every aspect of the traditional culture of Northern Europe. They speak of an age of agriculture, manual and craft work, sailing, animal power, and hand-to-hand combat, containing no reference to contemporary technology. But because they reveal principles rather than descriptions of physical objects, they are as useful now as they ever were. The principles present in the meanings of the runes still apply in the modern world.

The rune systems derived from the Elder Futhark have their own "personalities," which retain something of the place and time where and when they came into being. None is any better than any other, but one may be more appropriate under different circumstances. The choice is yours.

ABOVE A Viking chessman from a set originating from the Isle of Lewis, Scotland. Rune magic was often invoked in order to help the player win board games.

THE ELDER FUTHARK

★ ★ ★ ★ ★ ★ ★ ★ ★ ★ ★ ★ ★ ★ ★ ★

MOST RUNE USERS today work with the oldest and most widespread runic futhark, a rune-row with 24 characters. It has been studied more than any other version of the runes. This is the rune-row known either as the Common Germanic Futhark or the Elder Futhark. Like the letters of other alphabets, each of the runes has its own name that represents a sound. This is the basis of runic writing. But, since each runestave, or character, has a meaning, anything written in runes is also a combination of those meanings.

As with all alphabets, there is a definite order of letters in the Elder Futhark. In their correct order, the runes are a step-by-step development of meaning, a coherent whole made of 24 pieces. There is only one exception to the basic order. It is with the final two runes, Othala and Dagaz. In most versions of the Elder Futhark, Dagaz comes before Othala, which terminates the row. Occasionally, however, these two change places, making the last letters spell "OD."

RIGHT Rune meanings reflect the Norse way of life, with a rune for "harvest" but none for "city."

BELOW Rune names cover man, his property, and the natural world, featuring animals familiar to the Norsepeople, such as the elk.

Some see this as homage to the god Woden/Wotan (Odin) who discovered the runes. This order also fits in better with the cycle of the day and year because it begins again where it ends, with Dagaz, which signifies "day" or "dawn."

The main mystery of the runes lies in the rune names. They refer to various features of traditional culture. They include man and his property, as well as human artifacts and activities, such as the burning torch and harvest time. They tell of animals, such as the elk, cattle, and horses. Certain trees are there, including the yew and birch. Some of the runes are named after phenomena of the natural world, such as the sun, hail, and flowing water. The concepts of joy, need, defense, giving, and traveling are represented. Destruction is linked to the giants, as represented by the Thurisaz rune, while the power of creativity is conferred by other runes. The runes' names are only outward expressions, however. An animal or object also represents an inner quality. Each rune stands for the concept that its name represents. For example, cattle are literally a type of animal, but they also symbolize general wealth and strength.

Every system that attempts to describe the whole world has its own emphasis that reflects, at least in part, the time and place that it originated. The Elder Futhark is no different, for its rune-meanings have their own peculiarities. Because these meanings were set down in a male-dominated period,

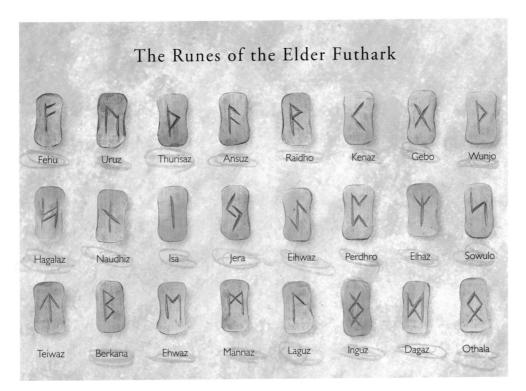

The Runes of the Elder Futhark

Fehu	Uruz	Thurisaz	Ansuz	Raidho	Kenaz	Gebo	Wunjo
Hagalaz	Naudhiz	Isa	Jera	Eihwaz	Perdhro	Elhaz	Sowulo
Teiwaz	Berkana	Ehwaz	Mannaz	Laguz	Inguz	Dagaz	Othala

the female principle is underrepresented. Although the runes include two gods – and the idea of "god" in general – there is no goddess directly named for a rune. There is no "woman"-rune at all, as there is for "man." There are no house-runes, weaving-runes, sweeping-runes, or other runes that refer to traditional women's work. The only reference to sexuality is male-oriented, while childbirth is implied by the birch-rune, which is associated with regeneration.

The Elder Futhark rune meanings focus on an outdoor life of agriculture, pastoralism, and raiding, rather than the more contained existence of the village or town. There are runes for land and harvest, but, just as there is no rune for "house," there are none for wall, bridge, temple, city, or castle.

Reflecting a simple, self-reliant society, there are no runes meaning "king," "queen," "priest," or "priestess." The Elder Futhark runes have a strong warrior influence. Though there is a rune that can mean the sword, there are no runes for the reaping-hook, ax, drill, saw, hammer, or plow. Weapon- and war-magic were some of the main concerns of runemasters in the first millennium after the runes appeared. Much of the documentation on runes from the Migration period (c.200–700 C.E.) to the Viking era (c.700–900 C.E.) tells of conflict and combat. Against such a background, in which a warlike way of life was celebrated, the runes understandably came to present a one-sided view of the world.

Since the 1970s, a new age of rune-use has dawned. Taking the original Elder Futhark as a starting-point, rune-workers in Europe and the United States have made significant steps towards overcoming this imbalance. Like all symbolic alphabets in use today, the runes have risen above their historical limitations.

BELOW A Swedish decorative plaque of the eighth century showing warriors. Runes date from an age that celebrated the warrior.

Interpreting the Elder Futhark
The First Aett

★★★★★★★★★★★★★★★★★★

The following eight runes belong to the first of the three aettir, or groups of runes, that make up the 24-rune Elder Futhark.

FEHU

The first rune of the Elder Futhark is Fehu. Its sound is "F."

As the primary rune of the first aett, Fehu symbolizes beginnings. Its literal meaning is "cattle," the same meaning as the first letters of the Hebrew, Greek, and Gothic alphabets. In Norse mythology, Audhumla, the primal cow, at the dawn of existence licked a block of salt from which emerged Buri, the father of the human race. On the earthly level, Fehu signifies movable wealth, for the herdspeople of ancient Europe measured their wealth in heads of cattle. Today, Fehu refers mainly to money and credit. In principle, Fehu is thus the power we need to gain worldly wealth, and to keep it, making it a rune of power and control. However, wealth brings responsibilities, as is stressed by a Norwegian rune poem: "Wealth causes friction between relatives, while the wolf lurks in the woods." Having wealth can lead to greed and envy, which divide society. Fehu is one of the few runes still present in the English language, in the word "fee," meaning a payment. It can also be found in *Jack and the Beanstalk*, in which the wealth-loving giant begins his well-known refrain "Fee, Fie, Fo, Fum, I smell the blood of an Englishman!" with the runic "fee" referring to his riches.

BELOW The shape of Uruz reflects the horns of the aurochs, a once-extinct, primitive form of ox now reintroduced by selective breeding.

URUZ

The second rune is Uruz. Its sound is "OO." This rune represents the great European wild ox called the aurochs, which was admired and feared for its awesome bulk and strength, and its long, sharp, curving horns. The Anglo-Saxon rune poem tells us: "The aurochs is bold, with horns rising high, a fierce horn-fighter who stamps across the moorlands, a striking beast!" The shape of the rune represents the horns of the aurochs. Unfortunately, the animal is now extinct. In Britain, it was exterminated in the 1200s, and the last aurochs of all was shot in Poland

ABOVE This primitive French clay figure captures the power of the primal ox, symbolized by Uruz.

in 1627. Symbolically, Uruz signifies the tameless power of the primal ox, the boundless power of the universe. Above all others, Uruz is the rune of inner strength, stamina, and perseverance. It is also a rune of healing. However, this empowering ability can never be used selfishly, never owned or controlled by a single individual for his or her own benefit. The influence of Uruz can bring personal success, but it will not be at the expense of others.

THURISAZ

The third rune is called Thurisaz. Its sound is "Th." In this form, Thurisaz is still part of the Icelandic alphabet. Thurisaz is protective. Shaped like a thorn, it symbolizes the power of resistance characterized by thorn trees, and the massive resistance of the earth-giants known as *thurses* or *moldthurs*. Thorns protect the plant on which they grow, but they do this passively, deterring attackers. Similarly, the Thurisaz rune channels defensive powers, and it can produce a sudden change without warning. It is the willful force of the generative principle, the masculine creative energy in action. Used effectively, it can significantly alter the way that things are going. Depending on how it is used, Thurisaz can represent defense or attack against adversaries. Thurisaz's trees are the blackthorn (*Prunus spinosa*), the may tree or hawthorn (*Crataegus monogyna*), and the bramble (*Rubus fruticosa*). The Thurisaz rune is still used in England. It appears in the rune's variant shape, "Y" (for "th"), in old inn-signs such as Ye Olde Cheshire Cheese, off Fleet Street, London.

RIGHT The thorns on hawthorn trees have a protective power, which is encapsulated in Thurisaz.

ANSUZ

The fourth rune in the Elder Futhark is Ansuz, the "god-rune." It also carries the newer names, As, Aesc, Asa. Its sound is "AA," as in "aah." Ansuz is the rune of divine force. It symbolizes the divine breath that powers existence, of which the gods and goddesses are the most perfect expression. Ansuz is also the divine source within human beings, an energetic controller of consciousness and of all intellectual activities. This rune is named for the ash tree (*Fraxinus excelsior*), one of the most sacred trees of the Northern Tradition and, specifically in Norse tradition, the tree of life, the World Tree, Yggdrasil, the cosmic axis that links all the worlds of creation. It is a symbol of stability, as the Anglo-Saxon rune poem tells us: "Humans love the ash tree, towering high. Though many enemies come forth to fight it, it keeps its place well, in a firm position." Ansuz thereby represents the divine order that stands firm no matter how difficult conditions may become. It is the divine stability that we can rely upon in difficult times.

ABOVE The ash tree was one of the most sacred objects in the natural world for the Norsepeople.

RAIDHO

The fifth rune is called Raidho or Raed. Its sound is "R." Literally, it represents the wheel and the motion that the wheel allows. Figuratively, it signifies the "vehicle" that we use to achieve an objective. But just as a wheeled vehicle cannot be used without a road on which to run, Raidho also represents the road or process itself. Raidho is both the way forward and the means to get there. Raidho is the rune of rites and ceremonies, events performed according to prearranged principles and plans. Raidho allows us to channel our energies in effective ways. This rune helps spirit, matter, or information to move or flow from one place to another, and so produce desired results.

The connected meanings of Raidho are "a raid" and also "music." Although these may seem very different from each other, they have in common that to perform either of them well requires dedicated practice and planning. Every circumstance, both inside and outside us, must be right. To take full advantage of Raidho, we must be in the right place at the right time, doing the right thing. This needs conscious awareness and foresight.

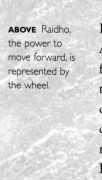

ABOVE Raidho, the power to move forward, is represented by the wheel.

KENAZ

The sixth rune is Kenaz, the rune of knowledge, as in the northern British dialect word "ken." Its sound is "K." Literally, Kenaz denotes a flaming brand, a fiery chip of resinous pine wood that in former times provided light. The Anglo-Saxon rune poem describes it thus: "The torch is living fire, bright and shining. Most often, it burns where noble people are at rest indoors." Because Kenaz gives us light in the darkness that surrounds us, it equally, on a symbolic level, brings the inner light of knowledge. Kenaz is a rune of teaching and learning, empowering all positive actions. It can be written in several different ways. Its most common form is a chevron (above left), and also a branch coming from a straight stem, (above right). The upright form is the shape of the ancient means of lighting, known in Germany as the *Kienspanhalter*, a floor-standing holder of the flaming pine-wood sliver. As the hearth fire, this rune represents the power of the forge in which material is transformed through the smith's skill into something new and useful, just as disordered raw materials are rearranged into an ordered form by the human consciousness. Kenaz can be used in meditations of personal illumination.

RIGHT Kenaz represents a flaming torch of pine wood.

GEBO

The seventh rune is Gebo. Its sound is "G," as in "gift." It is the X-shaped "sacred mark," the linking rune that symbolizes connections between people or gods. "Giving ... is an ornament that displays worth," the Anglo-Saxon rune poem tells us. It is "substance and honor." Literally, Gebo is a gift that brings about connections between people through exchange. It symbolizes unity between the donor and the person to whom the gift is given, creating a state of balance and harmony. Gebo is personified by the Norse goddess Gefn, "The Bountiful Giver." It gives us the power to link ourselves with other people, helping further a common cause or a business partnership. When illiterate people "signed" a document that bound them to an oath or contract, they used the Gebo rune to make their mark, signifying a gift from one to another. Gebo also links the human world with the divine. In rune work, we should write Gebo as a crossing of two lines only when we mean the general principle of giving. At other times, we should use a combination of two strokes, > and <. When these are written horizontally, they represent a link between two people on an equal basis. But when written one above the other, these strokes symbolize a connection between humans and other powers, either above in Asgard, or below, in Utgard.

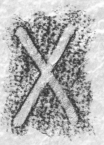

RIGHT Gebo symbolizes the harmony of exchange between people.

WUNJO

The eighth and final rune of the first aett is called Wunjo. Its sound is "W." Wunjo's shape represents a metal wind-vane, such as those used on Viking ships, pagan temples, and stave churches in Scandinavia. (Stave churches were early Christian buildings made of wood and supported on masts. No Scandinavian temples survive, but it is quite possible that stave churches were modeled on

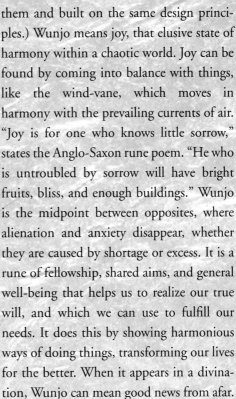

them and built on the same design principles.) Wunjo means joy, that elusive state of harmony within a chaotic world. Joy can be found by coming into balance with things, like the wind-vane, which moves in harmony with the prevailing currents of air. "Joy is for one who knows little sorrow," states the Anglo-Saxon rune poem. "He who is untroubled by sorrow will have bright fruits, bliss, and enough buildings." Wunjo is the midpoint between opposites, where alienation and anxiety disappear, whether they are caused by shortage or excess. It is a rune of fellowship, shared aims, and general well-being that helps us to realize our true will, and which we can use to fulfill our needs. It does this by showing harmonious ways of doing things, transforming our lives for the better. When it appears in a divination, Wunjo can mean good news from afar.

ABOVE Wind-vanes, with the same shape as Wunjo, feature in Scandinavia's unique form of religious architecture, the stave church.

The Second Aett

★ ★ ★ ★ ★ ★ ★ ★ ★ ★ ★ ★ ★ ★ ★

The following eight runes, together with their meanings, make up the second aett of the Elder Futhark.

HAGALAZ

The second aett begins with Hagalaz, the ninth rune. Its sound is "H." Like the other two runes at the beginning of this aett, all three of which are associated with the first part of winter, Hagalaz is icy and constricting. Literally, the name means "hailstone," which is water transformed for a short time from liquid into solid. During this time, the hailstone falls from the sky violently, often destroying crops or property. But once the damage is done, it melts. Transformation is the ruling principle here, like the sudden transformation that a snowstorm brings. Green fields and black roads are transformed rapidly into a sea of whiteness. Equally transformative is the thaw, when the colors of the land are restored. On a personal level, Hagalaz is the rune of the unconscious mind and of the formative processes of thought. On an impersonal level, Hagalaz lies at the roots of existence. Hagalaz is one of the major runes of Örlog, those laws of existence through which the patterns of events in our past shape our present. Hagalaz gives us access to energies originating in the past that are still active in the present. It offers us the power of evolution within the framework of present existence.

NAUDHIZ

The tenth rune is called Naudhiz or Not. Its sound is "N." Naudhiz represents the two balks of wood once used for kindling the need-fire, a powerful ritual fire that was only kindled at times of disaster, such as famine or an outbreak of plague in cattle. Naudhiz literally means "need," which is both scarcity and the absence of things, as well as the principle of necessity. All needs are constraints, and we see that Naudhiz restricts our possibilities. This is brought out in the Anglo-Saxon rune poem, which calls Nyd (the Anglo-Saxon name for Naudhiz) a "tight band across the chest." But within the Naudhiz rune is also the power to be released from need: "It can often be turned into a symbol of help," we are told, "if heeded early enough." Like Hagalaz before it, Naudhiz is a rune of change. When we use Naudhiz, we must be cautious, bearing in mind the ancient maxim "know thyself." In using it, we must not attempt to strive against our wyrd – fate – but should use it constructively. Then it may enable us to overcome difficulties. Normally, however, the rune binds and hinders us.

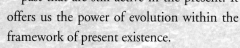

ABOVE Naudhiz stands for the two pieces of wood used to kindle the sacred need-fire.

ISA

The eleventh rune is called Isa. Its sound is "EE," as in "east." Literally, Isa means "ice," and its form is an icicle, straight, vertical, and unmoving. "Ice is too cold," says the Anglo-Saxon rune poem. "It shines like glass, just like a jewel ... fair to see." The Isa rune symbolizes static existence, the present time. Ice is beautiful to look at, but it does nothing, and it was of no use to the ancients. Symbolically, Isa is a rune that stops all activity. Ice forms because of the loss of energy that turns a liquid to a solid. The static resistance of ice replaces the fluidity of water. Isa signifies delay or a halt in the progress of something, or the termination of a relationship. Although ice is static, it sometimes moves in a mass. When it does so, as in a glacier, it flows with irresistible force. In this form, Isa represents inexorable processes against which we can do nothing. Also, when it is in the form of an iceberg, the depth of floating ice is deceptive, for we can see only one-ninth of the true mass above the surface. So the effects of Isa, which may seem insignificant, contain unsuspected implications and dimensions.

JERA

Jera or Jara is the twelfth rune. Its sound is "J," as in "jam." Meaning "year" or "season," Jera refers to the cycles of existence. It is the rune of completion at the proper time, for a plentiful harvest can only happen if the right things have been done at the right time. Jera cannot act against the natural order of things, but, when it is used properly, results will be beneficial, bringing – as the Anglo-Saxon rune poem states – "a bright abundance for rich and poor." The Jera rune is written in two different ways. One is on an upright stem, bearing a diamond shape. This form represents a stable state once it has been achieved. It symbolizes the cosmic axis surrounded by the four seasons in their correct order. Here, Jera is a pictogram of an actual object – the harvest garland, with its supporting pole. The other form is composed of two angled staves or characters, like two Kenaz runes that interpenetrate one another without touching. This is Jera's dynamic form, representing change toward completion.

LEFT Isa represents time captured in the eternal present, motionless and pure, like an icicle.

ABOVE One form of Jera, meaning "year" or "season," is based on the shape of the harvest garland.

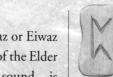

EIHWAZ

The rune called Eihwaz or Eiwaz is the thirteenth rune of the Elder Futhark. Eihwaz's sound is "EO." It is one of the most powerful runes, representing the yew tree (*Taxus baccata*). Early rune-magicians cut double-ended staves, or rods, of life and death from yew trees. Because it combines remarkable longevity with toxicity, the yew possesses both the powers of death and regeneration. Because it is the longest-lived of all European trees and is green throughout the year, the yew is a tree of life. Some ancient yews that have partially died are regenerated by their own daughter trees that grow in their decaying interiors. These, especially, are true symbols of life's continuity. Others, the so-called "bleeding yews," have never-healing wounds. Red resin flows like blood from these wounds, but the tree is unaffected. Bleeding yews are considered to be sacred, healing trees. But the yew has another side, for its bark, leaves, roots, fruit, and resin are all extremely poisonous. Thus the rune Eihwaz is sometimes called the "death rune," a power reinforced by its position in the rune-row as "unlucky 13." To the rune-masters of old, the Eihwaz rune is a magical protector and facilitator.

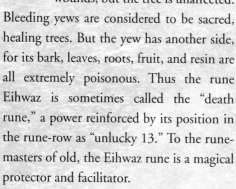

ABOVE Eihwaz represents the yew tree, which is remarkable for its longevity.

PERDHRO

The fourteenth rune is called Perdhro or Perthro. Its sound is "P." Perdhro's most common interpretation is the "dice cup" used to cast lots. Another possible meaning is a pawn or game-piece. Both dice and game-pieces symbolize the uncertainties of the game of life. As a game-piece, Perdhro symbolizes the interaction between personal freewill and the constraints of our circumstances. When we play, the pattern of the board and the rules of movement of the game-pieces are already laid down. But beyond these limitations the actual movements of our game are free. How the game is played depends upon the skill and will of the players, and their interaction. Perdhro is a also a rune of memory and recollection, problem-solving, and esoteric knowledge. It gives us access both to the inner secrets of the human world and also to the inner workings of nature. It empowers us with the ability to distinguish things of value from those that are worthless. Modern pagans see Perdhro as the womb of the Great Goddess that brings all life into existence. In this sense, it exposes things that previously were concealed, turning potential into physical reality.

LEFT Perdhro, which stands for the conflict between freewill and fate, is associated with gambling.

ELHAZ

At fifteenth position in the Elder Futhark rune-row is a powerful rune of protection called Elhaz or Algiz. Its sound is "ZZ," as in "buzz." Its shape symbolizes the stupendously resistant power of the elk, whose antlers strike fear into its enemies. Seeing the threatening antlers, none dare attack, and the elk wins without a fight. Elhaz also symbolizes the

ABOVE The power of the elk, with its mighty antlers, is captured in the protective rune Elhaz.

hardy "elongated" or "beaked" sedge plant (*Carex rostrata*), whose sharp leaves repel would-be eaters. To the runemaster, Elhaz is the most powerfully defensive sign of all, for it has the ability to repel all evil. Above all others, it is the rune of personal protection. Visualization of the rune around your body provides a potent shield against all kinds of physical and psychic attack. The Elhaz rune is equally effective in safeguarding property, especially buildings and vehicles. The supportive, defensive power of Elhaz promises protection against all of those forces or influences, known and unknown, which conflict with us. Symbolically, it represents the power of the human being striving toward the divine, with the assistance of otherworldly support.

SOWULO

The sixteenth and final rune of the second aett is called Sowulo or Sowilo. Its sound is "S." Like Elhaz, Sowulo is a rune of great force that embodies and channels the power of the sun, which it symbolizes. But it does not just stand for energy: it also symbolizes the illumination that the sun provides. Literally, Sowulo is the vital quality of daylight. Figuratively, it stands for the transhuman powers we need to achieve our objectives. Sowulo signifies power directed in a devastatingly straightforward way, without hindrances. Its shape resembles a flash of lightning, which describes its effects graphically. (Sowulo does not symbolize a lightning flash, however, which is the function of the Ziu rune.) Sowulo resists the forces of death and disintegration, heralding the triumph of light over darkness. Because of this, it is the rune that illuminates our goals. "To seamen navigating across the fishes' bath, the sun means hope," says the Anglo-Saxon rune poem, "until the horse of the sea brings them to harbor." Having clear vision and keeping our goals in sight in the light of Sowulo helps us to reach them.

BELOW The immensely powerful Sowulo is linked with the force and brightness of the sun.

The Third Aett

★ ★ ★ ★ ★ ★ ★ ★ ★ ★ ★ ★ ★ ★ ★ ★ ★

The third aett of the Elder Futhark is made up of the following eight runes.

TEIWAZ

The first rune of the third aett is the Teiwaz rune. Its sound is "T." Like Ansuz, Teiwaz is a god rune, being the rune of the ancient Northern European sky god Tîwaz. He was known in old England as Tîw and in Scandinavia as Tyr, and gave his name to the third day of the week, Tuesday. The power of Teiwaz is recounted in Norse myth when the courageous god sacrificed his right hand to allow the binding of the destructive Fenris-wolf that threatened the cosmic order. Thus Teiwaz is the rune of positive regula-

ABOVE Teiwaz represents personal sacrifice, in remembrance of the god Tîwaz, who sacrificed his hand in order to bind the Fenris-wolf. However, Fenris is destined to break free at the end of the world, as in this sixth-century helmet plate.

tion that needs personal sacrifice to carry it through to a successful result. Any success that comes through Teiwaz will be tempered by sacrifice, whether that means personal stress, hard work, or financial risk. The rune's spearlike shape represents the targeting of positive forces in the correct place for the greatest effect. Like the Sowulo rune, Teiwaz also promises successful achievement of our objectives. Teiwaz works especially well in legal matters. Here, however, success will come only if you are in the right to begin with. Travesties of justice do not happen when Teiwaz is empowered.

BERKANA

Representing the birch tree (*Betel pendulum*), the eighteenth rune is called Berkana or Birkana. Its sound is "B." The rune's shape represents the breasts of the Earth Mother goddess called anciently Nerthus, Berchta, or Frau Percht. The birch is a tree with white bark traditionally associated with purification. As the first tree to recolonize the barren land when the ice retreated at the end of the last Ice Age, it also symbolizes regeneration, springtime, and the returning warmth after coldness. Berkana stands for new beginnings, especially in the female sphere, where it is a birth rune. Berkana is powerful in all women's matters. In folk tradition, birch twigs are used for the "brush" part of the besom, or broom, used for sweeping away any bad luck. In some parts of Europe, whole birch trees are used as maypoles. Berkana's number – 18 – is double the sacred nine, being symbolic of completion and new beginnings on a higher, organic, level. It marks the point at which the primal laws of existence have been defined, and the stage is set for the play of life to begin in earnest.

RIGHT The Berkana rune stands for the birch tree, whose white bark makes it emblematic of purification.

EHWAZ

The rune called Ehwaz is the nineteenth stave. It is the horse rune, and its sound is "E," as in "every." Its shape is an ideogram of the horse. Horses were the most sacred animals of pagan Europe, being the steeds of several goddesses and gods. In the Baltic and Slavic countries,

ABOVE Ehwaz is the horse rune, recalling the trust between rider and animal.

they were used in divination, and holy horses graced the temples of Pomerania (on the southern shores of the Baltic Sea), Saxony, and England. The Anglo-Saxon rune poem tells proudly of the horse as "the joy of peers, stepping out with pride when talked about by wealthy riders everywhere, and to the restless, always a comfort." The horse rune symbolizes the forging of an unbreakable bond, like that between horse and rider. True partnerships require absolute trust and loyalty, so faithfulness is an absolute necessity for those who use this rune. Ehwaz demands a serious intention to carry a matter right through to completion. The horse is also a means of getting from one place to another, linking the connection between the starting point and the destination. Ehwaz enables us to create the impetus that we need to carry any task through from beginning to ending.

MANNAZ

The rune called Mannaz is the twentieth stave of the Elder Futhark. Its sound is "M." Mannaz represents the basic human qualities we all have, whether we are male or female: it signifies the shared experience of us all. Its shape represents the archetypal human being whom we see as a reflection of all things in existence. Symbolically, Mannaz stands for social order, without which we cannot achieve our full human potential. Its shape reflects the idea of mutual support. Its stems are linked by the Gebo cross into a rigid, stable, form, just as, when we support one another, we ourselves are stable. Because language is a prime faculty of human beings, Mannaz is classified as a *hugrune*, one of the runes of the mind. This rune is reflected in everything that is connected with language. By using it, we are able to gain advantage in disputes and academic examinations. A related meaning of Mannaz is the tree. This reflects the Scandinavian legend in which the first humans were made from trees. Askr, the first man, came from an ash tree, and Embla, the first woman, was a transformed elm.

BELOW This carving of a Viking warrior balanced on either side by his weapons, both recalls the shape of Mannaz and symbolizes its message.

LAGUZ

The twenty-first rune, Laguz represents water in its many phases and moods. Its sound is "L." Because water flows, Laguz represents fluidity. The power of this rune is embodied in the power of the tides and the force of waterfalls. The Anglo-Saxon rune poem tells us of this rune's danger: "To landlubbers, water seems troublesome if they put to sea in a tossing ship. The waves terrify them." The power of the sea is irresistible, and we must "go with the flow" or be destroyed. Laguz demonstrates the law of the unity of opposites present in many runes. Although we cannot live without water for long, neither can we live in water for long. A subsidiary meaning of Laguz is also embodied in the vegetable leek – a magical "herb" with a vigorous, upright power of growth – for the rune represents the abundant force of life present in physical matter and organic growth. But growth is not continuous. Organic growth proceeds in cycles, as can be seen in the growth rings of seashells and trees. The cyclical nature of growth is present in Laguz as the ebb and flow of the tide. Laguz clears blockages in progress, accelerating flows already taking place.

BELOW Laguz, the rune of the labial sound "l," is the rune of water, which played a major part in the life of seafaring Vikings.

INGUZ

The twenty-second rune is called Inguz or Ingwaz. It is a symbol of light, representing a beacon or firebrand. Its sound is "NG," as in "long." This rune can be written in two ways. One is a closed, contained form, shaped like the "diamond" in playing cards. This symbolizes the inner fire and appears

ABOVE The name of the god of fire, Inguz, survives in our word "inglenook," he is guardian of the hearth fire.

frequently on the walls of traditional buildings in Northern Europe. The second form is outgoing, with spreading lines denoting limitless expansion, carrying one's energy outward into the surroundings, showing its light far and wide. Like Teiwaz, the Inguz rune represents a god with the same name. He is the male consort of the Earth Mother, the goddess of fertility and nurture. Inguz is god of male fertility and the house hearth, the inglenook, so this rune is protective of households. More generally, Inguz signifies energy. Symbolically, the Inguz rune channels potential energy, bringing together and integrating previously separate things. However, although it is powerful, Inguz's energy is not immediate. It builds up gradually until it is so strong that it must be released in a single burst, like a male orgasm.

DAGAZ

Dagaz is the last but one rune of the Elder Futhark. Its sound is "D." Dagaz means "day" and its shape represents stable balance between polar opposites, especially light and darkness. It is the rune of the light of day, especially midday and midsummer, the high points of the light in both day and year. These are times of strength and well-being. The Anglo-Saxon rune poem says: "Day, God's message, is precious to people. The light of the Lord gives gladness and hope, to rich and poor, for the benefit of all." Some rune-users call Dagaz the "dawn rune." Its shape signifies balance between light and dark, enclosure and openness, ascending and descending powers. Dagaz has great protective power and is also a very beneficial rune of light, health, prosperity, and openings. It serves to stop harm from entering, while still allowing in those things that we need. Traditionally, to bring luck, this rune was painted or carved on doors, shutters, doorposts, and other uprights in the house.

In the spiritual realm, Dagaz gives people access to cosmic consciousness.

LEFT Dagaz, which means "day," is the rune for balance, such as that between light and dark.

OTHALA

The rune known as Othala or Odhil is the final rune of the Elder Futhark. Its sound is "O," as in "old." In the Frisian language, spoken in what is now northeastern Germany and The Netherlands, this rune was called *Eeyen-eerde*, meaning "own earth" or "own land."

LEFT
A traditional Danish farmhouse. Othala stands for family and clan property.

This name perfectly defines the rune's meaning of ancestral heritage in the form of family and clan land. In the traditional law of Northern Europe, this land could never be sold. It was eternal property, handed on from generation to generation. With this meaning, Othala's shape represents an enclosure whose contents cannot be taken away. Symbolically, the rune maintains the existing state of things. Othala resists arbitrary rules, preserving individual and collective liberty within the framework of natural law. This is true wealth. The position of Othala at the end of the Elder Futhark reflects Fehu at the beginning. Fehu is wealth that can be traded, while Othala is wealth that cannot be sold. Between them come all other aspects of human life. Othala is more than physical property. It also signifies the cultural and spiritual heritage that we received from our ancestors. It empowers our relationships with other people in our group or family.

ANGLO-SAXON AND
NORTHUMBRIAN RUNES

* * * * * * * * * * * * * * * * * *

As EARLY AS the sixth century B.C.E., rapid changes in language in Frisia brought a need for new letters. Runemasters responded to this by adding four new runes to the Elder Futhark. They were Ac, the oak; Aesc, the ash; Os, mouth or speech; and Yr, the yew, or yew bow. These 28 Frisian runes were brought to Britain by Frisian, Anglian, Saxon, and Jutish settlers from mainland Europe. There, around the end of the seventh century, a further, twenty-ninth rune was added to create the Anglo-Saxon rune-row. This new rune was called Ear, meaning "earth-grave." The Thames scramasax (*see page 28*) bears an early full example of this row. Another early Anglo-Saxon rune-row is in a manuscript known as the *Vienna Codex*, kept in the Austrian national library. There are also many other Anglo-Saxon runic inscriptions in existence today, found on stone and in manuscripts.

ABOVE The *Vienna Codex*, a ninth-century Anglo-Saxon manuscript, shows scenes of everyday life, and also includes a complete Anglo-Saxon rune-row.

When the scholars added new letters to the Elder Futhark, they also changed the rune order. Unlike the Elder Futhark, which was strongly fixed, the two main Anglo-Saxon examples are not the same. What the *Vienna Codex* and Thames scramasax rows have in common is that the fourth rune,

Ansuz ("A") is replaced by a new rune, Os ("O"). Ansuz, renamed Aesc, becomes the twenty-sixth rune. The remaining runes of the *Vienna Codex* row then adhere to the standard Elder Futhark order. The twenty-fourth rune is Othala, the last rune of the Elder Futhark, followed by the final runes Ac, Aesc, Ear, and Yr. In the Thames scramasax version, the last eight runes are in a different order, the final rune being Ear. Although the letters remain the same, the Anglo-Saxon rune poem offers yet another, third variation on the rune order from those in both the Thames scramasax and the *Vienna Codex* rune-rows.

Additional runes appeared in the Anglian kingdom of Northumbria, which covered the part of England north of the Humber River and southern Scotland. There was continuous interchange between Northumbria, Frisia, and Scandinavia at this period. There is also some Christian influence. The early eighth-century Ruthwell Cross, in Dumfries, Scotland, uses 31 runes in its Anglo-Saxon text of the Christian poem *The Dream of the Rood*. Two are unique forms not seen elsewhere, and another Ruthwell rune is from the Scandinavian Younger Futhark. The Anglo-Saxon rune poem describes a twenty-ninth rune, Iar, meaning a water beast. Finally, around 800 C.E., the Northumbrian rune-row stabilized at 33 runes. Some of the Northumbrian runes then found their way back to Frisia.

The later Northumbrian runes seem to have been influenced by Celtic tradition. Irish and Scottish monks taught the beliefs and customs of the Celtic Church in

Northumbria before they were banished by the Roman Catholics in 664 C.E. The Celtic Church had reinterpreted the pre-Christian lore of the Celtic Druids. This included the Ogham tree alphabet, in which each letter was named for a tree and symbolized its qualities. Runic codes used in Northumbria and Scandinavia worked on the same principle as the Celtic Oghams, where numbers of strokes of different kinds stood for letters. Runes and Ogham appear together in the *Book of Ballymote*, an Irish text of 1391.

Because there are 33 runes, the Northumbrian Futhork gives us a wider range of meanings than the Elder Futhark can. Some of the meanings are completely different, while others are extensions or refinements. The god rune Ansuz, for instance, is split up into two runes, Os and Aesc. The first means the godly function of speech. In Christian tradition, in the beginning was the Word, and the Word was God. The second rune, Aesc, has the godly meaning of stability, symbolized in the immobile World Tree, Yggdrasil. The new yew rune, Yr, takes over the meaning of the bow from the Elder Futhark rune Eihwaz. As in the Anglo-Saxon runes, the oak rune, Ac, is completely new, as are the final runes.

Today, the Northumbrian rune-row is not used as much as the Elder Futhark. Because it is more complex, it takes longer to learn the meanings and thus become a proficient rune-user. But it is worth the effort. Any technique described in the book for use with the Elder Futhark can also be used with the Northumbrian Futhork. Readings made with the English runes have a slightly different character from those using the Elder Futhark. Whichever we use is purely a matter of personal choice.

LEFT An inscription in the old Irish tree alphabet known as Ogham, on a stone from County Kerry.

RIGHT The eighth-century Ruthwell Cross in southern Scotland, inscribed with a Christian rune poem. This is the finest example of the early Northumbrian rune-row, still in transition from the Anglo-Saxon runes.

Interpreting the Anglo-Saxon and Northumbrian Runes

* * * * * * * * * * * * * * * * *

THE ANGLO-SAXON FUTHORK includes the runes of the Elder Futhark, plus four Frisian runes and one other rune to make a total of 29 staves in all. The Northumbrian Futhork builds on the Anglo-Saxon rune-row by adding a further four staves to make 33 in total. The Anglo-Saxon and Northumbrian runes therefore contain a fourth aett – which is known colloquially as the "aett of the gods" – in addition to the three aettir of the Elder Futhark (*see pages 50–61 for interpretations*). The runes of the fourth aett are interpreted below.

Ac

The fourth aett begins with the twenty-fifth rune, Ac. This has the sound of a short "A," as in "cat." Its literal meaning is "oak tree," the holy tree of the sky- and thunder-gods Tîwaz and Thunor (Tyr and Thor). It is a rune of usefulness. "Oak on earth, useful to men," says the Anglo-Saxon rune poem, "food for pigs, often it travels on the gannets' bath, as the sharp spears test whether the oak endures nobly." Ac is a rune that symbolizes great potential power, as exemplified by the acorn, from which grows the mighty oak. Seemingly insignificant, this seed contains the awesome capability of massive growth. Ac channels the power of strong, continuous growth from small beginnings to a mighty climax, assisting our creative and productive processes. Long-time endurance is the power of the oak. It is 300 years growing, 300 years mature, and 300 years in decline. Once dead, its wood can last indefinitely in the form of the timbers of a building.

Aesc and Os

The second rune of the fourth aett was originally Ansuz, the fourth rune in the Elder Futhark. When the Anglo-Saxons extended the Elder Futhark, they moved Ansuz into twenty-sixth place, called it Aesc and put a new rune called Os in its place, with the sound "O," as in "open." The Futhark thereby became a Futhork! However, there was still a close connection between the meanings of Aesc (Ansuz) and Os. Literally, Os means "mouth," and, by extension, speech, song, and language. Like Aesc, Os is also a god rune, belonging to the god Odin in his aspect as master of communication through language and writing. Os denotes the creative power of the word and hence wisdom itself. Speech is the fundamental ability that enables human culture to exist. All traditional knowledge, history, and cultural identity is expressed in poetry, song, oral saga, and written literature. More generally, Os signifies information in every meaning of the word. The Os rune is at its most powerful when called or chanted repeatedly during meditation, in what is known as *galdr*, or runic incantation, which is said to bring the powers of the cosmic breath into action.

Yr

The twenty-seventh rune is called Yr. Its sound is "Y," as in "yoga." Yr signifies a bow made from the wood of the yew tree. In the extended Northumbrian Futhork, Yr takes over this bow meaning from Eihwaz. Its shape may represent the *arbalest* or crossbow, a more powerful form of bow, used in ancient times by huntsmen and soldiers. Yr symbolizes the perfect combination of skills and knowledge applied to materials taken from nature. As well as being used as a bringer of death, the bow was used in divination to find special places. In medieval Europe, there were two ways that locators used the bow to find a special place. One was to shoot an arrow in a certain direction. Where the arrow fell, that was the place. This technique appears in the legend of Robin Hood: both his and Little John's burial places were defined by the fall of arrows. In 1219, the location on which to build Salisbury Cathedral was divined in the same way. The other method of location was to use the tensioned bow as a kind of water-divining rod. Whether representing a weapon or a divining tool, Yr is the rune of being in the right place – literally "on target." It is therefore most valuable for finding lost objects, or for locating a special spot.

ABOVE The bow could be used in divination; an arrow shot at random supposedly determined the burial place of Robin Hood.

IOR

Ior, the "water beast," is the twenty-eighth rune. Its sound is "IO," as in "helios." This rune represents the World Serpent, Iormungand, which, in northern mythology, circles the Earth at the bottom of the ocean. In its shape, the Ior rune resembles the Younger Futhark character Hagal, but there is no other connection. The Ior rune symbolizes dual natures, evident in the amphibious habits of many water beasts. According to legend, Iormungand is a formidable and dangerous beast whose violent movements cause earthquakes and tidal waves that threaten to destabilize the world. As an essential part of the world's structure, however, Iormungand cannot be destroyed. Even if it became possible to eliminate the qualities it represents, this would produce a catastrophe far worse than the monster's continuing existence. Thus the Ior rune signifies those unavoidable hardships and problems with which we must come to terms so that our lives can be tolerable. Ior tells us that we should not worry about things we cannot change.

RIGHT The World Serpent, Iormungand, was represented by the rune Ior, the "water beast."

EAR

The final rune of the Anglo-Saxon Futhork is Ear, which has the sound "EA," as in "hear." It represents the soil of the Earth, the "earth-grave" of human beings. Figuratively, this is "the dust" to which our bodies return at death. "To every noble, the dust is dreadful," says the Anglo-Saxon rune poem, "… the flesh starts to cool, the body must choose the earth." Symbolizing the grave that marks the end of all life, Ear provides a fitting end to the Anglo-Saxon rune-row. But death occurs only because there has been life in the first place. Without life, there is no death, and without time, there is no life. More generally, then, the Ear rune signifies the unavoidable end of all things in time. In rune magic, Ear speeds up the arrival of an inevitable end point. Like Eihwaz and Yr, Ear is a rune of the yew tree. It is the third "death rune."

CWEORTH

The following four runes, beginning with Cweorth, appeared in Northumbria. The first of these runes is called Cweorth. Its sound is "Q." The Cweorth rune symbolizes the climbing, swirling flames of fire. Specifically, it refers to the sacredness of the hearth and ritual cleansing by fire. Overall, it is the process of transformation through fire. In the case of the funeral pyre, one of the aspects of Cweorth, fire serves to liberate the spirit. Equally, Cweorth denotes the festival bonfire of celebration and joy. In this way, Cweorth is the opposite to the need-fire, represented by the rune Nyd.

ABOVE A chalice, or ritual offering cup, denoted by Calc, depicted in a fifteenth-century manuscript.

CALC

The thirty-first rune is called Calc. Its sound is "K." Literally, Calc denotes a ritual container or an offering cup. In its shape, Calc is an inverted Elhaz rune. When it is viewed as such, Calc is interpreted as symbolizing the death of the individual. However, it is not a "death rune" in the literal sense. It does not indicate the impending death of someone or something but, like Ear, signifies the natural conclusion of a process. This is not termination but rather the end of an old way of being, resulting in spiritual transformation. Calc connects us with areas of existence that appear to be accessible, yet cannot be touched – the ungraspable, unattainable, and unknown. In medieval myth, Calc is the rune of the Holy Grail, the otherworldly cup that restores and heals the wasteland.

STAN

The last but one Northumbrian rune is called Stan. Its sound is "ST." Literally, Stan means "stone," and symbolizes all aspects of this substance. Fundamentally, it denotes the "bones of the Earth," the rock beneath our feet. Figuratively, it represents an obstruction, such as a boulder at the entrance to a cave. It also means a stone or playing piece used in a board game. This meaning is reinforced by its shape, which is the same as the ancient playing pieces used in Northern Europe. Symbolically, Stan represents a link between human beings, earthly and heavenly powers, which, like the barrier stone, either provides protection, or impedes progress.

The runemasters of old used the Stan rune to obstruct and prevent, turning back opposition and driving away any assailants. The Norse poem *The Lay of Hamdir* tells of a Stan spell cast by the "High Gods' Kinsman" (Odin):

He roared like bears roar:
'Stones to the stout ones,
That the spears bite not,
Nor the edges of steel,
These sons of Jonakr!' .

GAR

The thirty-third and final rune of the Northumbrian Futhork is Gar. Its sound is "G," as in "gap." Gar has the literal meaning of a spear, specifically Gungnir, Odin's spear, which has a staff made of ash wood, making it a portable version of the World Tree Yggdrasil, on which Odin hung for nine days and nine nights before discovering the wisdom of the runes. Unlike the other 32 runes that are assigned to a particular aett, Gar does not belong to an aett in the Northumbrian system. It is a rune considered to contain all of the others. It is unique, representing the center point of space that is at the same time everywhere and nowhere. When the four aettir are written down in a circle, the Gar rune forms the central point. Gar represents the beginning of a brand new order of things.

LEFT A Viking chess piece, possibly representing Thor. One of the meanings of the Northumbrian rune Stan is a piece in a game. This posture is the "Iron Beard," a strength-producing technique of European martial arts.

LEFT A Viking spear. The final Northumbrian rune, Gar, refers to a spear – the spear's point represents the center point of space. Gar is always placed in the center of the rune row's four aettir.

THE YOUNGER FUTHARK

★ ★ ★ ★ ★ ★ ★ ★ ★ ★ ★ ★ ★ ★ ★

THE YOUNGER FUTHARK came into being through linguistic changes in Scandinavia during the seventh and eighth centuries. New sounds came into the language, and new letters were needed to write the new sounds down. When this happened in England, the 33-rune row was the final result. The Scandinavian runic scholars decided to take a different course. The carefully designed Elder Futhark was broken up. They got rid of eight runes, cutting down the original rune-row from 24 to 16 characters. At the same time, the letters themselves

ABOVE A Danish runic inscription in the Younger Futhark, introduced to incorporate new sounds emerging in the Scandinavian language.

were simplified wherever possible. Along with four others, the most complex runes, Gebo, Ingwaz, Othala, and Dagaz, were abolished completely. Where they were kept, runes with two uprights were reduced to a single stem.

The result of this revolutionary reformation was two slightly different versions of the Younger Futhark. Today they are called the Danish and the Swedish-Norse rune-rows, or Futharks. There are only small differences between them, so they are both classified as the Younger Futhark. The Swedish-Norse row is slightly later, and the runes are even simpler. Versions of this futhark appear on American runestones. Later, the process of simplification went further, producing the shorthandlike Hälsinge version.

Reducing the number of runes caused several problems. Instead of having one sound for each rune, the Younger Futhark had to give each rune several related sounds. Now a single rune could stand for up to six distinct sounds. This meant that, although it was shorter than the Elder Futhark, the Younger Futhark was far more complex and confusing. Condensing the rune-row also made it less explicit than the Elder rune-row had been. The Younger Futhark was a break with the tradition that each rune had a fixed meaning. Now meanings and sounds of the same rune had to change according to their context. Because the number of runes was reduced, some of the meanings also disappeared. Others were modified to include those that had been abolished.

In the Younger Futhark, the Elder Futhark god rune Ansuz was transformed into the rune Óss. In the Norwegian rune poem, this means "mouth of a river," a kenning for the "word of [a] god." The Elder Futhark rune Kenaz, "torch," acquired a different meaning in the Younger Futhark. It adopted the meaning given it by the Goths,

The Vikings

The Vikings were seafaring warrior-raiders who originated in Denmark, Sweden, and Norway. The Viking Age began with a seaborne raid upon the island monastery of Lindisfarne, off the coast of northeastern England, in the year 793 C.E. At first, Viking raids concentrated on the rich plunder available at poorly defended Celtic coastal and island monasteries in England, Scotland, and Ireland.

By 830, raiding and piracy had become a Scandinavian way of life. Manned by dedicated pagan warriors, armed with the most up-to-date weapons, and schooled in the northern martial arts, Viking ships were feared by everyone. Master mariners, the Vikings used traditional seafaring skills to navigate across the North Sea and Atlantic Ocean. As pagans, they used the runes to divine where they should attack and in which direction they should sail.

By the middle of the ninth century, Viking raids had developed into full-scale military invasions of the countries surrounding Scandinavia. Where they conquered, they settled. Viking settlements included the first towns in Ireland, northern and eastern parts of England, Normandy, and the founding of the state of Russia. They also settled in Iceland and Greenland.

ABOVE Some of the finest examples of Viking art, like this mythical animal's head, have been found in a ship burial at Oseberg in southern Norway.

Kaun, signifying an ulcer or abscess, which also signified spiritual illumination, but in a more obscure way. The Elder rune Uruz, symbolizing the primal power of the aurochs, or wild ox, and manly strength, became Ur, meaning "drizzle" or "slurry," the formless material of creation, a significant change in meaning. The only link between the two forms is on the symbolic level, since both relate to the primal energy.

Reducing the number of runes to 16 gave the Younger Futhark even less flexibility than the Elder Futhark and Anglo-Saxon and Northumbrian rune-rows. As in the Elder rune-row, the female principle is almost absent, but this already serious imbalance was accentuated even more by the Younger Futhark. Not only does it have no runes for life or love, and almost totally ignores nurture, but the scholars who invented it also abolished the Elder runes for "gift," "joy," "horse/partnership," and "ancestral property." They removed those runes that tell of nonviolent interhuman relations. The only

god rune left was Tyr. It cannot be a coincidence that the Younger Futhark was the Viking rune-row, used in a time when piracy and raiding was a way of life, and the warrior was applauded as the perfect role-model of manliness. Around 1150, the Younger Futhark was superseded by both the Roman alphabet and the longer rune-row known as the Pointed or Dotted Runes.

The Younger Futhark runes are not used much for divination. With only 16 meanings covering restricted possibilities, their usefulness is limited. There is

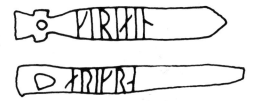

less chance to express fine points with so few combinations, so most diviners choose the Elder Futhark. But, ironically, these 16 Scandinavian runes did give rise, in the twentieth century, to the Armanen Runes, which remain influential in German-speaking countries, where the Younger Futhark had never previously penetrated.

ABOVE Drawings of *merkelapper* (wooden marking tags) from Bryggen, Norway, containing inscriptions of two of the simplified runes of the Younger Futhark, Kaun and Ar.

Interpreting the Younger Futhark

* * * * * * * * * * * * * * * * * *

THE DIVISION OF RUNE-ROWS into aettir cannot be effectively applied to the Younger Futhark. The 16 runes of this futhark have the following interpretations and associations.

FÉ

The first rune of the Younger Futhark is Fé (sound "F"). It has the same meaning as the corresponding runes in the Elder and Anglo-Saxon futharks – cattle and money – but also embodies the more specific meaning of gold. Fé is not all good, however, for it also warns against the divisiveness of unbalanced wealth, causing strife in families.

UR

Ur (sounds "U," "O," "Y," "W") means drizzle or slurry, the almost formless primal materials of creation. Ur is the lifeless volcanic ash that miraculously becomes fertile soil in which new things can grow. Symbolically, it is the emanation of the all from nothingness, the groundbase that all new things need to come into existence.

THURS

Thurs (sounds "Th," "Dh") means a giant, whose power overcomes all resistance. In legend, the giants have enormous power, carrying rocks to drop on their enemies. The runemasters of old used Thurs as a carrier rune, combining it with others in bindrunes or magic staves or signs called *galdrastafir*, such as the Icelandic *Svefnthorn* ("sleepthorn").

ÓSS

Óss (sound "O," as in "oh") means a god, with the subsidiary meaning of "mouth," both in the usual sense and that of an estuary, the "mouth" of a river. Symbolically, Óss signifies the commanding force of word or song, for it relates to Odin, also known as *Galdraföðhur*, "Father of Incantation."

RAEIDH

The Norwegian Raeidh or the Icelandic Reidh (sound "R") signify both the process of riding, as well as the means – horse, vehicle, and road. Equally, Raeidh can denote a physical journey or a spiritual pathway. Another reading is the sudden clap of thunder, ascribed in former times to Thor's wagon rolling across the heavens.

KAUN

Kaun (sound "K," "G") signifies a wound, sore, or ulcer. Kaun is the mystery of illness and illumination, where we gain new insights through suffering. This is the image of Odin gaining the runes through self-torture on the "windswept tree."

HAGALL

Like its Elder Futhark counterpart, Hagalaz, Hagall (sound "H") means hail, signifying a rapid transformation from a static to a fluid state. It is the rune of the goddess Holda or Frau Hölle, who covers the land with hail and snow, transforming its appearance.

NAUDHR

Like its Elder Futhark counterpart, Naudhr or Naudh (sound "N") signifies need or distress. But it has the more specific meanings of bondage and captivity, linked with need because we can all be enslaved by it.

IS

Is or Íss (sounds "I," "J," as in "year," "E") means ice, symbolizing the principle of contraction, the crystalization of spirit into matter. Static and unchanging, it embodies the resistant power of the ice-goddess Rinda.

AR

Ar (sound "A," as in "ah") signifies a good year. It is the rune of return. More specifically, Ar is the bumper harvest that comes from fertile land and healthy crops. Good results only come from application of skills at the right time.

SÓL

Sól (sound "S") stands for the goddess of the sun, called Sól in Scandinavia and Barbet in Germany and The Netherlands. Sól signifies directed action under spiritual control.

TYR

The rune Tyr (sounds "T," "D," "NT," "ND") stands for the god Tyr, the Scandinavian counterpart of the sky-god Teiwaz. Tyr signifies law and order in the human world and orderliness in the cosmos.

BJARKAN

The Bjarkan rune (sounds "B," "P," "V," "MB," "MP") represents a twig of the birch, the tree of purification and rebirth. As a woman's rune, Bjarkan symbolizes gestation and birth. Some maypoles – symbols of fertility – are made from birch trees.

MADHR

Madhr (sound "M") denotes a man. This means the generality of humankind and also the mythical ancestral "first man," Mannus or Mannaz. Madhr thus symbolizes continuity of the family and clan.

LOGR

Logr or Lögr (sound "L") denotes the power of the water in the form of both the waves of the ocean, and waterfalls. This is the irresistible power of flow, the life energy of the circulating blood within the body. Logr's symbolic meaning also signifies purification – a washing away of unwanted things, cleansing ourselves.

YR

Yr (sounds "Z," "R") denotes a bow made from the wood of the yew tree. It has the same meaning as the Anglo-Saxon Futhork rune Yr. Its shape symbolizes the three roots of the World Tree Yggdrasil. It is the entrance to the underworld, and in this form it is the "death rune" of Teutonic magic, where it is sometimes called Elgr.

GOTHIC AND MEDIEVAL RUNES

* * * * * * * * * * * * * * * *

THE GOTHS WERE one of the first peoples of Northern Europe to use the runes. The oldest complete rune-row is on a Gothic monument, the Kylver Stone. Gothic religion was Germanic in character. They worshiped the same gods as other northern nations, but when they settled in south-eastern Europe they adopted some of the Roman gods; they did not, however, adopt the Roman alphabet. They used runes for their religious dedications. For example, a Gothic pagan oath-ring, which was used in temples in the swearing of oaths and dates from the fourth century, was discovered at Pietroasa in Romania and was found to include runic inscriptions honoring "Jupiter, God of the Goths."

Because there is no Gothic rune poem, less is known about what individual Gothic runes mean. In 1928, in *Runorna i Sverige*, the Swedish researcher Otto von Friesen published a scholarly reconstruction of the Gothic runes. As well as their meanings, he also determined their genders. Compared with the Elder Futhark, they have a slightly different emphasis, but essentially they are the same.

Based in part on the Gothic runes, the real Gothic alphabet bears no relation to the decorative, medieval, "black-letter" Roman script often called "Gothic." Classically trained architects of the eighteenth century

ABOVE The Gothic invaders of the Roman Empire happily adopted the Roman gods, as shown by this drawing of a fourth-century oath-ring, whose runic inscription honors "Jupiter, God of the Goths."

considered all medieval architecture barbaric, so they called the style of the great cathedrals "Gothic" after the barbarian nation they supposed had destroyed Roman civilization. In fact, the Gothic alphabet was much older than high-medieval culture. It had originated in the middle of the fourth century, when Bishop Ulfila constructed a new alphabet so that he could write the Christian scriptures and prayer book in the Gothic language. Ulfila took the Gothic runes, based on the Elder Futhark, as the starting point for his new alphabet. Others were letters of the Greek alphabet, or new inventions. Ulfila added some new meanings, taken from Hellenic Greek, Gnostic Christian, and Arian Christian sources, thereby creating a distinct magical alphabet.

Ulfila's mission to the Goths largely failed, and he was sent away by their pagan king, Athaneric. He died in exile, but his alphabet proved useful, and the meanings then fed back into the Gothic runes. Most are related symbolically to the earlier meanings, but have a Christian flavor. They give us further insights into the overall meanings of the runes. Drawing on Greek cosmology, Ulfila added meanings relating to universal principles, symbolizing God's order. Daz, the rune of day, denoted the Holy City of God, the image of perfection. Eyz, formerly the horse rune, symbolized the *aether*, the cosmic medium that pervades creation. Thyth, equivalent to the rune Thurisaz, symbolized the crystal sphere of the heavens, on which the stars were believed to rest. Here, the cosmic order of God replaced the destructive power of the giants. Other

cosmic meanings include those of Pertra, the halo around the sun; Ezec, the Fifteen Stars of ancient astronomy, astrology, and traditional navigation; and Aza, the godly power of creation. The Goths gave up the runes when they converted to Christianity, brought by the missionaries who followed Ulfila. Just as the Arian Christianity adopted by the Goths replaced paganism, so at the same time the runes were replaced by the alphabet that Ulfila invented.

But the rise of Christianity did not eliminate the runes in Northern Europe. When the Christian religion was introduced there, it was often only the king and the ruling families who converted. During conversion, not all pagan cultural elements were abolished. Many were absorbed and renamed. Though the common people may have been baptized and induced to go to church on the great festivals, in everyday life various other gods and spirits had greater immediacy. In parallel with the God of the Church, people acknowledged deities of field and forest, the weather and the seasons, childbirth and healing.

Among them were the gods and goddesses who had not been assimilated with Jesus, the Virgin Mary, or the many saints who took over the functions of pagan gods and goddesses. They included figures such as Frau Percht, the goddess who rules over the wintertime. These goddesses and gods were invoked during traditional rites and ceremonies, usually in times of need. They had their own folksongs and dances, and were called upon by certain secret runes. These secret runes were not part of any runic futhark or futhork, but they acted generally as secret signs. Unusual runes that originated in official inscriptions continued much longer in folk tradition. Some even acquired phonetic meanings, but these runes are not used in divination.

For a definition and discussion of the medieval runes (*see page 77*).

LEFT The Gothic rune Thyth was associated with the crystal sphere of the cosmos, which was thought to hold the stars, above and around the Earth.

LEFT The runes reminded people of their pagan gods, whose powers they could see in the natural world around them.

Interpreting the Gothic and Medieval Runes

* * * * * * * * * * * * * * * * * *

THE INTERPRETATIONS BELOW refer both to the characters of Ulfila's Gothic alphabet and to the Gothic runes on which they were based. Interpretations of the medieval runes appear on page 77.

The First Gothic Aett

Collectively, the first three letters of the Gothic alphabet refer to different types and qualities of strength. Faihu/Fe is associated with creative strength; Urus/Uruz, earthy collective strength; and Thauris/Thyth, active bodily strength. The meanings of these and other runes and characters are as follows.

FAIHU/FE

The rune Faihu (sound "F") signifies well-being, prosperity, and fruitfullness. This rune is related to the mythic primal cow Audhumla, the Great Mother Goddess as preserver and nurturer. The equivalent Gothic letter Fe also signifies the generative principle, however, under the influence of Christian patriarchy it has become male, and is the phallus. The letter Fe symbolizes the accumulation of power and, through power, abundance.

URUS/URUZ

The rune Urus (sound "U") and the corresponding letter Uruz mean primal strength, the power we need in order to be creative. Persistence is worthwhile and produces useful things. Urus is the rune of Urd, the first of the three Norns, or three Fates. In the Christian tradition, she is personified as Eve, who is the ancestral mother of humankind.

THAURIS/THYTH

Thauris (sound "Th"), the rune of defense, is the thorn's power to resist attack without a fight. The Gothic character Thyth represents the crystal sphere, the symbol of cosmic order. Thyth denotes the eternal power of enclosure, a matrix that has the power to resist disorder and chaotic breakdown.

ANSUS/AZA

Ansus (sound "A," as in "cat") is the god rune, denoting human descent from divine beings. The Gothic character Aza signifies the divine power of creation, calling upon divine blessings.

RAIDA/REDA

The rune Raida (sound "R") means motion. The Gothic character Reda extends to include the feminine creative power of the Mother Goddess, Nerthus, bringing reproductive fruitfullness.

KUSMA/CHOSMA

The rune Kusma (sounds "C," as in "cake," "K") means illumination, knowledge, learning, insight, remembrance, and wisdom. The letter Chosma represents the dual phenomenon of illness and illumination, the borderline between madness and genius.

GIBA/GEWA

Giba and Gewa (sound "G," as in "gift"), rune and letter respectively, signify a gift, the act of giving, and the bond made between the donor and recipient.

WINJA/WINNE

The rune Winja and the character Winne (sound "W") signify joy. To the Goths, this was the pasture where contented animals graze – a place of perfect harmony, a haven in a chaotic world.

The Second Gothic Aett

The runes and characters in the second Gothic aett have the following meanings and associations.

HAGL/HAAL

The rune and character Hagl and Haal (sound "H") mean a hailstone, signifying constraint. It is the icy, primal seed of manifestation, symbolizing rapid and complete transformation from one state to another.

NAUTHS/NOICS

The rune Nauths and the character Noics (sound "N"), meaning need or necessity, are sacred to Nott, goddess of the dark night. Both also refer to an absence or scarcity of something, as well as "necessity." Noics also signifies the letter of justice.

EIS/IIZ

The rune Eis and the character Iiz (sound "I," as in "niece") represent an icicle, hanging vertically, which signifies unchanging existence, the eternal present. Iiz is linked with the Greek deity Kronos, the god with a cold character, who was called on by wizards in their spells to make their enemies cold by bringing death.

JER/GAAR

Jer and Gaar (sounds "J," as in "Frejya," "Y"), meaning "year" or "season," are the characters of nature's cycles. They symbolize completion at the proper time, bringing reward for good work.

AIHS/WAER

Aihs (sound "E," as in "egg") is the double-ended staff of life and death, cut from a yew tree. The corresponding letter, Waer, signifies sacrifice.

PAIRTHRA/PERTRA

The rune Pairthra (sound "P") represents a pot and, by correspondence, the womb. The equivalent Gothic character Pertra signifies the brilliant solar halo. It represents the powerful processes of nature that bring unexpected resolution to difficult situations.

ALGS/EZEC

The rune Algs (sound "Z") stands for the irresistible power of the elk. The Gothic character Ezec represents the Fifteen Stars of traditional European astronomy, the markers that link the human world with the divine cosmos.

SAÚIL/SUGIL

Saúil and Sugil (sound "SS," as in "hiss"), the rune and letter respectively, signify the ascendancy of light over darkness. This is the power of the sun, both physically and spiritually. Sugil's Greek roots are in the sigil, or sign, known as *Planeta*, referring to both sun and moon.

The Third Gothic Aett

The third Gothic aett is made up of eight runes, but nine Gothic characters. The final letter, Quairtra, is "outside of" the other letters but embodies the principles of them all.

TEIWS/TYZ

The rune and character Teiws and Tyz (sound "T") represent earthly power, victory, and achievement, attained through male power. Tyz is the character of the god of war, Mars.

BAÍRKANA/BERN

Representing the birch tree are the rune and character Baírkana and Bern (sound "B"), symbolic of birth, regeneration, and the power of woman. Birch twigs are favored for runic divination because the white birch symbolizes purification and the absence of harmful influences.

EGEIS/EYZ

The rune Egeis (sound "E," as in "egg") is the sacred horse. As well as riding them, the Goths used horses in divination, shamanism, and royal pageantry. The Gothic letter Eyz signifies the *aether*, the medium pervading the cosmos.

MANNAZ/MANNA

Mannaz and Manna (sound "M"), the rune and letter respectively, denote the basic qualities of humaneness that exist in every human, such as cooperative, supportive, and social abilities. Mannaz and Manna are the trees from which came the first man and woman.

LAGUS/LAAZ

Representing water in all its aspects are the rune Lagus and the Gothic letter Laaz (sound "L"). They signify fluidity and the power of growth.

IGGWS/ENGUZ

The Iggws (sound "NG," as in "long") rune symbolizes generative power, a channel for potential energy. This must be built up before release as a single burst of power. The letter Enguz denotes "becoming" – the eternal present.

DAGS/DAZ

The rune and letter Dags and Daz (sound "D") both mean "day." The rune is the symbol for the protection of entrances. Dags and Daz embody the archetype of wholeness.

OTHAL/UTAL

Othal (sound "O," as in "old") is the rune that denotes "our own land," meaning inherited territory and intellectual property. The Gothic character Utal (sound "U") represents riches.

QUAIRTRA

The final Gothic character, Quairtra (sound "QU," as in "quick") represents the swirling flames of the ceremonial fire and complete cleansing by the transmutation of things from one form to another. Quairtra is the fifth element or *quintessence* of alchemy, outside the realm of the other 24 characters, encapsulating and incorporating the essence of each one.

Medieval Runes of Magic and Healing

Although they are less well known than the previous rune-rows, there were a number of runes used individually in the Middle Ages, which are largely medieval Germanic and Dutch in origin. They are associated mainly with gods and goddesses who were worshiped in secret in Christian times. They were used for protection and healing, but not in runecasting. They are newer than the Gothic runes and form a separate category of their own.

WOLFSANGEL

The first of these runes is called Wolfsangel (sound "SZ," as in "ease"). It represents the wolf-hook, an ancient iron weapon used to catch and kill wolves. Wolfsangel channels magical energy for human use. First it binds all harmful influences and then it obliterates them.

ERDA

Erda (sound "OE," as in "er") is the rune of Mother Earth, our planet, which sustains us all. Her image is the orderly garden, where all good things grow in their proper season. Erda reintegrates human actions with the wider world.

UL

Ul (sound "UE," as in "ee" or "ö") is the rune of the old Frisian god Waldh, and means a turning point. Waldh is the forest-god of tranquillity who assists in crises of healing. The rune revives former powers.

ZIU

Ziu (sound "ZZ," as in "buzz") is the thunderbolt of the god Ziu. It signifies the irresistible power of the father of the gods, striking through all resistance. Ziu concentrates and channels cosmic energy to maintain right order.

SÓL

Sól (sound "SS," as in "hiss") represents the disk of the sun with a column of light linking it with the horizon. It is the rune of the goddess Sól, for the sun is considered female in the Teutonic tradition. The Sól rune brings us the pleasant and healing warmth of the sun.

WENDHORN

Wendhorn (sound "MM," as in "humming") represents the changing phases of the moon. Everything goes in cycles, and Wendhorn reminds us that we must experience good and bad alike.

FYRUEDAL

Fyruedal (no given sound) represents the fire-fan or bellows. This is the mover of the air needed for fire to burn. Fyruedal symbolizes motivation, the power to get going.

WAN

Wan or Irings (no given sound) is the rune of emptiness. It represents Ginnungagap, the yawning void from which existence arose and all the spaces in which solid matter exists.

THE ARMANEN RUNES

★ ★ ★ ★ ★ ★ ★ ★ ★ ★ ★ ★ ★ ★ ★ ★ ★

THE ARMANEN RUNES were the invention of the Austrian Guido List (1848–1919), who was the founder of the main school of German rune-work in the twentieth century. Although his ideas appear to follow the researches of the seventeenth-century scholar Johannes Bureus, List argued against the theories of the origins of the runes that Bureus and other scholars had maintained, and which were widely held to be true. Instead, List maintained that his own 18 characters were the most ancient script of the Aryan race and were even older than the 24 runes of the Elder Futhark. Moreover, he identified each of his runes with one of the 18 spells of the Old Norse poem *Hávamál* in the *Poetic Edda* (a collection of poems written by unknown Norwegian poets from the ninth to twelfth centuries), thereby giving them magical meanings.

Although the *Hávamál* spells are genuinely ancient, there is no historical evidence for List's claim that his are the original form of the runes. Neither do they have anything at all to do with supposedly ancient civilizations. Guido List's "Armanen Runes" are clearly a version of the 16 Mixed Runes that were once used in Scandinavia (*see pages 30–31*). All List did was to add two more, and give them new meanings in line with his own personal ideology. Nevertheless, their fallacious origins did not prevent his runes from being very influential.

The forms of Guido List's runes were more rigid than those of previous systems. He based their shapes on the six branches of the Hagal "hailstone" rune, or the "mother rune." According to his contemporary followers, the shape of the Hagal rune imitates the hexagonal lattice underlying the structure of matter. The most striking example of this pattern in nature is the clear quartz crystal, which List and his followers saw as the "frozen light" in which the Armanen Runes are encoded. It is said that all of List's 18

BELOW An example of the Armanen Runes. Guido List based the 18 characters of his Armanen Runes on the 18 spells of the Old Norse poem *Hávamál.*

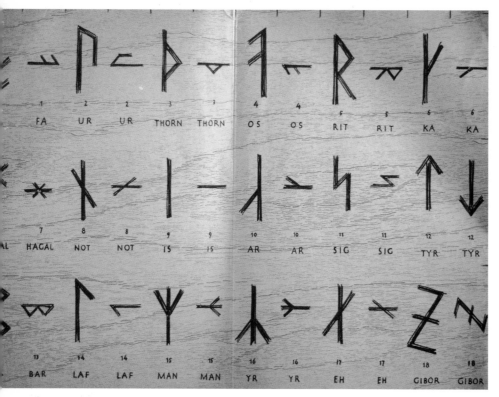

1	2	2	3	3	4	4	5	5	6	6
FA	UR	UR	THORN	THORN	OS	OS	RIT	RIT	KA	KA

	7	8	8	9	9	10	10	11	11	12	12
AL	HAGAL	NOT	NOT	IS	IS	AR	AR	SIG	SIG	TYR	TYR

	13	14	14	15	15	16	16	17	17	18	18
	BAR	LAF	LAF	MAN	MAN	YR	YR	EH	EH	GIBOR	GIBOR

runes can be projected by shining a light through a hexagonal crystal at certain angles. According to this theory, when light is shone vertically through a crystal, the full, six-branched Hagal rune is then projected. When it is shone at right angles to the crystal, the straight ice rune, Is, is then revealed. Correspondingly, the other runes are made by shining light at the appropriate angle. This means that the special geometrical angle that produces each rune also expresses its magical relationship to the cosmos. Looked at in this way, each rune can be viewed as a form of spatial energy-mathematics.

Guido List's runes give similar results to those of the Younger Futhark, on which they are based. He also reversed the runes by turning them the other way around and thereby gave them additional meanings. A rune that is thus reversed is called a *daemonium*. Not only did they have another meaning, but these reversed runes also had a change of name.

Although List's influence was at its greatest in Germany up to the fall of Hitler and the Nazis, his legacy continues today. In 1969, the Guido von List Society, originally established in 1908, was refounded and is still functioning, and in 1988, his book, *The Secret of the Runes,* was translated into English and published. Although their origin is often unknown to those who use them, the Armanen Runes remain very influential in present-day Germany and German-speaking countries, where they seem to be even more widespread than the Elder Futhark. However, most present-day users appear to have dropped the more overtly racist elements from the interpretations of the Armanen Runes.

List also wrote about other signs, symbols, and runes, which he linked with his original 18 characters. However, they were neither part of his rune-use programs, nor did they catch on in the way that the Armanen system did. However, with his Armanen Runes, List successfully established his ideas within the repertoire of Germanic occultism. His followers have continued to develop spiritual techniques based on the 18 runes. The most important of these is the so-called "runic yoga" of posture-magic, whereby people adopt postures that mimic the shape of certain runes in order to experience and use the runes' power. The principles of runic yoga are explained in more detail on pages 130–33.

LEFT In the Armanen system, Hagal reflects the hexagonal shape that runs through much of matter, as exemplified by the quartz crystal.

RIGHT Followers of the Armanen system often practice runic yoga. Adopting the shape of a particular rune confers its quality on the practitioner. Shown here is Othil.

Interpreting the Armanen Runes

* * * * * * * * * * * * * * * *

The meanings of List's runes are virtually the same as those of the Scandinavian rune-rows, but their names differ slightly. Modern users ignore or alter some of the unacceptable elements of List's meanings.

FA

The first of List's runes is called Fa (sound "F"). Fa represents primal fire and the fire-borer anciently used in making ceremonial fires. Symbolically, it signifies the creative power of the primordial Word, the power of spirit, and change.

UR

Ur (sound "U") represents eternity, continuity, resurrection, and what List called the "primal soul." Ur is the physician's rune and has the power to channel "telluric magnetism."

DORN

Dorn, Thorr, or Thurs (sound "Th") is the rune of lightning and thunder, the threatening thunderbolt. It also signifies activity, targeting goals, and the "horn of life," the phallus. In Armanen earth mysteries it transfers the supposed earth energy called Od from person to person.

OS

Os, As, Ask, or Ast (sound "O" as in "old") is the mouth and signifies the power to rise up. Os also represents the breath and the word. It is spiritual power working through speech, breaking through boundaries. It is said to radiate the supposed Od-energy to its surroundings.

RIT

Rit, Reith, or Rath (sound "R") is close in meaning to Raidho in the Elder Futhark. Rit represents ritual, primal laws, things done correctly, and right orderliness in the world. It also denotes cyclical events and rescue from adversity.

KA

Ka or Kaun (sound "K") stands for the World Tree, which List saw as the Aryan tribal tree. Modern interpreters see Kaun representing artfulness, power, generation, and general ability.

HAGAL

Hagal (sound "H") is the rune of enclosure, containing the primal seed of things. Contemporary users call this the "mother-rune" and see all other runes as derived from it. Its sixfold form may signify the midpoint of order in the cosmos.

NOT

Not, Nuath, or Noth (sound "N") denotes the necessity of fate. This is the rune of *karma*, the Hindu concept that states that what we do in this or previous lifetimes determines and colors our present and future existence.

IS

Is, Ire, or Iron (sound "I" as in "niece") stands for obedience to the compelling will and for personal power and control. It does not mean "ice," as in the ancient futharks, but the ego. Its power is used to control oneself – and others!

AR

Ar or Ar-Yans (sound "A" as in "aah") represents nobility and leadership. It is the sunlight or the power of God destroying physical and spiritual darkness. List's alternative name, Ar-Yans, linked it to the Aryans, whom he believed to be the "master race." Modern users make it stand for beauty, wisdom, fame, and virtue.

SIG

Sig, Sol, Sal, Sul, or Si (sound "S") is the rune of sun power. It stands for victory, success, the conquering energy of the creative spirit. The Nazis used this as Sieg, the "victory rune."

TYR

Tyr, Tar, or Turn (sound "T") is a rune that can turn a situation around. It symbolizes concealment and the magic cap of invisibility, but also the rebirth of the sun god. Modern readers ascribe to it generative power and wisdom, spiritual development spiraling upward toward the realm of the gods.

BAR

Bar or Beor (sound "B") is the Armanen rune of birth, more specifically the eternal future life in the sense of predestination. Current interpretations include the power of becoming and the creative power of song.

LAF

Laf, Lagu, or Logr (sound "L") represents primal law (Örlog).

This includes the concepts of downfall and defeat, and also List's view of the essential laws of nature. Today it is often linked with primal law, life, and water.

MAN

Man or Mon (sound "M") is a mother-rune, the holy sign of the propagation of the human race. Contemporary readers see it as man, maleness, increase, and health. In Armanen tradition, this rune is used to denote a birth and is written alongside a person's birth date.

YR

Yr or Eur (sound "Y" as in "tiny") is the bow or the rainbow. To List, it signified anger, error, falsehood, and the opposites of the Man rune. Contemporary interpretations are femaleness, instinct, night, death. In Armanen tradition, this rune is used to denote a death and is written by a person's death date.

EH

Eh (sound "E" as in "every") is the rune of love, marriage, trust, and duality, where a pair is bound together by the primal laws of existence. List's interpretation was essentially the same as the Elder Futhark Ehwaz.

GIBOR

Gibor, Ge, or Fyrfos (sound "G") is the giver of life, the divine principle, the cosmic consciousness, the giver, and the gift. The Fyrfos form of this rune given by List is the swastika.

PART THREE

THE MYSTERIOUS WORLD OF RUNES

★ ★ ★ ★ ★

Runes connect the visible, physical world and the invisible otherworld. According to the runic worldview, there are no real barriers between the two. With their origins in nature, the runes found their way into every area of human existence. They were present in every aspect of Northern European traditional culture, especially the realms of magic and mystery. The sagas, legendary Icelandic tales, tell us that there were runic spells "against sorrows and ordeals and every grief there is." Runemasters knew "how to blunt swords and to quell sea-waves."

Through the runes, we are told, they talked with birds, put out fires, soothed sorrow, and stilled the senses. Farmers used runes as calendars, while merchants carried runic talismans to protect them against the hazards of their journeys. Wizards' and wayfarers' staffs were carved with runes, which gave their users strength in traveling, warding off evil influences. Runemasters endowed swords and other weapons with runic power. Runes appeared on houses to protect them from bad luck and intruders.

ABOVE A Viking clasp in the shape of a bird. Symbols of birds in Viking art are often associated with the god Odin.

THE SAGAS

* * * * * * * * * * * * * * * *

THE RUNES APPEAR in many places in ancient literature. In the old Norse tale, *Rigsmal*, Rigr, also known as the god Heimdall, creates the classes of traditional European society. He visits three human couples. First, the ancestors, then the grandparents, and, finally, the parents of the human race. The ancestors give birth to Serf, "with hairy and harsh hands." The grandparents bring forth Churl – "Houses he made, homesteads he held, Plowed the land and led the wagon." Finally, the parents produce Earl, a warrior-nobleman, to whom Rigr gives the runes.

RIGHT A modern statue of the Nordic god Heimdall, a creator-god in the sagas.

BELOW According to the *Volsunga Saga* Brünnhilde taught Sigurd the secret of the runes by giving him a loving cup of mead and shaven runes.

The *Volsunga Saga*, set in ancient Germany, tells how the Valkyrie Brünnhilde taught the hero Sigurd the runes. She brought him a loving-cup, filled with mead into which the runes had been "shaven and sheared." Drinking, Sigurd absorbed the magic of the runes. Then she told him of the kinds of rune for use in different circumstances.

The runes came from the gods. They were written on the shield "that stands before the shining god." They were on the ears and hooves of the horses of the sun's chariot. They appeared on the teeth of Sleipnir, Odin's horse, on the traces of his sleigh, and the point of his spear. Runes empowered the tongue of Bragi, god of

The Lay of Rigr

The Norse saga *Rigsmal* tells how Earl was the first to receive the runes from the gods.

Right from the wood came the brave Rigr
To teach him runes, to tell him truth,
Seeking a name for him, called him Son.

Konur, Earl's descendant, was such an adept runemaster that he took the name Rigr:

Konur the young knew the runes,
Bygone runes and runes of the future …
Knew how to blunt swords, to quell sea-waves.
Talked with birds, quenched burning brands,
Soothed sorrow, stilled senses.
Wrestled in rune lore with Old Rigr.
Waxing in wisdom, won the wager,
Became Rigr, the runic sage, himself.

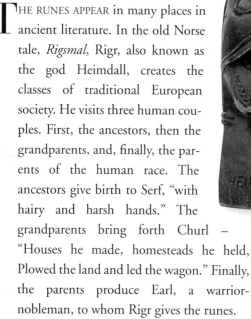

poetry. They marked the hub of the world, the "Norn's nail." According to Brünnhilde's poem, the runes are dispersed among the worlds. Some remain with the Aesir, the gods led by Odin. Others are held by the wise Vanir, the gods and goddesses of wild nature, flocks, and fields, and the elves. Yet others are possessed by humankind.

The Viking sagas give a first-hand account of how rune magic was used. The saga of Egill Skallagrimsson tells us how the eponymous hero used runes to detect poison in a drink. To do this, he cut certain runes onto the drinking horn. Then, as he colored the runes, he recited a spell. At that, "the horn burst asunder, spilling the drink down into the straw." In another episode of the same saga, Egill was at the house of a man named Thorfinnr, where he was taken to a woman who was seriously ill in bed. On a whale bone by the bed, he saw some runes carved by a previous visitor in an attempt to heal her. Egill read the runes and realized that the person who had written them was incompetent.

He took away the useless runes, saying, "I saw ten dark letters scored on a scraped whale bone: they have brought an over-long sickness to the leek-linden." Then, skillfully, he carved some appropriate runes on a piece of antler and laid them underneath the bolster of the woman's bed. Soon she awoke, as if from a sleep, and said that she was healed. This story tells us that not every rune user of old was competent. Not every ancient runic inscription is necessarily an example of good or effective rune use. Just like Egill, contemporary rune users must

develop the understanding to distinguish good rune use from bad.

Another saga, featuring a hero by the name of Gretti the Strong, set around the year 1023, tells how he went looking for a giantess who had killed some men. He was accompanied by a priest; however, the priest was so frightened that he ran away. Gretti found the giantess and killed her, then discovered the remains of the men in her cave. He wrapped up their bones and took them to the priest's church, where he left them along with a runestaff on which he carved a poem describing the events. When the cowardly priest came to the church the next morning, he found the runestaff that told him what had happened.

ABOVE The sagas tell tales of humans and the gods, and how warriors who die in battle will be received into Valhalla by Odin, shown here on his eight-legged horse, Sleipnir.

BELOW The binding of a giant with runic fetters, engraving from Olaus Magnus, 1555. It is the power of the runes that makes the fetters strong.

HÁVAMÁL

★ ★ ★ ★ ★ ★ ★ ★ ★ ★ ★ ★ ★ ★ ★ ★ ★

THE LITERATURE OF the Northern Tradition tells us of the scope of rune-magic. For example, the words of Odin, recorded in the poem *Hávamál*, speak of 18 different power spells, covering all eventualities: there are binding spells, love spells, battle-magic, protection against magical attack, and the means to distinguish beneficial gods from harmful spirits. The spells of *Hávamál*, set out below, are the basis for all contemporary rune magic.

Runes you will find, and skillful characters;
Very great characters, very strong characters;
That a mighty thule painted, and great gods made,
Carved by the prophet of the gods.

Odin among the Aesir, but Dain for elves
And Dvalin for dwarfs,
Asvidhr for giants:
Some I carved myself.

Do you know how to carve them?
Do you know how to read them?
Do you know how to paint them?
Do you know how to prove them?
Do you know how to pray with them?
Do you know how to sacrifice with them?
Do you know how to send with them?
Do you know how to offer with them?

ABOVE
A dwarf at work, depicted on a Viking font. Dwarfs were thought to possess remarkable creative powers, and several are mentioned in *Hávamál*.

It is better not to pray at all than to
*   sacrifice too much:*
A gift always demands a repayment.
It is better not to send at all than to
*   offer too much:*
Thus Thundr carved before the birth
*   of nations*
At that point he began when he
*   came back.*

I know those spells which no lord's wife knows,
Nor any man's son.

One is called Help, and it will help you
Against sorrows and ordeals and every grief there is.

I know the second, which those sons of men need
Who wish to live as healers.

I know the third: If my need grows dire
For binding my deadly enemies, I dull the blades
Of my foes – neither weapon nor deception will bite
*   for them.*

I know this, the fourth:
If warriors tie up
My arms, I call this,
And I can go free: the shackles break from my feet,
And the handcuffs from my hands.

I know this, the fifth:
If I see an arrow shot in combat,
Shot deadly straight,
None flies so hard that I cannot stop it
If I catch sight of it.

I know this, the sixth;
If a lord curses me by the roots of a fresh young tree,
The man who calls down curses on me
Misfortunes will destroy him, rather than me.

I know this, the seventh:
If I see a high hall on fire around my comrades,
None burns so ferociously that I cannot rescue them;
I know the spell to chant.

I know this, the eighth:
Which is useful for everyone to learn,
Whose hatred grows for a war-king's sons:
I can soon alter that.

I know this, the ninth:
If I need to keep my ship afloat,
I can calm the wind, smooth the waves,
And lull the sea to sleep.

I know this, the tenth:
If I see the hedge-riders magically flying high,
I can make it so that they go astray
Of their own skins, and of their own souls.

I know this, the eleventh:
If I must lead old friends to battle,
I call under their shields, and they go empowered,
Safe to war, safe from war, safe wherever they are.

I know this, the twelfth:
If I see a corpse swinging from a noose high in a tree,
Then I carve and I paint the runes,
So that the man comes down and speaks with me.

I know this the thirteenth:
If I should sprinkle water on a young lord,
He will not fall, no matter if he goes to war –
The hero will not go down beneath the swords.

I know this, the fourteenth:
If I should preach of the gods at a moot,
I will know how to distinguish between
    all gods and elves:
Few of the unwise know this.

I know this, the fifteenth,
Which the dwarf Thjothrerir
Called before Delling's doors.
He chanted power to the gods and strength to elves,
And foresight to Hropta-Tyr.

I know this, the sixteenth:
If I want to have the wise woman's spirited games,
I steal the heart of a white-armed wench
And I turn all her thoughts.

I know this, the seventeenth:
So that the young woman will not want to avoid me.
Loddfafnir, you will be long in learning these lays,
Though they will do you good if you get them,
Be usable if you can grasp them,
Handy if you have them.

I know this, the eighteenth,
Which never will I teach maid or man's wife
(It is better to understand it alone – the end of the
    poem follows),
Except that woman who folds me in her arms,
Or perhaps my sister.

Now are the Hávamál sung in Hávi's Hall,
Essential to the sons of men, useless to the son's
    of giants.
Hale he sang, hale he who understands.
May he use them well who has grasped them,
Hale those who have listened.

FOOTNOTE
thule = wizard; Dain =
dwarf who made Freyja's
gold-bristled boar,
Hildisvini; Dvalin = dwarf
who helped to make
Freyja's necklace,
Brisingamen; Asvidhr =
another name for Odin;
Thundr = another name
for Thor; hedge-riders =
witches; moot = assembly;
Delling = the third hus-
band of Night (Nott),
whose son is Day; Kropta-
Tyr = the god Tyr;
Loddfafnir = "Everyman,"
a human being from
Midgard; Hávi = "The
High One," or Odin.

RUNESTONES

* * * * * * * * * * * * * * * *

THE RESTING-PLACES of the dead have always been protected from interference on the part of humans, animals, and malignant spirits alike. Before the runic alphabet was introduced, graves in Scandinavia were marked with uncarved boulders known as "bauta-stones." Erected from the Bronze Age onward, these bauta-stones can measure between 3 and 20 feet (1 and 6 meters) high. It is likely that they were once painted, and when the runes reached Scandinavia runemasters began to inscribe protective formulas upon them.

The power of writing was held in such high regard that many runic inscriptions on bauta-stones name the runemaster rather than the dead person. Because of this, we know the names of several runemasters: Soti, Asmund Karason, Gaut Björnsson, Öpir, Toki, Lifstein, and Balli.

An eighth-century gravestone from Eggjum, in Sogndal, Norway, describes how the runes for the dead were carved. It tells how neither stone nor runes saw sunlight, and that iron – a material believed to frighten away spirits – was not used to carve them. It warns that the stone must never be brought into the light of day, or its power will be destroyed at once. Frequently, the runes were not visible to passersby, but were concealed below the stone for the benefit of the dead alone. A good example is a sixth-century runestone from Noleby in Sweden.

Other runestones are simple memorials with inscriptions commemorating the dead person, who may or may not have been buried there. Most runestones have a formula such as this one at Glavendrup, Denmark:

Ragnhild erected this stone in memory of Alli Sölvi, priest of the Vé, most worthy captain of the militia. The sons made this monument in memory of their father, and his wife in memory of her husband. Soti carved these runes in memory of his lord. May Thor consecrate them …

Sometimes a runestone contains a genealogy, such as "Freymund erected this stone in memory of Fe-Gylfi, son of Bresi. And Bresi was the son of Lini. And Lini was the son of Aun. And Aun the son of Ofeig. And Ofeig the son of Thori." Sometimes runestones were put up to commemorate landowners' good works for the community. The builders of public roads and bridges are remembered in such texts as: "Thririk's daughter made this bridge after Astrid, her daughter. She was the most skillful woman in Hadeland."

Early runestones bear plain runes without ornament, but on later ones they are written between parallel lines. These lines are sometimes in the form of the Lindorm serpent, an undulating pattern made up of two lines, with a snake's head at one end and a tail at the other, with the runes in between. Another, more formal, layout, is the *Irminsul* (Tree of Life) pattern. Here, the runes are written vertically up the stone. The first line of script begins at the foot of the tree, written from left to right. When the runes reach the top, they make another line on the right of the first one, which reads from top to bottom. If there is another line of script, it begins to the left of the tree and is read from the bottom. Any additional lines follow on in the same sequence. The whole inscription is written as a *deosil* (sunwise) spiral.

Sometimes magical formulas accompany commemorative texts, each complementing the other. The memorial of a *thule* (wizard) at Snoldelev in Denmark has a series of solar symbols accompanied by the inscription: "The stone of Gunnvald, son of Hroald, Thule in Salløv." Often there are curses warning would-be grave-robbers. A runestone text at Tryggvaelde in Zealand, Denmark, ends with "… a rati be he who destroys this stone or drags it from here." According to ancient belief, a *rati* is a cursed person, whose soul is robbed from the body by the Wild Hunt, a supernatural host that rides on windy nights, led by the Wild Huntsman, Odin, or the goddess of wintertime, Frau Percht or Perchta. Another Danish runestone inscription ends "… a rati be he who destroys this stone or drags it for another." In regions where stone is scarce, there is a possibility that someone will take away a memorial stone to reuse it as a tombstone or for building material. Cursing them in advance is a practical way of preventing it, and the runes were the perfect vehicle for the curse.

The tradition of memorial runestones flourished for many centuries in every place with a Scandinavian presence, from Ireland to Russia. They were made in large numbers, though many have been destroyed over the years. But there are still over 3,000 runestones in Sweden alone.

ABOVE A runestone from the eleventh century, found near Uppsala in Sweden. It is common for runes to appear in borders.

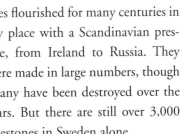

LEFT Runestones were almost certainly painted, as in this restoration of a stone in Stockholm.

RUNES IN ACTION

* * * * * * * * * * * * * * * * * *

RIGHT The god Thor with his hammer Mjollnir, "the crusher," his constant companion. Runemasters invoked him when inscribing tools or weapons.

BELOW Two ravens, Hugin and Munin, habitually perched on Odin's shoulders. Odin used them to find out what was happening in the world. Hugin lent his power to the *hugrunes*, the runes of mind-power.

IN THE EARLY days of rune use, runemasters divided the runes into categories according to their uses, and gave these categories names. Some had practical, constructive effects; others played a more defensive, protective role.

Of the various categories of runes, the most useful and widely applicable are those that enhance memory and speech and increase mental agility. The power of these runes can be brought into action through both the spoken and written word. Spoken runes are the most immediately effective. In the Norse text *Sigrdrífumál*, which records the many uses of the runes, these are called *malrunes*. The word *malrune* comes from *mal* or *maal*, which means speech, a word that can be found in the title of several Old Norse texts, such as *Hávamál*, the text that Odinists believe is the divine word of Odin, the spoken runes of the god of consciousness.

Generally, malrunes are any rune whose magic is connected with the spoken word – they are runic formulas spoken, called, or sung to achieve a desired result. These runes are powerful in the word-magic of poetry and invocation, and are effective in all areas of life where words are important. Traditionally, malrunes are used to gain compensation for injuries, especially in legal actions. When they are used for this purpose they should be written upon the walls, pillars, and seats of the place where the case is being tried.

Hugrunes or *hogrunes* are closely related to malrunes, because they are the runes of thought and mind-power and enable the user to excel mentally. Hugrunes are one of the most powerful and effective means of mind-concentration in the northern European spiritual tradition. Traditionally, hugrunes were written upon the runemaster's chest and "secret parts." The use of the hugrunes is related symbolically to the name of one of Odin's two attendant ravens, Hugin, or "Memory."

Other needs were served by other runes. In order to gain success in any action, ancient runemasters used the *sigrunes*. These are named after and contain the solar power

of the rune Sowulo or Sigel. These runes were written upon the runemaster's tools, clothing, instruments, or weapons before the event in which success was needed. While they wrote the runes, the runemasters invoked the thunder-god Thor twice.

For restoring sick people to health, runic healers used the *limrunes*, which drew upon the nurturing power of trees. They were carved ceremonially on the south-facing bark or leaves of the tree. The *biargrunes* are more specialized healing runes, related to a specific tree, the birch. They call upon the goddess of childbirth, known as Berchta or Frau Percht, to ensure a safe birth. They were also used to protect mothers and their babies after the birth. The biargrunes include the goddess's rune, Biarg or Berkana. This is the rune that represents purity and new beginnings.

When runes are used magically, they are called *ramrunes*. These strong runes are empowered by magical ritual. The word "ram" means strength, as in the male sheep, which, with the power of its horns, can batter its way through difficulties. *Wendrunes*, which are any runes written "backward" from right to left so that their shapes are reversed, are also considered to possess magical properties. Runes written upside-down are similarly called wendrunes. The runes that can help to bring us into communion with otherworldly realities include the *trollrunes*, used in divination. Their name comes from an ancient teaching that prophecy originates with the trolls, who have knowledge of the future. Trolls are literally earth-spirits, the elemental forces that appear at places of power in the land. In addition to prophecy, the trollrunes were used in enchantment. Related to the trollrunes are the *swartrunes*. These are literally the "black runes," necromantic characters used by sorcerers to speak with the dead.

LEFT A birch tree. Runes carved on birch bark gave protection to mothers and babies, both in childbirth and afterward.

LEFT A Viking silver amulet in the shape of Thor's hammer. Sigrunes were associated with Thor, but other runes were linked with a range of magical powers, creatures, and other objects.

RUNES FOR PROTECTION

* * * * * * * * * * * * * * * *

DEFENSE IS AN important area of rune use. The runemasters of old used runes to ward off harm emanating from both the physical and nonmaterial realms. This aspect of rune magic was the sphere of the warlock, the cunning man skilled in the magical arts of *vardlokkur*, the techniques of protecting people and binding, or constraining, spirits. There are several sorts of rune that are used in binding-magic. In ancient times, for example, men employed *alerunes* in order to block the magical enchantments of strange women. Alerunes were written inside the cup from which the woman would drink, and also on the back of the man's hand. The man would then scratch the Naudhiz rune (the rune of need and constraint) upon his fingernail in order to activate the rune power.

Runes also play a part in traditional weather-magic connected with hunting, sailing, and farming. This sort of magic tries to anticipate the weather and to control its forces. The runemasters used the *brunrunes* – literally the "fountain runes" or "surf-runes"– to deal with bad weather. Brunrunes are staves that connect the runemaster harmoniously with the power of flowing and running water, including the ocean. To protect a Viking ship against harm during a voyage, for example, brunrunes were carved upon the stern, steering-oar, or rudder. There are brunrunes carved on a late-eighth-century yew amulet, or charm, found at Westeremden in Frisia, which gave power over the waves. The story of Canute, the Dane who became the king of England and who unsuccessfully ordered the tide to go back, may have been an attack on the earlier, pagan use of brunrunes.

A number of ancient Frisian wooden amulets, including the Lindholm stave and another from Wijnaldum, are shaped like tusks. Tusks have been revered as magical objects for thousands of years. Mammoth tusks were used as magical objects before the last Ice Age, and the cult continued into the Middle Ages, ten thousand years after the last mammoth died. A mammoth tusk still hangs in St. Michael's Church at Schwäbisch Hall in southern Germany, where it was believed to be a unicorn's horn. Boars' tusks were also used as amulets in ancient times, being made into necklaces and even helmets. Another powerful material used in rune magic is bone, which, like wood, contains the life-essence of the being from which it was taken.

BELOW Brunrunes, seen here carved on this eighth-century yew amulet found at Westeremden in Frisia, were used to protect the Vikings during sea voyages.

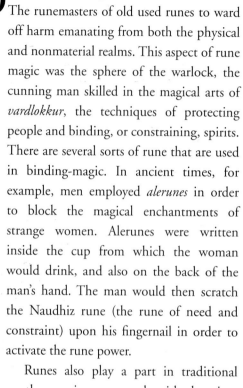

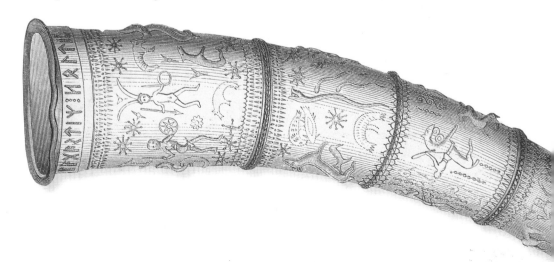

RIGHT An inscribed horn from the fourth or fifth century. Because they contain some of the essence of the creatures from which they came, bone and horn were thought to have particularly strong magical powers.

How to Make Runic Talismans

Making a runic talisman, or magical charm, is straightforward. According to custom, we should make constructive or protective talismans during the waxing moon, in a runic hour corresponding with the required power.

Once this is done, we enclose the talisman in darkness, wrapping it in a black cloth or placing it in a container. Then we carry the talisman in a sunwise circle nine times, chanting the runic name of power Laukaz, for growth and empowerment.

After this, we bring back the talisman into the light of day. This is its symbolic birth and is the time when the talisman is named and empowered. By naming an object, we give it a personality, a sort of life of its own. Traditional names are kennings or allusions to the power within the empowered object. Named objects include ships, swords, spears, banners, musical instruments, and many other tools and implements. Only in recent times have names become a means of advertising and publicity

When deciding on a name for the talisman, we should choose one that is related to its intended function – a kenning from Norse mythology may be appropriate. For example, if it is to be a protective talisman, it could be named *Dragvandil*, or "draw-wand" – the kenning for "sword." The talisman is named over a flame. As we do this, we call upon the powers of light and life to bring the talisman's qualities to their full strength. Then we scatter water over the talisman and call its name. The talisman is ready after we have spoken its function.

Making a Talisman

1 Prepare the materials, working out any designs and inscriptions in advance. Consecrate the working place by sprinkling it with salt and water, and then light incense and a candle to symbolize fire.

2 If the talisman is to be made of wood, stone, or metal, you will need an engraving tool called a burin or *ristir*. As you carve the runes, call out their names, visualizing their power entering the work.

3 To perform the naming of your talisman, first of all you must pass the talisman slowly over a candle or incense in a *glódhker*, or small incense-burner, three times.

4 Finally, give the talisman the power to carry out its task by speaking its function out loud. The talisman is then ready for use.

RUNIC INSIGILS

* * * * * * * * * * * * * * * * *

RUNIC LETTERS AND related signs can be arranged to make powerful amulets known as insigils or runic wheels. From a central point, four, six, seven, or eight lines are drawn to make a "star." Runes are written along these lines, and a circle is drawn around them, making what is called an insigil. A runic insigil may be worn around the neck, when it is known as a bracteate.

This basic form offers almost unlimited possibilities for runic insigils, which are customarily made using runes that symbolize power and protection. A number of bindrunes put together in a runic wheel, for example, creates a very effective amulet. Your own name, or a runic title such as Erilaz ("runemaster"), written in runes, makes a good insigil for a rune user. One of the most powerful insigils of all is based upon the Heavenly Star, an eight-branched figure symbolizing the eightfold division of space and time. The Heavenly Star itself is a symbol of balance and right orderliness, and can be used as an insigil on its own.

In Irish tradition, letters arranged as an insigil are called *Feisefín* (Fionn's Shield). They are named for the ancient hero Fionn MacCumhaill, who used them to protect himself against otherworldly assailants. Protective signs like this were painted on Celtic warriors' shields in ancient Ireland. Those called *liuthrindi* dazzled opponents who saw them.

The most powerful insigil of all is thought to be the Norse *Aegishjalmur* or Helm of Awe. It represents an irresistible power. Those who wear it can disempower their opponents by using both physical and psychic force. In legend, the *Aegishjalmur* was one of the treasures that the hero Sigurd (also known as Siegfried) won by killing the dragon Fafner. The Helm of Awe is a powerful insigil because it is formed from eight Elhaz runes combined with 24 cross-arms that represent all the runes of the Elder Futhark. It thus embodies the combined power of all the 24 runes of this futhark, projected outward from the center.

RIGHT Two examples of runic insigils: bindrunes in a runic wheel (right) and the Helm of Awe (far right) – this sigil is especially powerful because it draws on all the runes of the Elder Futhark.

In ancient Iceland, Helm of Awe amulets were made of lead, the metal ruled by the awesome power of the thunder-god, Thor. When a warrior preparing for combat used the insigil, he pressed a small lead Helm of Awe between his eyes. According to custom, this is where this insigil should be worn, in the place where its power is greatest. The warrior then made the affirmation "I bear the Helm of Awe between my brows." Visualizing the insigil and feeling its power, he went fearlessly into battle.

In medieval France and England, this runic insigil became a heraldic emblem called the escarbuncle or lilienhaspel. It was used in the coat of arms of the English knight Sir John de Warenne in the 1320s. At Windsor Castle in England, the oldest enamel shield of a knight of the Garter, in St. George's Chapel, also bears an escarbuncle. Dating from 1390, the badge of Ralph, Lord Bassett, has a bleeding heart at its center, which may be an allusion to the dragon's heart in the Sigurd legend.

Although knights used empowering symbols on their shields, not every insigil was so visible. It was also customary to write runic signs and formulas very small, so as not to attract attention. They were often inscribed in an invisible place, such as on the backs of brooches, inside the bosses of shields, and on the underside of stones. Because of this, it is likely that many ancient objects in museums might bear still-undiscovered runes.

Often, runes were inscribed on any precious or magical object that came to hand. The runes had the power of transforming the power of the object according to the runemaster's wishes. A remarkable example of this is an Islamic Cufic (Arabic script) coin that had been minted in Samarkand. This coin was found in an eleventh-century burial place in Denmark. This has inscriptions in Runic that are Christian prayers for eternal life. By any account, it is an outstanding magical object, because the coin combines in one small place pagan, Islamic, and Christian talismanic traditions. To the magicians of old, there were no boundaries between different belief systems, only successful outcomes.

RUNIC GAME-SPELLS

* * * * * * * * * * * * * * * *

RIGHT Medieval
wrestlers. To win
their fights, Nordic
wrestlers might
inscribes sigils on
the soles of
their feet.

FAR RIGHT Game-
players combined
use of the runes
with magic spells,
in which a wagtail's
tongue often
featured.

BELOW The runes
were used to bring
luck in games of
chance.

IN FORMER TIMES,
game-players used
runic formulas to
give them an
advantage over
their opponents.
Some particularly
important examples of this practice have
been found in Iceland. Although the runes
went out of use in early medieval times in
most of Europe, in Iceland they lasted
longer, and folk tradition there has magical
runic formulas for use in almost every area
of life. Many runic spells and diagrams were
collected by folklorists from Icelandic
country folk during the nineteenth century,
when they were still in everyday use,
including those used by contestants in
sports and games.

Among the remarkable magical survivals
he recorded, the folklorist Bishop Jón
Árnason was shown two magical symbols
called Gapaldur and Ginfaxi. These were
used in the wrestling-magic called
Gimagaldur. In order to win his
match, a wrestler would write
the Gapaldur sigil under his
right heel, and the Ginfaxi sigil
under his left big toe. Then he
recited a spell that invoked both the
runic power of the sigils and his
guardian spirit. Having done
this, the wrestler was supposed
to become unbeatable.

Rune magic was not
only used in the mar-
tial arts but in
board games,
too, for these also
had their magic.
In his book *Chess
in Iceland*, pub-
lished in 1865,
Daniel Willard
Fiske, the noted
authority on Icelandic board games, tells of
the spells used there to win at games: "There
still exist in Icelandic old magical formulas to
enable one to win at *kotra* [backgammon]
just as there are others applicable to chess.
One of them runs thus: 'If thou wishest to
win at backgammon, take a raven's heart,
dry it in a spot on which the sun does not
shine, crush it, then rub it on the dice.' "
This spell uses the spirit-power of the raven,
the oracle bird of the god Odin, along with
the runes. It is intended to influence magically the roll of the dice, which, according to
folk tradition, were invented by Odin.

In another magical
operation for *kotra*
players, a wagtail, rather
than a raven, was
involved, as described by
Árnason: "In order to win at
kotra, take the tongue of a
wagtail and dry it in the
sun; crush and mix it
afterward with commu-
nion wine, and apply it to the points of the
dice, then you are sure of the game."

Sometimes words of power called upon
spirit-powers, including famous Norse
kings, to bring success in the game. Árnason
wrote of one in which "the backgammon
player should cry 'Olave, Olave, Harold,

Harold, Erik, Erik'" before playing. Royal names or other spells were also written in runes and hidden beneath the backgammon board or in the player's clothes. Yet another technique was for a player to hold a runic parchment between his or her knees.

The magical preparation of runic talismans for winning at backgammon involved complex operations, including visiting a crossroads, which was seen as a place of magic power. One Old Icelandic text recommends that you should write a certain runic formula on new parchment and wrap a silver coin in it. Before midnight on a Sunday, take it to a crossroads, bury the coin there, and stamp three times on the ground with your left foot, calling out the runes you have written. Make the runic sign between each word, nine times in all. Then leave without looking back. On the next day, go and recover the coin, which you can then carry with you to the gaming-table as a lucky charm. But, the text reminds us, users of gambling-magic should always remember to donate ten percent of their winnings to the poor in thanksgiving. If they fail to do so, they will never win again!

Many of these runic talismans, called *kotruvers*, were composed of bindrunes and other diagrams containing runes. Some *kotruvers* included Christian elements, as in the spell described opposite recorded by Árnason, which substitutes Church communion wine mixed with powdered wagtail's tongue for the raven's heart. Because game-players used this sort of magic, the Church in Iceland attempted to stamp it out. So, in 1639, the runes were prohibited, and people found in possession of runes were executed. Also, the laws known as the Jónsbok Code prohibited the making and use of *kotruvers*. But, of course, this did not put an end to the practice, and some people suffered the death penalty for their disobedience. In 1681, for example, Arni Pétursson was burned alive in the presence of the Icelandic Althing (parliament) for using *kotruvers* when playing backgammon.

ABOVE The chess pieces preserved on the Isle of Lewis, off the western coast of Scotland, are the most famous physical survival of the Viking love of games.

ABOVE The site of the ancient Althing, the Icelandic parliament, where a spellcaster was executed in 1681.

RUNESTAFFS

★ ★ ★ ★ ★ ★ ★ ★ ★ ★ ★ ★ ★ ★ ★ ★

MANY ANCIENT ARTIFACTS used in rune magic are still in existence. In ancient times, as now, rune magic used wood extensively. Wood is magically potent, for it was once a living material and it still contains the vital

RIGHT A drawing of a magical wooden sword from Arum, West Friesland, inscribed with a runic charm.

essence of the tree from which it came. But relatively few ancient wooden artifacts exist, because wood is very perishable and rarely lasts for over a thousand years. But there are enough to show us how the ancient rune-masters worked. Most of the known wooden runic objects have come from waterlogged

ABOVE A wood engraving of late-medieval magicians, with runes clearly marked on their magic staffs.

ground, which preserved them. In The Netherlands, excavations of the *terpen*, artificial mounds on which people once lived in wetlands, have brought to light numerous wooden runic objects. Others have been unearthed from the old harbor districts of

Bergen in Norway, Dublin in Ireland, and from Danish bogs.

One well-known magical wooden object, familiar from ancient legends and modern fantasy novels, is the staff – the "mark of office" of wizards and wise women. Staffs of power are no fantasy, however, because they were used in reality in ancient and medieval Europe. As early as the second century, we know of a Germanic wise woman who was named Waluburg after her *walus*, her magic staff.

Many ancient runestaffs bear runic formulas that promise protection in difficult circumstances, such as travel and battle. One such object is the wooden sword discovered at Arum, near Harlingen in west Friesland, in The Netherlands. Dating from around 650 C.E., this is a magical object, with an inscription in runes that reads EDAEBODA, which is interpreted as "return, messenger." Clearly, this is a magical amulet intended to protect a traveler on his or her missions.

Another wooden wand, discovered at Britsum, also in Frisia, and dating from the sixth or seventh century, bears a runic inscription that translates: "Always carry this yew in the battle-host." Yet another Frisian yew wand, from Westeremden, contains a reference to the Frisian warlord known as Amluth, who was probably the original of William Shakespeare's Hamlet. Dating from around 800 C.E., its magical inscription promises power over the waves of the ocean. Many of the runes carved on these staves were inscribed with great deliberation. Some of them have a number of repeated strokes, especially in their uprights, which appear to have been cut with great energy, presumably so as to give maximum power to the runes.

Another important use of the runes is in healing. A pine wood stave, one foot (30 centimeters) in length, which was found at Ribe in Denmark, bears a spell intended to exorcise the disease that was called "the Trembler," probably malaria. Made around the year 1300, its inscription utilizes both pagan and Christian words of power:

"I pray, guard Earth and Heaven above; Sól and St. Mary; and Himself the Lord God; that he grant me the hands to make whole, and words of remedy, to heal the Trembler, when treatment is necessary ... A stone is called Swart [black]: it stands out to sea. On it are nine Needs.

Neither shall they sleep nor warmly awaken until you have recovered from it."

The spell is empowered with the formula "Thoet se" – "so be it," equivalents of the ceremonial affirmations "So mote it be" and "Amen."

In the days before printing, wooden staves were used as perpetual calendars, known as "clog almanacs." There were two kinds. One was flat, with runes and marks on both sides. The other was square and had markings across the corners. Important days of the year and other vital information were carved on these almanacs, and they were hung next to the fireplace.

Today, rune users still make runestaffs and wands. Generally, they are called *gandr*, and are painted or carved with runic formulas. Contemporary wands are usually modeled on the ancient Frisian amulets. They are personal to the user, and their sizes are determined by the bodily dimensions of the user. Each one should be no smaller in diameter than the user's index finger, no larger than the circle made by the index finger and thumb, and no longer than the ell, which is the distance from the fingertips to the elbow. Runestaffs usually measure the equivalent of the user's height, and are larger in diameter than wands. Both wands and staffs may have all 24 runes of the Elder Futhark written on them.

ABOVE A drawing showing a wand made of yew, from Frisia. The wand drew power from the living material from which it was hewn as well as from its inscription.

LEFT A modern *gandr* or runestaff. Such staffs are personalized, being sized according to the dimensions of the owner.

WEAPONRY

* * * * * * * * * * * * * * * *

THE PRE-CHRISTIAN WARRIORS of Northern Europe empowered their weapons with runes. The kind of sword they used was a development of the long swords of the ancient Celts. It had a flat, broad blade, with two cutting edges that were almost parallel with one another, and it was a highly sophisticated product of the sword-smith's craft. The blade was composed of three parts. The edges were forged separately, and the central section between them was made up of many narrow strips of iron. These strips were woven and welded together into various symbolic patterns by the swordsmiths, who then forged them to

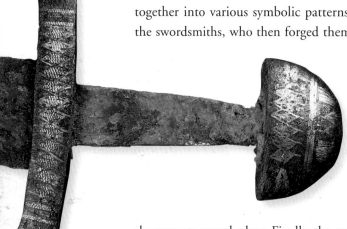

BELOW The Vikings often decorated their swords to give them special powers and would inscribe on them the names they had given them.

the separate sword edges. Finally, the sword was sharpened and burnished, leaving the central section with a fluid pattern. These pattern-welded or damascened swords were greatly regarded, being "patterned like a snake." One such sword was celebrated in the Anglo-Saxon poem *Beowulf*:

RIGHT A Celtic sword from between 500 and 100 B.C.E., from Grimston in northeastern England. Viking swords were derived from styles used by the Celts.

Not the least or worst of his war equipment
Was the sword the herald of Hrothgar lent
In his hour of need – its name Hrunting –
An ancient heirloom, trusty and tried;
Its blade was of iron, with an etched design
Tempered in the blood of many a battle …

The snake pattern was seen as the power within the sword. The Norse *Kormacs Saga* tells us how the hero borrowed a sword named Sköfnung to duel with his enemy, Bersi. Before the duel, Kormac was told by its owner how to empower the sword with his breath: "When you come to the fighting-place, go off alone to one side, then draw it. Hold up the blade and blow on it; a small snake will crawl from under the guard; slant the blade, making it easy for the snake to creep back again."

The Vikings recognized various blade-pattern styles and gave them descriptive names. The Old English *waegsweord* pattern they called *vaegir*. *Ann* resembled swathes of mown grain, and *blodidha* blood-eddy, or swirling blood. *Blodvarp*, blood-warp, and *idvarp*, intestine-warp, are styles whose pattern comprises long, parallel stripes running lengthwise. *Varp* is "warp," as in weaving, and the lines along the blade are likened to the warp of a weft that was completed when the blade was embedded in the enemy's body.

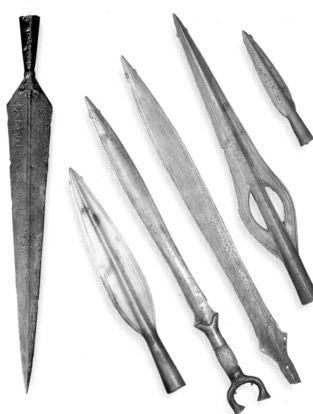

In the Viking period, around 900 C.E., the swordsmith Ulfberht of Solingen, in the Rhineland of Germany, created an improved sword. These new swords were designed so that their center of gravity lay nearer to the hilt. This was achieved by making the blade taper more markedly than before. Swords of this design gave swordsmen better maneuverability and speed.

It was traditional to inscribe the sword's name in runes upon the blade, hilt, or scabbard. Some have invocations of godly powers. *Sigrdrifumál*, a poem in the *Volsunga Saga*, recommends the rune of the god Tyr (Teiwaz) for successful combat: "Learn victory-runes if you seek victory, and have them on your sword's hilt ... some on your sword's guard, and call upon Tyr twice." A third-century scabbard from a Danish bog has a runic inscription meaning "Servant of Ull," god of archery. *Magnus Barefoot's Saga* tells how King Magnus carried a sword named Leggbitr ("Leg-biter"): "Its guards were of walrus tusk, and its hilt was covered with gold. It was one of the best of weapons."

Describing a battle, *Egils Saga* tells us "Thorolf had ... a sword which he called Lang ["The Long One"], a large and good weapon. Also, he had a spear in his hand ... Egil had the same equipment as Thorolf. He had a sword which he called Nadr ["The Adder"], which he had from Kurland. It was an excellent weapon."

Like swords, spears were also named. Their names were inlaid in runes. Runic spears excavated from warriors' graves include Raunijar ("The Tester"), from Øvre-Stabu (150 C.E.) in Denmark; and Rannja ("The Assailer"), from a grave at Dahmsdorf, Brandenburg (c.250 C.E.) in Germany.

Runic weapons were buried with warriors, a practice that had a twofold function. The departed warrior, going to Valhalla, the heavenly abode of heroes, needed the weapon in the next world. It also prevented a fine and famous weapon from passing on to those not worthy to bear it.

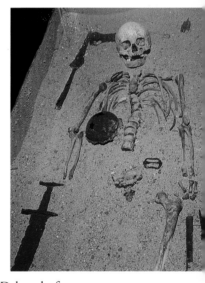

ABOVE The owner's weapons would be buried with a Viking warrior, to serve him in the afterlife.

OWNERS' MARKS

* * * * * * * * * * * * * * * * * *

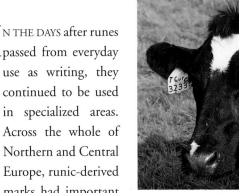

RIGHT Norse farmers identified their cattle with inscribed ear clips, in much the same way as they are marked today.

BELOW In this engraving, a horseman pulling sacks on a sled shows how owners commonly identified their goods by using runes.

I N THE DAYS after runes passed from everyday use as writing, they continued to be used in specialized areas. Across the whole of Northern and Central Europe, runic-derived marks had important applications. The most widespread of these were the family-marks, the *hof*-marks of nobles, and house-marks, all of which were the insignia by which a particular individual or group were known. In Norway, these insignia were called *bumerker*. They belonged to landowners, trades- and craftspeople, and were used in all areas of trade and business. Many are still in use today as family signs and trademarks.

The purpose of these runic marks was to act as a stamp of ownership on all kinds of property. Farmers used runic marks in order to identify their livestock, branding, clipping, or painting them on the animal. They were also cut into ears of domestic animals, and onto the beaks and webbed feet of geese, swans, and ducks. Lots used in the runrig divinations that allocated the division of land (*see pages 16–17*) sometimes carried individuals' runic marks. Plowmen starting a new field would plow their own signs into the earth to bring good luck and a bumper harvest.

Merchants and millers painted and printed their marks on their sacks, or attached wooden tags with runes – known in Norway as *merkelapper* – to them. Personal marks were branded onto carts, wagons, sleds, and boats. Loggers punched them into the bark of timber floated on rivers, so that individual owners' trees could be sorted out at the saw-pits. Hunters' weapons and prey were similarly marked, as were fishing-floats. Owners' house-marks were painted onto the outside of houses and carved into the woodwork of mills. They can still be seen all over Central Europe today. Sometimes, as is the case in East Anglia, in the east of England, wrought-iron wall-anchors were also made in the shape of the owner's house-mark. These identifying marks were woven into rugs and tapestries, stamped into metal cutlery, plate, and cups, and proudly displayed on personal rings and jewelery.

They were also used to decorate stained-glass windows in churches and halls, where they appeared in the heraldic crests of the nobility. They are still prominent in Central European burghers' coats of arms. Berne Cathedral, in Switzerland, has some fine examples. Finally, they appeared on the caskets and tombstones of their owners.

The most secretive of these mystical marks were used by the operative freemasons of medieval and later times, who worked the stone for churches, castles, and bridges. Many Central European masonic signs are runic in origin. Each individual mason had his own mark that was derived from the sign of the lodge and city to which he belonged.

Traditional family-, *hof-* and house-marks include the whole range of runes. Some house-marks are runic ideograms of tools and implements. In German-speaking lands, for example, they depict the key, flail, pothook, arrow, windmill, ladder, hanger, and hourglass. Some signs are long bindrunes containing the letters of family and personal names. Others range from elegant and simple runic forms to ferociously complex combinations. They can all be analyzed as bindrunes – combinations of various runes that give the house-mark both its own identity and its esoteric meaning.

In former times, each property-owning family possessed its own house-mark that was recognized throughout the local area. It was also possible for each individual in the family to have a mark that varied in a specific way from the basic form. By the addition of extra marks – such as double or treble crosses, points, dots, or small circles – next to the original sign, the signs of the sons, grandsons, and other relatives of the "founder" of the family dynasty could be created without destroying the basic unity of the original house-mark. In this way, the identity of individual property within the family group could be be defined.

Unlike heraldry, which is controlled by law in several European countries, personal marks are a matter of individual choice. If your trade or family has not already given you a personal mark, it is possible to create your own mark using runic letters.

LEFT A shield over a door in Wildberg, in Germany, displaying tools of the owner's trade, his initials, a runic house-mark, and the date, 1653.

LEFT The guildhall in Bamberg, Bavaria, Germany, which displays gilded-metal trade emblems and marks above the door.

TRADITIONAL BUILDINGS

* * * * * * * * * * * * * * * *

RUNIC TALISMANS, in the form of real objects or their corresponding runes, are used on traditional buildings, to deflect bad luck and evil or to draw in beneficial energies. Traditional European builders still have special protective rites and ceremonies that they perform during construction. There are ceremonies for selecting the site of the house, laying the foundations, building the fireplace, erecting the walls, and for topping-out the roof.

In former times, many builders' rites and ceremonies used symbolic objects. When laying the foundations, they often buried animal skulls. They believed that the skull of a cow brought the power of Fehu, wealth, while an ox skull had the runic power of Uruz, primal strength. Skulls were buried to protect the threshold and the hearth, the places of entry into the house. Horse skulls were also buried where sound needed to be amplified. They have been found beneath the floors of barns, where they assisted the men threshing grain with flails. If the threshing floor

RIGHT Odin's eight-legged horse was often invoked by carvings of horses' heads for protection.

ABOVE A Primitive Methodist chapel in the remote fens of Cambridgeshire, England. A horse's head was buried beneath it on its foundation in 1895, "to keep away witchcraft and evil."

RIGHT The familiar horseshoe is a symbol of good luck because its shape reflects the rune Uruz, the rune of strength, and its iron wards off evil spirits.

"rang" as a result of the buried skull, the threshing was held to go better. They are also found in the walls of some church chancels, where they were said to amplify the sound of the choir's singing. Today's custom of burying bottles may have substituted the earlier use of skulls. Many other protective items are buried in walls, under floors, or beneath wall-plaster.

Not all builders' talismans are hidden. Attached to the outside of buildings, horns invoke the power of Fehu and Uruz. In northern Germany, traditional buildings have twin wooden horse heads that refer to the horse rune Ehwaz. They invoke the protection of the sacred horse of the god Wotan (Odin). In shape, horseshoes resemble Uruz, the runic of primal strength, thus combining the magical power of iron, considered effective against evil spirits and bad luck, with the power of Uruz. They are nailed on or above doors with the points uppermost "to keep the luck from running out."

Nails themselves symbolize the power of the god Thor as the keeper of order in a chaotic world. To bring good luck, they are hammered into the front-door frame and the main

beams of a building. Nails resemble Isa in shape, the rune of changelessness. They are thought to bring good luck and protection from fire and intrusion.

Runes themselves are part of the repertoire of spiritual house-protection. The most common ones used in this way are Inguz, Dagaz, Gebo, Gar, and Othala. They appear frequently in contrasting-colored brickwork, or they may be carved or painted on the outside of a building in appropriate positions. Inguz, Gebo, Gar, and Othala are used in walls, while Dagaz, Gar, and Othala protect door- and window-frames. Structural posts of timber buildings are marked with the Gebo or Inguz runes. Inguz sometimes takes the form of "God's Nail," the common six-petaled flower pattern, when a flower is carved in the center of the rune. This symbolizes the Midnight Sun, seen at midsummer north of the Arctic Circle – a time where the power of light conquers all darkness. Old houses with inglenook fireplaces often have posts with this sign, protecting the place of fire and light. As well as symbolizing God's Nail, this flower pattern also represents the Younger Hagal (Hagalaz) rune. It stands for stability and continuity. The "hex," or "magic," signs

on traditional Pennsylvanian Dutch buildings are also mainly runic in origin. According to Pennsylvanian tradition, a building should have seven hex signs to be fully protected against all harm.

Old brick buildings in Northern Europe often have iron wall-anchors that tie the walls to wooden structural beams inside. Most wall-anchors are reverse S-shaped. This shape is the protective Eihwaz rune that symbolizes the spirit of the house, resisting attack by lightning and fire. Other common wall-anchors are Gebo shaped. Windows are protected by the Inguz and Gar runes, in the form of glazing lattices. The "leaded lights" of country cottages, castles, and churches are expanded Ing (Inguz) runes. Traditional English thatching, using straw or reed, also incorporates runes. The Ing rune appears as part of roof ridges and gable ends. Othala and Ing runes appear in contrasting-colored roof tiles in Britain, Ireland, and France, while in Germany and The Netherlands the Othala rune is used as a finial on the end of roof ridges.

LEFT The patterns in timber-framed buildings would often contain runes, as in this seventeenth-century house in Weobley, Herefordshire, England.

BELOW A lockup and clock tower with an Inguz rune in color-contrasting brickwork at Fenstanton, eastern England. Rune patterns have been found in buildings throughout the world in areas once colonized by the Vikings.

TWENTIETH-CENTURY BUILDINGS

* * * * * * * * * * * * * * * * * * *

IN 1912, PHILIPP STAUFF (1876–1923), the leading disciple of the Armanen theorist Guido List, published a book entitled *Runenhäuser* (*Runehouses*). In it, he claimed that the patterns of beams in timber-framed *Fachwerk* ("half-timbered") houses, built according to a particular style of structural timberwork, were runes. Stauff believed that the master-carpenters deliberately used combinations of patterns that rune users could read. To Stauff, each "rune house" contained a hidden message. It was a fasci-

Although many of them were destroyed in World War II, there are still 1½ million timber-framed buildings in Germany alone. The oldest buildings still standing date from the thirteenth-century, and the technique of building them is still known and practiced by the carpenters' guilds. New timber-framed buildings are built every year in the traditional way, especially in Austria and the south Tyrol. However, although Central European timber-framed buildings do appear to contain runic patterns, their structure is strictly practical. The forms come from the necessity of reinforcing the building frames at certain key points. These styles of building frames have proved so durable that they have remained unchanged for over 800 years.

In Germany, a number of local styles of *Fachwerk* exist, such as the Lower Saxon type that is common in Westphalia. In southern Germany, there are three main styles, these are *Alemannischen Fachwerk* (Alemannic), *Fränkischen Fachwerk* (Frankish), and Bavarian *Bundwerk*. Each style has very specific forms of carpentry. Frankish work has panels infilled with reinforcing crosswork that resemble Gar runes. Bavarian *Bundwerk* forms complex, trellis-like structures. There are traditional names for the joints and forms, but none of them are runic. The

ABOVE There are over 1½ million timber-framed buildings in Germany. New ones are still being built, like these farmhouses in Bavaria, which are modeled on ancient designs.

nating possibility, but his claim could not be backed up with any objective evidence. He did not mention that there was no tradition of this in the carpenters' guilds. But the idea caught on. Despite the absence of any proof that this was a historical reality, looking for "rune houses" became a popular pastime for the members of the Guido von List Society.

The Haus Atlantis

Perhaps the most remarkable of all German runic ornament of the twentieth century was found on the Haus Atlantis in Böttcherstrasse, Bremen, Germany. Part of an artistic building development, this ornament was designed by the pioneering architect and sculptor Bernhard Hötger (1874–1949). It was finished in 1931.

The structure of the Haus Atlantis was totally contemporary and forward-looking. It was the first building in which rolled steel was used in its construction. Inside the Haus Atlantis, the elaborate décor incorporated metal runes and Tree-of-Life motifs, but its most notable feature was the beautiful wood-carving on the façade. This displayed a huge Tree of Life including a representation of the god Odin's discovery of the runes. The carving showed the god crucified on a wheel inside the quotation from the Icelandic *Edda* that told of Odin's self-sacrifice. There were also 24 roundels that were carved with the Elder Futhark runes. These were wendrunes, which ran in a counterclockwise direction. However, the runes in the carving were not Armanen, and this image did not please the Nazis. Fearful for his life, Hötger was therefore forced to flee to Switzerland in 1933. Later on, his work was publicly condemned by Adolf Hitler himself. However, the building and sculpture survived until 1944, the twelfth year of Nazi rule. Then it was burned down, not by the Nazis but as the result of an Allied air-raid. When the Haus Atlantis was rebuilt in the 1950s, the carving, unfortunately, was not included.

ABOVE The runes around the edge of the sculpture were Elder Futhark runes carved in roundels.

LEFT The original façade of the Haus Atlantis in Bremen, Germany, showing Odin on the World Tree surrounded by runes.

nearest is the mainly Alemannic strengthening structure called *Mann*, which rune-house enthusiasts always look out for. But the inner mysteries of the timber-frame masters are not in the supposed runic patterns of beams. They are much more subtle than that. Where runic patterns do appear, they are carvings and painted signs that are intended to protect the building against evil spirits and bad luck.

After World War I, the numerous decorative possibilities of runes were recognized by modern architects. Runes and related craftsmen's marks from the *Zimmermann* (carpenters') guild tradition were carved visibly to symbolize continuity with old times. The Zipfer Bierhaus in Salzburg, Austria, which was built in 1931, is a fine example of this. It has a series of runic signs that have been carved on the ceiling rafters.

RIGHT A traditional runic Tree of Life painted on the walls of the living room of an old farmhouse in Saxony, Germany, around 1910.

HIDDEN CODES

★ ★ ★ ★ ★ ★ ★ ★ ★ ★ ★

MOST RUNIC INSCRIPTIONS are straightforward, and can be read by those who know the runes – the old language in which the inscriptions are written. But quite a few ancient runic inscriptions cannot be read in the normal way because there are no known words in them. Clearly, they are most unlikely to be nonsense, since no one would take the time and effort to carve runes into hard stone without reason, especially without wishing to communicate something. In fact, inscriptions that cannot be read directly are in some sort of code. The runes have the most complex cryptology of any ancient kind of writing. Because runes were used for magic, the runemasters of old often put their formulas in code that prevented others from reading the meaning. It also stopped other rune-users from changing the inscription and thereby altering the effect of the magic.

Wendrunes, which are written from right to left in the "wrong" direction, provide the simplest form of encoding. In times when many people could only read a little, even the idea of writing backward was secret, and this was enough to stop people from reading them. An important wendrune inscription may be seen in Sweden, carved on the standing stone at Möjbro, near Uppsala. It has a carving of a

RIGHT The Möjbro Stone of around 500 C.E., from near Uppsala, Sweden. The inscription over the rider is to be read from right to left, rather than the normal left to right, and from bottom to top.

horseman holding a wand or lance. Above him are two lines of wendrunes. Although the Younger Futhark was then in common use, this magical inscription contains all 24 letters of the Elder Futhark, suggesting that the carver considered the earlier form of runes to be more powerful.

Most runemasters went a lot farther than just writing backward. A widespread method of code substitutes one letter for another. In its simplest form, this involves moving the whole alphabet one letter in either direction. So the word "cat" – C-A-T – will be written RThS if the preceding letter is substituted. CAT will be GRB if the following letter replaces each one. Either technique forms an apparently meaningless row of letters. The runemasters often used this method to encode individual names. A good example of this can be seen on the church font at Kareby, in Bohuslan, Sweden, where an inscription in Norwegian runes says: "Read who can the name Orlaski." The final name, "Orlaski," is a code, which, by moving the whole alphabet back one by letter, reads Thorbjørn.

Another kind of character substitution was done either rune by rune or in groups of runes. There are almost limitless ways of doing this. One ancient method was discovered on a runic code-stick that was found in the Bryggen district of

Bergen, Norway. The stick is the key to a code that uses multiple letters to represent individual ones. It encodes the 16-character Younger Futhark. The runes read f, ff, ffo, oo, oooh, hh, hhha, aa, aaab, bb, bbb, which are equivalent to f, u, th, o, r, k, h, n, i, a, s, t, b, l, m. Code-sticks such as this allowed runemasters to exchange secret messages. They are similar to the Ogham code-sticks carried by the Celtic Druids and the sett-sticks of Scottish plaid-weavers that encode the colors for the clan's tartan.

Lonnrunor is another encryption technique that was used by the runemasters of old. It uses number symbols to denote the position of any letter in a prearranged group. As with the other cryptic systems, there are several variants. *Lonnrunor* can be produced simply by indicating the number of the letter from the beginning of the futhark. For example, in the Roman alphabet, the number 7 represents the letter "G." But the runic system offers greatly subtlety and flexibility, because the futhark is divided into three aettir, which allows for a "two-tier" numbering system. First, the three aettir are

numbered 1, 2, and 3. Then, within each aett, each rune is given a number. In this way, only two numbers are needed to define each letter. It is usual to write the aett number first, and then the rune's number within the aett.

Most commonly, the number code is written on an upright stave that has side branches that point upward – a branch rune (*kvistrúna*). On one side of the stave, the number of branches is the number of the *aett* containing the rune. On the other side of the stave, the number of branches denotes the number of the individual rune in that aett. Thus, a branch rune that bears two strokes to the left and six to the right represents the sixth rune of the second aett. Encryption can be made more complex by prearranging a different rune order. The numbers 1 to 3 can be given to any of the three aettir, and within the aettir the order of the letters can be changed.

Number Symbols

A simple code used to represent words by numbers uses the position of letters in each of the three aettir of the Elder Futhark. The first digit defines the aett, the second the letter's position in the order of the aett. Thus the name "Maria" is 34 (Mannaz), 14 (Ansuz), 15 (Raidho), 23 (Isa), 14 (Ansuz). The numbers can also be represented by branches on a stave, with the number of strokes on the one on the left giving the aett, and those on the one on the right giving the position of the letter in the aett.

M	A	R	I	A
34	14	15	23	14

SECRET MESSAGES

* * * * * * * * * * * * * * * *

THERE ARE MANY ways of encoding the information that is contained in the aettir, other than those already mentioned on pages 108–9. Other codes used by the runemasters of old include *hahalrúnar* (hook runes), *tjaldrúnar* (tent runes), *Iis* runes, and *Lagu* runes. The side branches on branch runes point upward, while those of the *hahalrúnar* point downward. Whichever way they are written, the principle is exactly the same. The aett number is shown on one side and the rune number is shown on the other. Tent runes are similar, but do not use the vertical stem. They are based on an X-shape. Tent runes are usually read sunwise, beginning on the left.

The *Iis* runes use numbers to denote individual runes, but unlike the branch, tree, and tent runes, these runes are made up of unconnected, single strokes. To represent the number of the aett, the *Iis* runes use short strokes. The number of each rune within the aett is shown by longer strokes. The *Lagu* runes are related closely to the *Iis* runes, using the *Lagu* runes in the place of the single strokes.

Further codes using other runes have been found, but they are much less common. One interesting example is a runic code-stick found at Narssaq in Greenland, which used a version of the Younger Futhark Kaun rune. Other systems use groups of dots or lines, combinations of dots and lines, and alternate short and long lines attached to an upright stem. It is possible that some systems in Northumbria may use the techniques of the Irish Ogham tree alphabet. Undeciphered runic cryptograms also exist on certain ancient artifacts, such as the fragment of a Christian stone cross that is kept in the church at Hackness, near Scarborough in Yorkshire, northern England. This stone cross also has signs resembling Ogham. There are many more cryptic stones in Scandinavia, but most are yet to be deciphered.

A different type of runic code that was popular during the medieval period uses the basic meanings of individual runes in order to spell out their corresponding letters. These are then combined to spell out a hidden word. An example of this is found in the eighth-century Old English poem, *Elene*, written by the poet Cynewulf to encode his own name in Anglo-Saxon runes. Three of his four signed poems contain his name in this way:

RIGHT Tent runes, or tree runes (shown on bottom row) were one of the many codes used by ancient runemasters. These codes are based on the shape of a cross.

BELOW Heimdall, the gods' herald, from a carving in the Isle of Man. Viking hunters would send hidden messages by blowing their horns according to a code based on kloprunes.

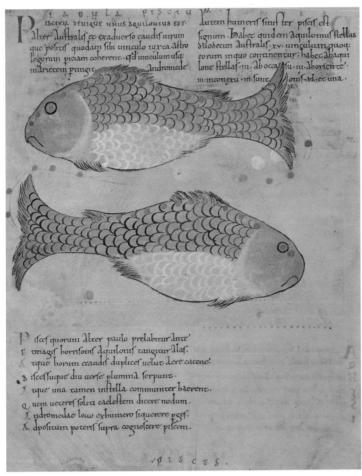

Nyd; and "aurochs," Ur, is both a kenning and a pun.

By using such methods, poets and runemasters were able to hide messages for those who could decode them. Runic codes also gave a way of transmitting messages through walls or over long distances. The method called *kloprúna* used sounds in groups representing rune and aett in the same way as written codes. These kloprunes were the forerunners of the nineteenth-century Morse Code. In close use, they were sent by clapping hands and knocking, and over longer distances by wooden clappers, drums, horns, and bells. It is likely that horn codes used by medieval huntsmen were based on *kloprúna*. An ancient Greek technique was also used to send encoded messages at night. Flaming torches were shown in groups on either side of a board or shield. Those on one side represented the aett, and those on the other the number of the rune in that aett. It is also possible that a kind of runic semaphore was used on the battlefield and between ships at sea.

Until then, the man had always been attacked by waves of sadness: he was a burning torch *[Cen, C], though in the Mead-Hall he was given treasures, apple-shaped gold. He lamented the* evil *[Yr, Y], he the brother of* sorrow *[Nyd, N]; he suffered affliction, cruel secret thoughts, though for him the* horse *[Eh, E], measured the mile-paths, ran proudly, adorned with ornaments.* Joy *[Wyn, W] diminishes, and pleasure too, as the years pass by; youth has gone and former pride. Once, the glory of youth was* ours *[Ur, U]. Now, with time, the old days have passed away, life's joys have slipped away, even as* water *[Lagu, L] drains away, the flowing floods.* Wealth *[Feoh, F] is transitory for all people under heaven: the Earth's ornaments disappear beneath clouds like the wind when it blows loudly ... [author's emphasis].*

In this extract, "evil" is a kenning for "yew" or Yr; "sorrow" is an aspect of "need,"

CALENDARS

✱ ✱ ✱ ✱ ✱ ✱ ✱ ✱ ✱ ✱

THE OLD WOODEN runic clog almanacs recorded time in the Julian Calendar, which was the standard calendar used from Roman times until 1582–1921, depending on country. Within the Julian Calendar are cycles that are only used now by churchmen for the calculation of Easter Sunday. Easter is defined by the correspondences between the spring equinox, the day of the week, and the phase of the moon. To figure out such complex cycles, mathematicians in Imperial Rome established a system of notation using the so-called "Golden Number" in combination with a "Dominical Letter" (*see opposite*). In the year 325 C.E., a Church conference at Nicaea, in what is now Turkey, ruled that Easter Day should be celebrated on the first Sunday after the full moon following the vernal (spring) equinox. If this is a Sunday, however, then Easter must be celebrated a week later.

The runic calendar codes are based on the interaction between two sequences of

RIGHT Julius Caesar devised the Roman calendar, which was the basis of old runic calendars.

BELOW A Swedish runic calendar of 1755. This calendar is unusual in being printed on paper; most were carved in wood.

numbers. First of all, there is the sun-moon period of 19 years. This covers all of the phases of the moon, after which the new moons fall on the same cycle of dates as defined by the sun. This is usually known as the Metonic Cycle, after the fifth-century B.C.E. Greek sage Meton, who first described it. Each year in the Metonic Cycle is given a number from 1 to 19. This is known as the "Golden Number" or "Prime." It can be found by adding 1 to the year date, and then dividing it by 19. The remainder is the Golden Number. The Golden Number sequence is thus an "endless chain" of the numbers 1 to 19. These numbers do not run in the normal sequence, however, because the number 8 is added to the preceding number. (This "code" enables those who know how to calculate the 19-year concordance of the moon's cycles with the solar year.)

On wooden almanacs, the numbers are represented by the 16 letters of the Younger Futhark, with three other, new runes called Aurlaugr (for 17), Belgtzhor (for 18), and Twimadur (for 19) added in. The sequence runs: Fé; Is; Aurlaugr; Kaun; Logr; Thurs; Sól; Belgtzhor; Naudhr; Yr; Raeidh; Bjarkan; Ur; Ar; Twimadur; Hagall; Madhr; Óss; Tyr; and then again Fé, etc.

The cycle of the Julian Calendar also contains the Dominical letters. In the Norse wooden almanacs, these seven letters are represented by the runes Fé, Ur, Thurs, Óss, Raeidh, Kaun, and Hagall. These runes tell

The Golden Number

Runic calendar codes are based on the correspondence between the lunar and solar cycles. Every 19 years there is a recurrence of the dates on the solar calendar on which the phases of the moon occur exactly. Each year in this 19-year cycle is numbered accordingly.
• To compute this number take the date, add 1, divide by 19, and the number left over is the Golden Number.

• Thus for 2001:
2001 + 1 = 2002 ÷ 19 = 105 with a remainder of 7.
If there is no remainder, the Golden Number is 19.
• However, in the code the numbers do not follow each other simply, but in series of eight.
Thus the sequence beginning with 1 goes:

1 – 9 – 17 – 6 – 14 – 3 – 11 – 19 – 8 – 16 – 5 – 13 – 2 – 10 – 18 – 7 – 15 – 4 – 12 – 1

us when Sundays fall in any given year. This is calculated by adding to the year date a quarter of it, omitting remainders, and also the number 6. Then the sum is divided by 7. If there is no remainder, the Dominical letter is Fé. If there is a remainder, then there is another Dominical letter that year. The remainders from one to six define the other days, thus: 1, Hagall; 2, Kaun; 3, Raeidh; 4, Óss; 5, Thurs; and 6, Ur. Leap years have two Dominical letters, one before February 29, and another after it.

The whole sequence of letters and numbers makes a 532-year cycle, composed of 28 x 19 years. Within this cycle, any individual day can be defined by a combination of the Golden Number, the Dominical Letter, and another number that is the number of days remaining in that year. These were used on runic memorials.

Runemasters used these sequences to record dates. Sometimes, they gave numbers that corresponded with a position on the Perpetual Easter Table, a list of Golden Numbers and Dominical letters that was used by priests. These were encoded in runic inscriptions. As well as recording dates, these number sequences were used to find the magical, numerological qualities of days. Although most Protestant countries had, by the eighteenth century, adopted the Gregorian Calendar, which the Roman Catholic Pope Gregory XIII had introduced in 1582, in the rural areas people continued to use the older Julian Calendar. When printed calendars and almanacs became available, most of these used the Gregorian Calendar, and the wooden almanacs went out of use. Then runes ceased being used for Golden numbers and Dominical letters. Estonia, however, did not change to the new calendar until 1921, when it had just gained independence from the Soviet Union. Runic calendars remained in use there until that year. Although the runic almanacs are no longer used, New Year is still celebrated according to the old calendar in Cwm Gwaen in Pembrokeshire, Wales, and at Burghead in Morayshire, Scotland.

ABOVE Pope Gregory XIII introduced the calendar that is essentially the one we use today.

PART FOUR

WEAVING THE WEB OF WYRD

★ ★ ★ ★ ★

The runes can help us in every aspect of life. As well as having the basic meanings already described, the runes interweave with every aspect of the spiritual world. Every rune is connected with the powers of a god or goddess of the old Northern European pantheon. Each one also expresses a precise aspect of human psychology that speaks directly to us. Because they reflect the human psyche, the runes are valuable tools in meditation, and because they relate to the human body, too, we can use them in body work, including runic yoga and dance.

The runes are versatile in other ways. They correspond with colors and numbers, the directions of the compass, the times of day and night, and the turning wheel of the year. There is even a form of astrology that is based on the runes and their place in the cycles of time. Even more is possible, for advanced rune work also combines them in special ways, enhancing their potential even further. Through the runes we are given many possible ways to live more conscious and harmonious lives.

ABOVE A tenth-century Viking amulet of Thor's hammer. Each of the runes was associated with a particular god or goddess. The Thurisaz rune is related to the thunder-god Thor.

THE THREE ASPECTS OF FATE

★ ★ ★ ★ ★ ★ ★ ★ ★ ★ ★ ★ ★ ★ ★ ★

IN THE NORTHERN Tradition, of which the runes are part, everything is composed of three aspects. This idea is the core of existence. Everything has a beginning, a middle, and an end. Everything present in time is ruled by this triadic law. The cycle of the day is threefold, starting with sunrise, flourishes at midday, and ending with sunset. We, as humans, must experience this cycle in our own lives through the three events of birth, life, and death. In life itself, there is a threefold structure of youth, maturity, and old age.

There is an old English saying, "The present is the daughter of the past, and the mother of the future," which expresses our presence within time. Traditionally, this presence has also been seen as a threefold unity, with the present as the moving middle link between the past and the future. European mythology depicts these three temporal states as three female figures, who, by extension of the same idea, become the three goddesses of fate who rule human destiny – past, present, and future.

Sometimes their triple role is combined in a single figure. In ancient Rome, for example, the goddess of fate was known as Fortuna, a figure downgraded in modern times to "Lady Luck." Classical tradition, however, depicts three goddesses of time and fate. In ancient Greece they were the Moirai: Clotho, Lachesis, and Atropos, the three daughters of Night. Images of the Moirai show Clotho holding a distaff, Lachesis handling a spindle, and Atropos carrying shears. Clotho spins the thread of life; Lachesis uses her ruler to measure it; and Atropos finally cuts it.

To the Romans, these three fates were the Parcae, from a Latin word meaning "to bring forth." They are called None, Decima, and Morta, meaning "nine," "ten," and "death." To the Romano-Celts, there were three similar goddesses, the Matrones (the "Mothers"), who watched over humankind. In ancient pagan Germany, they were the "Three Eternal Ones," Einbet, Barbet, and Wilbet. Their Northern European equivalent, are the three Norns, whose power rules the runes. The first Norn is Urd, "that which was"; the second, Verdandi, "that which is becoming"; and the last Skuld, "that which

RIGHT Teiwaz, Fehu, and Isa from the first, second, and third aett of the threefold structure of the Elder Futhark.

BELOW In Nordic tradition, everything is governed by the rule of three. Thus the main aspects of the day are dawn, midday, and sunset.

is to come." Like the three Greek fates, the first Norn, Urd, spins the thread of existence. She passes the spun thread on to Verdandi, who weaves it into the present pattern of existence, the Web of Wyrd. This is seen as a woven fabric composed of myriad strands or threads, "woven by the decrees of fate." Verdandi passes the woven web to Skuld, who rips it apart and disperses it back into the void. In old England, they were called the "Weird Sisters," mentioned in Geoffrey Chaucer's *The Legend of Good Women* (1385). Later, they appeared as the three witches in William Shakespeare's play *Macbeth* (1606), describing themselves as "the weird sisters, hand in hand, posters of the sea and land."

Whatever they called them, people have tried to question these goddesses of time and fate. Writing around the year 1200, the Danish commentator Saxo Grammaticus tells us that in his time pagans who wished to know their children's future would consult the goddesses through the priestesses who represented them. "Three maidens sitting on three seats," impersonating the Norns, went into a trance and answered questions about things to come. These beings are personifications of the three parts of time. However, although the mythical fates may appear equal, the three parts of time are not equivalent to one another. The past, the realm of Urd, is fixed, and cannot be changed. It is known, or at least partially recorded, and its effects are present. Verdandi's time, the present, is in a state of constant change. We are experiencing it now, and it is here, even when our perception of it is imprecise. But the future, the domain of Skuld, has not happened yet. It is totally unknown, though its shape is determined both by past and present events. Ever since the rise of human consciousness, the shape of things to come has been a major human preoccupation. Runic divination is one way of finding out what that future may look like.

THE GODDESSES AND GODS
OF RUNECRAFT

★ ★ ★ ★ ★ ★ ★ ★ ★ ★ ★ ★ ★ ★

HE RUNES BELONG to the Teutonic world-view, which has its own gods and goddesses. Traditionally, each deity rules over a specific aspect of life. The northern deities are grouped into three main dynasties. The

ABOVE Combining fire, water, and air, the rainbow symbolizes the gods who rule those elements: Loge, Hler, and Kari.

oldest represents elemental powers. They include the ice-, fire-, and earth-giants, and formless elemental beings. The more human deities of nomadic hunting and fishing are called the Vanir. Both these dynasties were superseded and absorbed by those representing the settled life of agriculture, the Aesir gods and Asyniur goddesses, headed by Odin, Thor, and Frigg. Having been discovered by Odin, the runes are mainly associated with this dynasty.

Particular runes are associated with, or shared by, these different deities and elemental beings. But they do not all come from the same futhark. Since the personae of the gods and goddesses were never formally established in written texts, they were never fixed in people's minds. Consequently, over

the years, people understood and worshiped them in various ways and attached runes from different futharks to them.

The elementals represent the basic forces of material existence. They are Loge, god of wild-fire; Kari, air; and Hler, the water-god. Their symbol is the rainbow, made of fire, water, and air. The fourth and fifth elements, earth and ice, are represented by Erda, the fruitful earth-goddess, and Rinda, goddess of the frozen earth. Collectively, they are represented by Uruz.

The main deities of the Vanir are Freyr and Freyja, whose rune is Fehu. Freyja's two daughters, Hnossi and Gersemi, rule all things bright and beautiful in the natural world. Their rune is Wunjo.

The Aesir and Asyniur are represented by the "god rune" Ansuz. Their chief god is Woden/Wotan or Odin, the Allfather. Odin's runes are Othala and Óss. Together with his two brothers, Vili and Vé, they signify spirit (Odin), will (Vili), and holiness

RIGHT The chief of the Aesir, Odin, or Woden/Wotan, was usually depicted with his two ravens, one eye, and a dark hat.

(Vé). The sons of Odin have specific functions. Hermod is the messenger of the gods. His runes are Raidho, Ehwaz, and Laguz. Vidar, whose task is to destroy the demonic Fenris-wolf, has the runes Stan and Wolfsangel. Vali the archer, god of lovers, has Gebo and Yr.

Frigg, Odin's consort, is queen of heaven, "most magnificent." She rules over food, clothing, and married sexuality. Attending her is Sága, the goddess of events in time. Her rune is Perdhro, for recalling hidden things. Gná is Frigg's messenger, while Hlí is the goddess of infinite compassion. Sjöfn, goddess of love, and Hlí both share the Gebo rune with Gefn, goddess of giving. Gefjon is goddess of unmarried women, and Lofn (for whom there is no appropriate rune) brings together lovers under unfavorable conditions. The goddess of healing and medicine is Eír. Her runes are Berkana, Laguz, Ul, and Sól. Vor witnesses oaths, and Var punishes people who do not keep their word. The goddess Syn guards the door. She admits desirable people and things, while keeping out the undesirable. Her rune is Dagaz.

The Aesir gods rule the traditionally masculine aspects of humanity. Tyr (Tîwaz), sky-god of battle and victory, is the sword-god. His name is also the name of a rune. Thor, deity of thunder and lightning, defense and strength, is the god of the working man, laboring in the fields and forges. His rune is Thurisaz. His consort, the golden-haired Sif, rules over the bright, fertile days of summertime, bringing peace and happiness, with the runes Berkana and Inguz. The god Ing represents male sexuality, enclosure, protection, and regeneration. His runes are Inguz and Raidho. Bragi, the bardic god of poetry and eloquence, has Ansuz, Kenaz, and Óss. The rune of Baldr "the beautiful" is Sowulo. The goddess Sól is his female counterpart. Forseti, the ax-god, son of Baldr, is champion of justice, with the runes Sowulo and Teiwaz.

Chief of the Aesir water-deities is Aegir, god of the stormy sea. His consort, Ran, destroyer of ships, is goddess of death for all who perish at sea. Their rune is Laguz. Njord is the Vanir god of coastal waters who stills storms. His runes are Fehu and Laguz. Njord is the consort of Skadi, whose name means "shadow." She is the destroyer-goddess of wintertime. Her runes are Eihwaz, Hagalaz, and Isa. Hela is the ruler of death, and keeper of the underworld. Her runes are Eihwaz, Hagalaz, Naudhiz, and Isa. Ullr is the yew-tree god of midwinter, skiing, sleds, and archery. His runes are Eihwaz and Yr. Finally, the trickster-god Loki and the Fenris-wolf are bound in the underworld. Their dangerous powers remain unresolved.

LEFT An Icelandic bronze figure of Thor, in the warrior's "Iron Beard" posture, from around 1000 C.E.

ABOVE Loki, the trickster-god and precipitator of the cosmos's final catastrophe, depicted here bound in the underworld during the Last Days.

LEFT A Viking silver pendant, showing Baldr, the most handsome of the gods, on a horse.

THE FEMALE MEANINGS
OF THE RUNES

* * * * * * * * * * * * * * * * * *

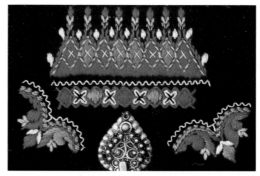

RIGHT Norwegian embroidery. Such crafts have traditionally been done by women and included runic patterns.

WRITTEN RECORDS OF the runes come mainly from the times of the Vikings, which was a male-dominated patriarchal society. Also, our basic knowledge of the runes' meanings comes from the three rune poems. Because of this, the runes are sometimes criticized for having little connection with women. However, this is a misunderstanding. There are specifically feminine meanings to most of the runes. The runes are a universal system, which are part of the Europe-wide goddess tradition, having their place in women's mysteries. As mothers and teachers of children, women have always been the main carriers of human language. Women have also been the main guardians of human signs and symbols, through the handicrafts of pottery, weaving, knitting, and housekeeping.

The runes contain a logical progression of creation, from the first rune to the last rune: beginning with Audhumla, the primal creatress, and ending with Gar, representing mystic union. Fehu represents Audhumla, the primal cow of the Norse creation myth. She is the first being, the creatress of all material things. As the white, horn-bearing, milk-giving Moon Cow, she symbolizes the Great Mother

ABOVE Fehu, whose feminine side is associated with Audhumla, the sacred cow that fed the first beings on Earth.

ABOVE Raidho, whose feminine aspect lies in its link with the seeress who oversees human existence.

as the preserver of all life. Uruz represents Mother Earth, the origin of life and awareness. Thurisaz is the rune of the goddess Thrud, whose name means "power" or "strength." Thurisaz is the archetype of the strong woman.

The god-rune Ansuz signifies the Asyniur, the goddesses, who are "no less important than the gods." Raidho is the wheel of existence, the symbol of the seeress who oversees all human life. Kenaz is the fountain of wisdom, ruled over by the three Norns. Gebo is the rune of Gefjon, the freely giving goddess of abundance. Wunjo is the otherworldly "fairy flag" that is carried by the servants of the queen of Elfland, Titania. This sign brings advantage to all who recognize it.

Hagalaz and Hagall are the runes of the underworldly goddesses Holda and Hela, who are beings of transformation. The Naudhiz rune signifies Nott, the goddess of the night, and the necessity of sleep for regeneration. Isa, ice, is personified by Rinda, the freezing goddess of immobility. Jera represents the Moon in all her phases and the goddess of harvest, Sif. Eihwaz is the rune of Skadi, the merciless, wintry, destroyer-goddess.

LEFT A Swedish figure of a priestess. Although Scandinavian culture was male-dominated, women were thought to have particular magical and spiritual powers.

Perdhro symbolizes both the womb and the holy jar that is sometimes used as a burial-vessel, promising rebirth. Elhaz is the protective rune of the Disir, the Divine Grandmothers who serve as our spiritual guardians. These goddesses are the "fairy godmothers" of folktale. Sowulo represents Sól, the goddess of the sun, "the glory of elves." She brings the warming, nurturing sunlight. Teiwaz represents the Pole Star, sacred to the goddess Zisa. It is the spindle star of Frigg, the queen of the heavens.

The shape of Berkana represents the breasts of the nurturing Mother Goddess whose sacred tree is the birch. Ehwaz is the rune of the White Mare, or the horse-goddess who is known as Epona or Horsel. Mannaz tells us that all human beings are the children of Mother Earth. Laguz is the flowing water, ruled over by the dangerous sea-goddess Ran. Inguz is the rune of the Earthly goddess of fruitfulness, Nerthus, who keeps all the good things of the world in a basket in her lap.

Dagaz is the rune of the door, controlled by the goddess Syn, who admits only those who should come in. Othala is the hearth, nurturing and containing the spirit of the household, symbolized by the goddess Hertha. Closely related to Othala is the later rune Erda, the symbol of the Earth Mother. Ac is the acorn, the symbol of potential. It is the woman's rune of pregnancy and childbirth.

Óss is the speech-rune. It signifies the female role in carrying language, which most of us learned at our mother's knee. The female version of the yew-tree rune, Yr, represents the loom, the implement of the weaving sisters who create our destiny. Ior is the rune of the female World Serpent, Iormungand, who represents the primal forces of existence. The rune Ear is the earth-grave, where Erda, Mother Earth, receives back her children. Cweorth, as the funeral pyre, is another means of Mother Earth taking back her dead. Next, Calc is the caldron of rebirth.

Stan signifies motherstone, a type of stone also called puddingstone. This stone was used traditionally to mill grain into flour, so it is a vital component in making bread. Gar, as a woman's rune, represents mystic union – the gathering-in of all created things – at the end of the runic cycle.

ABOVE AND LEFT
In its female aspect, Teiwaz represents the spindle star of the goddess Frigg.

THE AETT DEITIES

* * * * * * * * * * * * * * * *

IN THE NORTHERN Tradition, the different groups of runes are ruled by various gods and goddesses. The first aett, beginning with the rune Fehu ("F"), is ruled by Freyja and Freyr. The second aett, beginning with the rune Hagalaz ("H"), is ruled by Heimdall and Mordgud, while the third, beginning with the rune Teiwaz ("T"), is ruled by Tyr (Tîwaz) and Zisa. The deities of the first aett are the chief goddess and god of the Vanir, the gods of nature, while the other two aettir are under the goddesses of the Asyniur and gods of the Aesir, deities of human order.

The names "Freyja" and "Freyr," who rule the first aett, mean "The Lady" and "The Lord." According to the medieval Icelandic writer Snorri Sturluson, Freyja was the most renowned of the goddesses. She rules over the plants of the Earth, the trees and animals of the forest, natural love, female sexuality, and magic. Freyja is the goddess of love between men and women, and her assistance may be called upon in love affairs. In ancient times, women giving birth called on the goddesses Freya and Frigg in order to ease their pains.

Freyja wears a magical necklace called Brisingamen, made of amber or quartz. She travels through the worlds wearing a falcon skin, or in a chariot pulled by cats or bears. As well as being

pulled by cats, Freyja may also ride one – a twelfth-century wall-painting in Schleswig Cathedral, Germany, shows her astride a large, striped cat that may be a Siberian tiger.

The god Freyr rules over fertility, sexuality, prosperity, sacred kingship, and, in a lesser capacity, battle and death. Freyr is the god of growth, male sexuality, and the fruitful rain. In Sweden, Freyr was held in the highest regard, being called Blótguy Svía, the blessing-god of the Swedes. He was also called Veraldar Gudh, "God of the World." The swine and the horse are his holy animals, especially the magic boar, called either Gullinbursti (the "gold-bristled") or Slíthrugtanni (the "cutting-tusked"). The characteristics of the boar or sow give the animal powerful symbolic associations. It roots in the earth, it is highly fertile yet may also eat its own offspring – like the earth-mother Gaia, who both gives life and takes it back into herself – while Freyr's golden boar, Gullinbursti, evokes the archetype of Sol Invictus, the "Unconquerable Sun," who at the Winter Solstice on December 21 is "reborn," a symbol of the irrepressible power of regeneration. In England, Freyr is still ceremonially honored at Yuletide, when a boar's head is eaten, a seasonal custom that continues to this day at Queen's College, Oxford and at the Swan Hotel in Bedford.

The second aett is ruled over by the guardian god and goddess Heimdall and Mordgud. Heimdall is guardian-watcher of the gods and keeper of Bifröst, the rainbow bridge between

ABOVE The treasures found on the Oseberg ship, used for the burial of an aristocratic woman, show Freyja on a sled pulled by cats.

RIGHT A Swedish bronze statuette of Freyr, the god of fertility.

Earth and heaven. Disguised as Rigr, Heimdall organized the classes of traditional society – bondsman, yeoman, and lord (*see page 84*). His power is to "rig" things, arranging matters according to their proper order. His rune is Hagalaz in its structural aspect. Just as Heimdall rules Bifröst, so Mordgud guards the bridge leading downward into the underworld.

The third aett is ruled over by the god Tyr and the goddess Zisa. As the sky-father Tîwaz, Tyr was the chief god of the ancient Germanic tribes. In the later Norse religion his position as Allfather was taken over by Odin. His loss of power is seen in the Old Norse language, where the name Tyr came to mean just "god." Before Tyr was superseded, he was god of order and justice. The *Prose Edda* says: "There is a god called Tyr. He is the boldest and most courageous, and has power over victory in battle; it is good for brave men to call upon him."

The god's name probably means "shining" or "resplendent." The Anglo-Saxon rune poem refers to the rune Tyr as a star that "keeps its faith well with nobles, always on course through the dark of night, it never fails." This is probably the sailors' guiding star called "God's Nail" (the North Star, and also its emblem, the six-petaled flower). The Old Icelandic rune poem describes Tyr as "ruler of the temple." In the eleventh century, the Suebi of southern Germany worshiped him as Ziu. His consort, the goddess Cisa or Zisa, had a shrine at Augsburg, where they celebrated her festival annually on September 28.

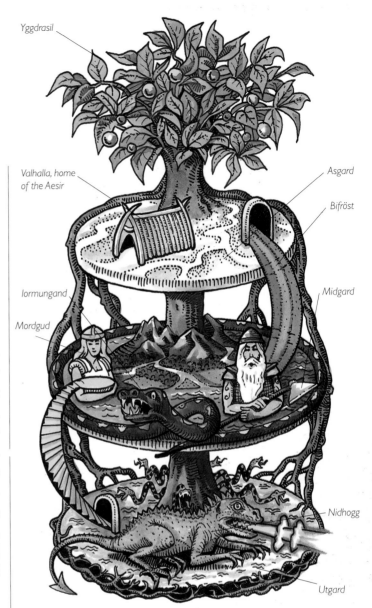

Yggdrasil

Valhalla, home of the Aesir

Asgard

Bifröst

Iormungand

Mordgud

Midgard

Nidhogg

Utgard

In the later rune-rows, the name of the leading rune of the third aett is Tyr. The poem *Sigrdrifumál* tells us to use the rune Tyr in order to ensure victory in combat: "Learn victory-runes if you seek victory, and have them on your sword's hilt … some on your sword's guard, and call upon Tyr twice." This rune is also associated with burial. It appears as early as the third century on artifacts from the Galgenberg, at Cuxhaven in Germany. In England, this rune was stamped on cremation urns that date from the fifth and sixth centuries, which were buried in Anglian cemeteries in Norfolk and Lincolnshire.

ABOVE The aettir are each ruled over by one of the most important deities, binding the written language to the essence of the cosmos itself. This consists of the three worlds: Asgard, home of the gods, Midgard, home of humanity, and Utgard, the realm of the dead, as shown above.

RUNIC INITIATION

* * * * * * * * * * * * * * * * *

A GOOD WAY IN which to begin working with the runes is through the ceremony of the runemaster's initiation. This involves a 24-day-long series of meditations, where each of the runes is meditated upon in the correct sequence. The meditation for day 1 will be on the first rune, Fehu. That for day 2 will be on the second rune, Uruz; for day 3, the third rune, Thurisaz, and so on, until the 24th day is the day of the final rune, Othala.

The initiation also involves baking 24 cookies or cakes, each of which bears one of the runes. For breakfast on each of the 24 days, the initiate eats the corresponding runic cookie or cake while concentrating upon its meaning.

Using the runes well is like any other skill. To use them properly you must learn about them. When interpreting runic readings, it is necessary to be able to call up any rune in your mind at once without difficulty. The simplest way in which to get to know the runes is to make your own set of runecards. Printed runecards, while useful in divination, are not so good when learning the runes. It is also beneficial to make your own cards, because they will then contain your own energy from making them.

Draw each rune carefully on an individual card, thinking about the meaning of the rune as you do it. It is best to draw the rune in red ink upon a white cardboard about 9 inches (23 centimeters) square. You can call or sing the name of the rune as you draw it. Start with the 24 runes of the Elder Futhark, which are the basic runes. When you have mastered these, you can, if you want to, go on to draw the remaining runes.

To start using your runecards, you should sit comfortably, in good, but not dazzling, light. Go through the cards in order, beginning with Fehu and ending with Othala. Put a runecard in front of you in a place where you can see it without holding it. Then look at the rune in front of you, concentrating on its form and thinking of the rune's meaning as you view it. When you shut your eyes, you should continue to see the rune for a short time. This will help you to develop the ability to see the rune without the help of the rune card.

Another way of getting closer to the runes is to look for them in nature. Because they have their origins in nature they are present everywhere in the natural world – if only we can see them. Seeking them here is a valuable meditation that is possible only with the runes. No other alphabet or symbolic system can be used in this way.

ABOVE Cakes or cookies decorated with runes are baked especially for the initiation of runemasters.

RIGHT Making your own cards is an excellent way of getting to know the runes.

To start the meditation, go into the outside world and banish unwanted thoughts. Then look for runes wherever they appear to you. You may see them in the branches of trees, the cracks in the earth, the shadows and shafts of sunlight, or the patterns made by flying flocks of birds. They also exist in the human-made world in cracks, flaking paintwork, rust, dust, stains, and the patterns made by leakages and spillages of fuel and water. But although they are ever-present, we can only see the runes when our minds are receptive.

Once you have developed this way of seeing, it is time to take the next step. This is an awareness meditation, and involves seeing all of the runes in order in nature, one by one. To do this, take a walk, all the time looking for runes. It is best to do this in the country if you can, but it is also possible in an urban environment, especially where there are trees. Once one rune has made itself known to you, go on to the next one. Although some runes may come easily, occasionally one cannot "find" all of the runes in their correct order. Sometimes the next rune does not appear for a long time – this can be very frustrating!

If you cannot discover the next rune in the sequence, do not be tempted to cheat. Not seeing a rune is as important as seeing one. The "failure" to see a certain rune tells us something about ourselves.

The rune that we cannot find represents something that is repressed or blocked inside us, so this exercise is an effective way of discovering what this block is. Once we realize what the nonappearance is telling us, then the rune will appear, almost miraculously.

The runes allow us to access the patterns of nature in two ways. In the meditation above, we open ourselves to runes that are already "out there." This is an "incoming" technique, where we see and interpret what the world gives us. When we divine with the runes, we create the patterns ourselves, in what is an "outgoing" technique. The runes we use here exist either in the form of stones, slivers, or cards, or are created when we throw sticks.

LEFT Runes can be seen in tree branches or the patterns of bark.

BELOW Runes can equally well be drawn on cards, inscribed on stones, or produced by casting-sticks.

RUNIC MEDITATION

* * * * * * * * * * * * * * * * * *

IT IS ONLY possible to make real progress with the runes through inner discipline. Runemasters see the runes as the medium through which we can draw knowledge from within. The runes thereby involve traditional spiritual techniques that bring us into communion with the other levels of reality that they symbolize.

Mastering the runes is not simple, but it can be achieved through dedicated effort. But before starting runic meditation you must have worthy intentions. You should commit yourself to using the powers you gain only for needs that do not subvert the freewill of other people. Also, so that you do not raise the wrong sorts of energy, it is necessary to perform runic spiritual exercises that raise you to a state of "purification." Only after you have performed some form of cleansing and protection ritual should you encounter the runes. This involves personal cleanliness, and wearing clean clothes. Many rune users set aside special clothes that they wear only in meditation.

Once you have finished the runic exercise, you should not just get up and walk away. You must complete it properly, in a "re-awakening" to reenter the world of normal consciousness. The best way in which to do this is to use the methods to the right in reverse order. Consciously order each part of your body, in turn, to function normally once again. This technique should be used for a few minutes each day, and in divination whenever a runecast is to be made.

After initiation, the relationship between the rune user and the runes can be developed by other runic meditations.

Basic Meditation

There are five basic elements in runic meditation. They are: 1, posture; 2, breathing; 3, banishment of unwanted thoughts; 4, concentration, and 5, the runic calls.

STAGE 1

Each time you meditate, you must sit or stand in a definite posture. You should feel relaxed, yet alert. There are two ways of sitting for runic meditation. The first is with crossed legs, the so-called "Celtic Posture." The other has the legs beneath the body, as if kneeling. Meditation can also be performed standing up. Some rune teachers recommend standing in a posture that imitates the shape of the rune being meditated upon, as in runic yoga. In another, called the "Crane-stance of Clarity," you stand on one leg with one eye closed; in this way you emulate the one-eyed god, Odin.

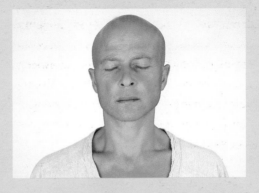

STAGE 2

Control your breathing. Quiet, deep, regular breathing creates the correct physical conditions. When you control your breath, you become calm. First, inhale deeply and slowly for nine seconds. Then hold your breath for three seconds. Next, exhale for nine seconds, and finally hold your breath for three seconds. This makes a cycle of 24 seconds for a complete breath.

STAGE 3

Once you are spiritually calm, you must banish all unwanted thoughts. This is one of the most difficult parts of meditation, at least for the beginner. First, withdraw your attention from external objects and other distractions. Next, close your eyes and ignore the mental images you see. Once you have done this your bodily sensations will fade and eventually you will lose consciousness of them.

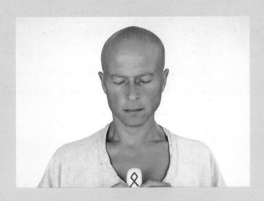

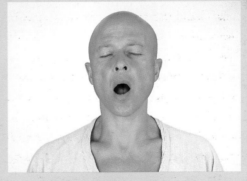

STAGE 4

Once you have mastered stages 1–3 without difficulty, you can move on to stages 4 and 5. Concentrate on the rune. You can do this by visualizing it. You can either look at a runecard set up in an appropriate place or visualize the rune with closed eyes. You should meditate upon it until it becomes part of your awareness.

STAGE 5

Make the runic call. Speech and song release the psychic energy present in sound. Runic calls are composed of the name of a deity or a sacred formula, broken down into its sounds. As you breathe out, repeat these while visualizing the corresponding rune. Do this for a few minutes until you have felt the inner essence of the rune.

Five Elements Meditation

* * * * * * * * * * * * * * * * *

EACH RUNE IS RELATED to one of the elements. Runic meditation recognizes five elements: Earth, Water, Ice, Air, and Fire. They symbolize the five different ways in which the material world behaves. The Five Elements meditation can bring insights into the nature of each element, and how it relates to each rune. Each elemental meditation has the same technique. It starts with the densest element, Earth, and progresses toward the lightest one, Fire. The order is Earth, Water, Ice, Air, Fire.

As well as symbolizing the five expressions of physical existence, the elements represent the directions of space. Earth stands at the center. Water is located in the West; Ice occupies the North; Air is in the East; and Fire is in the South. The sequence of meditation is thus Center, West, North, East, South, which creates sunwise spiral of expanding consciousness.

N

W

E

S

After each meditation, direct your consciousness away from the elemental object. Then return your mind and body to a full awareness of the things around you. It is best to work several times with each element until you feel that you are ready to move on to the next one. Once the whole program has been completed, you will find your relation to the runes greatly empowered.

1 EARTH MEDITATION

Put some earth into a bowl, and locate the bowl in a convenient place. This is the focus for your meditation on the element of Earth. Explore in your mind the many forms of the element that are symbolized in this small sample, such as soil, rock, sand, crystals, and dust. Now imagine yourself at one with the earth, and experience the feelings that this brings. Finally, concentrate upon the runes that relate to the Earth element: Fehu, Uruz, Wunjo, Jera, Berkana, Ehwaz, Inguz, Othala, Ear, Calc, Stan, Wolfsangel, and Erda.

2 WATER MEDITATION

Pour some water into a bowl. Use natural water, from a spring, well, or stream, not from the mains supply, which has been altered chemically. Put the bowl in a convenient location and focus your meditation upon the water in it. Explore the many forms and qualities that water can have, such as rain, ocean, springs, rivers, waterfalls. Imagine yourself at one with the water and experience the feelings this brings. Later, concentrate upon the runes related to the element of Water: Perdhro, Laguz, Inguz, Ior, and Wendhorn.

3 ICE MEDITATION

If it is a cold winter, bring in some ice from outside. Put this in the meditation bowl. As with water, it is always better to use natural ice. But when this is not possible you may freeze some natural water. Never use water from the mains supply. Focus your meditation upon the ice in the bowl. Explore its coldness, its crystalline patterns, and the many forms that ice takes, such as icicles, snowflakes, ice crystals, ice sheets, glaciers. Imagine yourself at one with the ice, experiencing the feelings that this brings. Finally, concentrate upon the runes that relate to the Ice element: Hagalaz and Isa.

4 AIR MEDITATION

Light some incense. Burn it in a fireproof dish, watch the spiraling smoke rise, and explore the many forms and qualities that air can take, such as clean, fresh air, gentle breezes, cold winds, storms. When you have done this, imagine yourself as part of the air, experiencing the feelings this brings. Finally, concentrate upon the runes that relate to the element of Air: Ansuz, Raidho, Gebo, Elhaz, Sowulo, Teiwaz, Mannaz, Dagaz, Óss, Ziu, Ul, and Fyruedal.

5 FIRE MEDITATION

Although you can use any form of fire, it is best to use a candle, preferably a deep-orange or red one that evokes the color of fire. Watch the brilliant flame, and focus your meditation upon the many forms and qualities of fire and flame, such as heat, flickering flames, red-hot metal, volcanic lava, the sun. Then imagine yourself as part of the fire, experiencing the feelings that this brings. Finally, concentrate upon the runes that relate to Fire: Fehu, Thurisaz, Kenaz, Naudhiz, Dagaz, Ac, Cweorth, Ziu, and Sól.

6 SUBTLE POWER MEDITATION

Finally, meditate on the "subtle element" that embodies the other five. In the Northern Tradition this is called Nwyvre. It is the natural empowerment of everything, including your own consciousness. Nwyvre is the flowing energy-matrix of the universe upon which all things are patterned. You can visualize it as flowing patterns of colors, forming ever-changing spiral and geometrical shapes. Nwyvre contains the runes of all the elements, most specially Eihwaz, Yr and Gar, and also Wan, emptiness.

LEFT A candle is best for fire meditation because it gives a simple flame on which to focus.

RUNIC EXERCISES

★ ★ ★ ★ ★ ★ ★ ★ ★ ★ ★ ★ ★ ★ ★ ★

IN THE 1920s, the German rune-master Friedrich Marby developed a system of physical exercises that he called *Runen-gymnastik* ("rune gymnastics"). They probably originated in the "biomechanical exercises" devised by the avant-garde Russian theater director Vsevolod Meyerhold for the training of actors. Marby's techniques were refined by Siegfried Kummer, founder of the List-inspired Runa, a rune school near Dresden. In the early 1930s, Kummer published his ideas under the title *Runenyoga* ("runic yoga"). The technique involves making your body take the shape of a rune, concentrating on its meaning, and calling out its sound. In some ways, it is derived from Indian yoga, but there is also some evidence that people in Northern Europe practiced some kind of posture exercises in ancient times. Because of this, the Norse word *stadhagaldr* is sometimes used to describe runic yoga. Marby claimed that those who practice runic exercises increase their vital energy and physical strength, act more effectively, think more clearly, and rejuvenate their souls.

RIGHT Runic dancers start by adopting the shape of their chosen rune, then move around clockwise in small steps.

ABOVE Runic dancing has a similar effect to that of the spiritual whirling practiced by Islamic dervishes.

Although there are no historical records of dances in the shape of runes in ancient times, German and American runemasters have devised techniques of dance that can generate altered states of consciousness. Friedrich Marby may have invented runic dance in the early twentieth century when he made his runic yoga postures mobile. It is likely that he was influenced by the spiritual *Eurhythmy*, a system of harmonious body movement taught by the philosopher Rudolf Steiner. Going beyond Marby, Siegfried Kummer claimed that these dances were actually recreations of heathen religious dances performed by ancient Germans. These dances, he asserted, were performed naked by ordinary folk, but the priests and priestesses wore magical robes, decked with splendid, symbolic jewels. However, although there are many traditional European folk dances, the runes play no overt part in them.

Runic dances are described by Edred Thorsson, founder of the American Rune Guild, as a form of runic yoga. When it is performed as a spiritual exercise, runic dance has the same spiritual effect as that of the circular dance of the "whirling dervishes," members of an Islamic brotherhood. According to Thorsson, runic dances involve standing in the posture of a certain rune and then moving in a clockwise direction with short steps. As the dancer moves, he or she must hum the sound of the rune whose shape is being held. Turning progressively faster and faster, the runic dancer's final aim is to reach a state of higher consciousness. It is possible to dance all of the runes in this way.

Runic Mudras for Meditation and Healing

The Indian tradition of yoga uses a series of symbolic hand gestures called mudras. Runic yoga also has mudras, in the form of the 18 runes of List's Armanen system. They were devised by the German runemasters who developed runic yoga. In parallel with whole-body postures, hand mudras are another way of calling upon the power of individual runes. To perform runic mudras, you must first prepare in the usual way, clearing your mind of unwanted thoughts and becoming spiritually calm, as for runic meditation (*see pages 126–27*). Then make the shapes of the runes with your hands. Runic mudras should be made in front of the eyes, about one foot (30 centimeters) from the face. The hand should be an equal distance from the pineal gland in the middle of the brain – the "third eye" – and the throat. In this position, it is believed that the mudra is charged with the energy of the voice and empowered by the body's inner

eye. Sing the corresponding runic mantras while making the signs. Holding a shape for the recommended time of ten minutes requires great willpower and concentration.

Runic mudras are used in spiritual healing, as well as for meditation. In runic mudra healing, the afflicted part of the body is touched by the healer's hands in the shape of appropriate runes. Although the Armanen mudras are the best-developed runic hand-signs, we can make runic mudras based on any other rune-row or individual runes. In general healing, for instance, it is best to use the non-Armanen healing-rune Ul. Specific Armanen runic mudras are, however, said to bring relief to related parts of the body. For example, runic healers use Fa for fevers, head ailments, and bone injuries; Eh for depression; Ur and Os for chest problems; and Not and Laf for infections.

Runic healing is practiced by only a few expert healers. Mudras should not be used alone to treat illnesses without consulting an appropriate medical practitioner.

BELOW Hand mudras were developed as a way of representing the Armanen Runes.

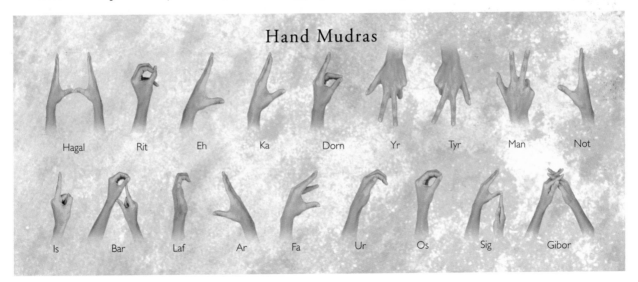

Hand Mudras

Hagal	Rit	Eh	Ka	Dorn	Yr	Tyr	Man	Not

Is	Bar	Laf	Ar	Fa	Ur	Os	Sig	Gibor

PRACTICING RUNIC YOGA

* * * * * * * * * * * * * * * * *

IN HIS *RUNENYOGA*, Kummer used 13 postures based on 12 runes and a cross. The postures are as follows: Is, Ka, Man, Ur, Cross, Not, Eh, Sig, Tyr, Laf, Os, Fa, Hagal. According to Kummer, these different postures affect the way in which runic currents enter the body, as the force moves from the right (east) to the left (west). Each posture is to be carried out daily for 14 days before performing the next one. Kummer claimed that the order he used is a natural sequence in which one posture leads to the next. Once you have performed all 13 exercises, then you should do two or three each day.

Is

Before starting, you must get yourself into a proper frame of mind and bodily relaxation, as for runic meditation (*see pages 126–27*). Once you have achieved this, first make the Is rune by facing north and standing upright with your hands by your sides. Chant the sound *iiisss* and feel power flowing in through your feet and the crown of your head.

KA

To do the Ka-posture, begin by standing in the Is position, as described above. Then lift your arms in front of you to a 45-degree angle, keeping them straight. In this position, chant the sound *kaaaa* and visualize the force flowing in through the palms of your hands to the solar-plexus region of your midriff and out again through the soles of your feet.

MAN

To do the Man-rune posture, stand upright and raise both arms outward away from the body to a 45-degree angle. The palms of your hands should face upward to receive power from above. Power also enters through the crown of your head and flows down through your body to your feet. As you stand, chant the mantra *mmmmm*.

UR

For the Ur-posture, bend at the waist, and then point your fingers toward the ground. Sing the mantra *uuuuu* in order to draw force into your body from the Earthly realm. Visualize the force flowing in through the soles of your feet and then out through your fingertips.

CROSS

The next posture is the Cross. Stand upright, holding your arms away from your body at right angles. There is no chant for this posture. Visualize the force flowing into your body through the back of your head and your right hand, and out through your feet and your left hand.

NOT

For the Not posture, stand upright with your right arm pointing upward away from your body at 45 degrees. Point your left arm downward. Chant the mantra *nnnnnn* and visualize the force flowing into you through your right arm and head, and out through your feet and left arm.

EH

The Eh-rune posture is the reverse of Not, with your left arm raised and your right lowered. Chant the mantra *eeeee* and visualize the force flowing from your left arm and your head

SIG

Sig is performed by squatting with your heels together and your arms resting on your thighs. Chant the mantra *zzzeeeeg* and visualize the energy flowing through the top of your head to your solar plexus and out through your feet.

TYR

For the Tyr posture, stand upright stretching your arms outward and downward from your body at 45 degrees. Hum and focus on the "T" sound. Visualize the energy flowing upward from your feet in a spiral to the crown of your head.

LAF

Laf's posture involves standing upright with both arms held out in front of you at a downward angle of 45 degrees, chanting *lllll*. Visualize the power flowing through the soles of your feet, upward through your body and out through your fingertips.

OS

Os is performed by standing with your feet apart with your hands above your head. Press your palms together and make the sound *ooooo*. Feel the energy flowing up from the ground through your right foot, around your body, up your left arm and down your right and back to earth through your left foot.

FA

The Fa posture is performed standing upright, facing the sun and with your arms held out in front of you. Your left arm should be at an angle of about 40 degrees, with your right arm at 50 degrees, imitating Fa's shape. Make the sound *fffff* and visualize the power flowing in through your head. Power also flows in through the palms when you breathe in, and outward when you breathe out.

HAGAL

The final posture is Hagal. It consists of a series: first the Cross, then Not and Eh, Is, Man, and Tyr, and finally another Cross. Chant *ha ha ha ha ha* and visualize the energy flowing according to the position you are in.

RUNIC COLORS

★ ★ ★ ★ ★ ★ ★ ★ ★ ★ ★ ★ ★ ★ ★ ★

PEOPLE HAVE NOT always called colors by the same names that we do. It is even possible that in earlier ages people perceived colors in a completely different way. Some colors that we distinguish as separate were included within other colors in former times. During Viking times, for example, the rainbow was seen as having only three distinct colors – red, green, and blue. In those days, colors called "red" included some that we now see as separate. Similarly, early heraldry recognized only a few shades. Brown, orange, orange-yellow, and the yellow of the rainbow were all included as types of red. This is not so surprising when we realize that even today it is common to talk of a person with "red" hair, a "red" fox, or a "red" cow. Neither the person's hair, the fox's fur, or the cow's hide is red in modern terms.

In order to empower the runes, the runemasters of old would "make them red." Blood or red pigment made from the madder plant was rubbed into runes that had been scratched on wood or stone. This coloring material is called *tiver*, a word meaning "magic." Although it is traditional to color all runes red, modern rune users have developed color correspondences that express the power within individual runes. Today rune colors use the traditional rune names but follow the modern perceptions of colors. These colors are particularly useful in visualization and runic meditation. Moreover, in modern rune use, each color has a symbolic meaning and its own associated runes.

There are two main systems of runic colors. The general system is based on the Northumbrian Futhork and its additions. Some of the color correspondences and meanings come from ancient writings. Others have been discovered intuitively over the years. An alternative interpretation is from Guido List's Armanen Runes, using other colors, such as bright violet. Runic colors are used by healers to stimulate parts of the body.

Red stands for power, strength, and vitality. It is the color of blood, the carrier of life. Its element is Fire, and it brings warmth

RIGHT The madder plant was used by runemasters for a red pigment with which they would color their runes.

BELOW Red runes are associated with power and are linked to the element of Fire, two associations familiar to Vikings, who had seen volcanic eruptions on Iceland.

134

and excitement. In runic color healing, red runes are used to stimulate the circulation of the blood and the sensory nerves. The red runes are Fehu, Fa, Laf, Thurisaz, Raidho, Kenaz, Teiwaz, Mannaz, Wolfsangel, Ziu, and Fyruedal. The Armanen system recognizes deep-red, whose rune is Not. The Armanen rune Man is purple-red, the color that is associated with sexual energy.

Tawny or orange symbolizes the transformative powers of material existence. In color therapy, orange runes are used to treat muscular cramp and spasms. The color is believed to strengthen the lungs, spleen, and pancreas. Its runes are Cweorth, Ul, and the Armanen rune Ur.

Gold or yellow symbolizes the divine power of sunlight, and the power of the intellect. Yellow is the color of conscious mental energy, and it is used in healing to activate the motor nerves and to aid digestion. Psychologically, the color yellow helps to lift feelings of depression. But yellow must be used sparingly; too much of this color is likely to trigger violent reactions. The yellow runes are Wunjo, Sowulo, Inguz, Othala, Sól, and the Armanen rune Eh.

The color green represents the living power of plants, symbolizing fertile growth, and ecological balance. This color is associated with muscle buildup and stimulation of the pituitary gland. The green runes center on what is known as the subtle body – a person's very "essence" – when suffering fatigue, illness, or shock. The green runes are Uruz, Berkana, Ac, and the Armanen Hagal. Laguz is dark green.

Blue is the heavenly power of the sky. Sky-blue promotes growth and healing, reducing stress. It is the color of intuition and higher consciousness. The sky-blue runes are Hagalaz, Jera, and Dagaz. Dark-blue or indigo is used in runic healing to work on the parathyroid glands in the throat, to purify the blood, and to tone the muscles. The dark-blue runes are Ansuz, Gebo, Eihwaz, Os, Gar, and the Armanen runes Is, Sig, and Gibor.

The color violet has the power to calm the nerves, to restore balance, and to aid concentration. This color brings the feeling of being secure. The violet rune is the Armanen Os rune.

Silver or white denotes the power of the moon, which represents light in darkness, and purification. The silver runes are Elhaz, Ehwaz, Calc, and Wendhorn. Ka is white with a yellow tinge.

Brown signifies the nurturing power of the earth, and has the runes Yr, Ear, and Erda. The color that rune users call Stone (gray) represents the immobile strength of stone. Its runes are the Northumbrian Stan and the Armanen Tyr.

Black is the color of hidden things, gestation, and potential power. It symbolizes constraint and limitation, also the void and nothingness. Its runes are Naudhiz, Isa, Perdhro, Ior, and Irings (Wan).

ABOVE White and silver represent the power of the moon, which stands for purification and light in darkness.

LEFT The color green's strong association with growth and a healthy environment builds both a person's body and his or her energy.

RUNIC NUMEROLOGY

* * * * * * * * * * * * * * * * *

NUMEROLOGY IS THE art of deriving symbolic numbers from the letters of the alphabet. Through these numbers, names are given meaning. Numerologists believe that existence is the outward expression of archetypal ideal forms. We can access these through numbers. Originally, the concept of ideal forms was the basis of neoplatonic philosophy, but it has also been applied to runes.

Numerologists give a value to each letter of the alphabet. Because the letters of different alphabets have different numerical values there are many variants of numerology. There are also different ways in which to ascribe numbers to letters. Numerology arose with the Greek and Hebrew alphabets, which also served as numbers in their own right. The first eight letters of the Greek alphabet stood for the numbers 1–8, the second for 10–80, and the third for 100–800.

Present-day runic numerologists use a number of current systems that have been developed for the Roman alphabet. They range from the system developed by the late-nineteenth-century magical "order" of the Golden Dawn, in which letters only have the values 1 to 9, to the "Ulian Schemata" of D. Jason Cooper, published in his book *Understanding Numerology* (1990), which has number values from 1 to 800.

Usually, when analyzing a name using the Roman alphabet, the numbers are added together repeatedly until a single digit remains, for example, 725 may be reduced as 7 + 2 + 5 = 14; 14 = 1 + 4 = 5. The name then has the symbolic meaning of the resulting number. However, this kind of numerology is very limited, having only nine possible interpretations. Runic numerology need not work in this way: there are alternative systems. For example, the numerology for your name may be related to the name numbers of other beings. So, for instance, 31 is the number of the first man, Askr; the primal Norn, Urd; the goddess Frigg; and the thunder-god, Thor.

The most popular system numbers each letter of the Elder Futhark according to its position in the rune-row. This means that Fehu is 1, Uruz is 2, Thurisaz is 3, Ansuz is 4, and so on. Each rune therefore represents a number from 1 to 24, and each number has a symbolic meaning. These symbolic numbers reinforce the standard rune meanings, giving them special emphasis. As well as using this system for the Elder Futhark, the runic calendars of Scandinavia and the Baltic use Younger Futhark runes to represent the numbers 1–16, with three extra runes to make up the 19-year cycle of sun and moon.

The Elder Futhark has the following numerical meanings. Fehu, number 1, stands for unity. Uruz, 2, the ox's two horns,

The Numbers of the Elder Futhark

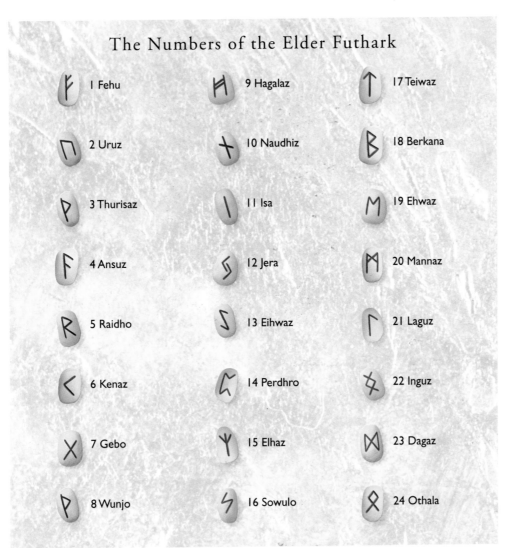

1 Fehu	9 Hagalaz	17 Teiwaz
2 Uruz	10 Naudhiz	18 Berkana
3 Thurisaz	11 Isa	19 Ehwaz
4 Ansuz	12 Jera	20 Mannaz
5 Raidho	13 Eihwaz	21 Laguz
6 Kenaz	14 Perdhro	22 Inguz
7 Gebo	15 Elhaz	23 Dagaz
8 Wunjo	16 Sowulo	24 Othala

LEFT Each of the runes of the Elder Futhark has a numerical equivalent.

signifies spiritual substance. Thurisaz, 3, is the triangle, symbolizing enclosed energy. Ansuz, 4, is the number of universal creation. Raidho, 5, signifies universal life. Kenaz, 6, denotes divine intelligence. Gebo, "lucky" 7, is the good fortune of a gift. Wunjo, 8, is the number of balance.

Hagalaz, 9, refers to the nine worlds of Norse cosmology, the essential substance of existence. Naudhiz, 10, is potential force, while Isa, 11, is static force. Jera, 12, is the number of a complete group – the dozen and the 12 months of the year. Eihwaz is "unlucky" 13, representing the destruction of the old to make space for the creation of the new. Perdhro, 14, bears the number of involution or entwinement, the entry of spirit into matter. Elhaz, 15, denotes the Fifteen Stars of ancient astronomy, signifying destiny. Sowulo, 16, stands for divine power

Teiwaz, 17, is the number of wisdom and immortality. Berkana is 18 or twice 9, symbolizing new beginnings on a higher plane. Ehwaz is 19, the number of the solar/lunar cycle, the interweaving of two variables. Mannaz, 20, is actualized force. Laguz, number 21, represents flow, facilitating human willpower. Number 22, Inguz, represents connection and expansion, while Dagaz, number 23, denotes day, and vision. Othala, 24, is the number of the completion of the cycle, as in the 24 hours of the day.

RUNIC SPACE

★ ★ ★ ★ ★ ★ ★ ★ ★ ★ ★ ★ ★ ★ ★

THE NATURAL DIVISION of the horizon around us is into four parts: front, back, left, and right. This division appears elsewhere in nature. The four seasons of the year and the apparent motion of the sun and moon are also fourfold (heavenly bodies rise in the east, set in the west, and have their highest and lowest points directly above or "below" us).

There are two kinds of fourfold divisions. First, we can divide the hemisphere with lines that run from the center to the four "directions" or cardinal points: North, East, South, and West.

This is the basic arrangement according to Northern Tradition myth. The second possible division is along lines running to the intercardinal directions, northeast, southeast, southwest, and northwest. The northern quarter runs from northwest to northeast; the eastern quarter from northeast to southeast; the southern quarter from southeast to southwest, and the western quarter from southwest to northwest. This is the basic four-square orientation of traditional architecture.

When we combine these two kinds of fourfold division, we make an eightfold division. This eightfold is the basis of European direction- and time-measurement. It is the basis of runic astrology and of a runic divination technique. The Norse word "aett" basically means a group of eight, but it has other meanings, too. An "aett" is, as we have seen, a group of eight runes, but it is also one of the eight sectors into which the sky and space are divided, as well as denoting a "family." The point midway along each aett, or spatial sector, is the cardinal or intercardinal direction, called an *aetting*.

The eightfold division is also the basis of the traditional year-cycle of

BELOW A color wheel created by the author, showing in the outer circle the runes with their traditional colors, then the directions, time, and the phases of the moon.

ARIADNES
HESPERIDES
ANTHERIDES
HYADES

Northern Europe. There are eight major festivals: the equinoxes and solstices and the four "cross-quarter days" of the harvest cycle. They are the Autumnal Equinox (September 23); Samhain (November 1); Winter Solstice or Yule (December 21–25); Brigantia, Oimelc or Candlemas (February 1); Vernal Equinox (March 21); Beltane or May Day (May 1); Summer Solstice (June 21); and Lughnasadh or Lammas (August 1).

Guardians of the Quarters

In rune lore, particular goddesses and gods guard the quarters. The northern quarter is ruled by Odin and the three Norns, and the eastern by Frigg and Tyr. The southern sector has Iduna and Thor, and the western Freyja and Njord. Each of these quarters also has a power-object. The northern quarter has Odin's spear, Gungnir, and the Norns' threads; the eastern quarter has Frigg's distaff and Tyr's sword; the southern quarter has Thor's hammer, Mjöllnir, and Iduna's apples of immortality; the western has Freyja's necklace and Njord's ax.

The 24 runes of the Elder Futhark are divided among the quarters, so that there are five whole runes and two half-runes for each. One

of the five whole runes is the ruling rune for each quarter. The central, ruling, rune of the northern sector is Jera. The eastern is the "goddess-rune", Berkana. In the south is Dagaz, and the west, Kenaz. The other runes are arranged in order around the circle. This quartered circle of space defines every runic time-cycle, however short or long: the hour, the day, the season, or the solar year.

Magically, there are also four supernatural beasts that act as guardians of the directions in the Northern Tradition. We know them from a story about the Norwegian king, Harald Gormsson. Harald wanted to invade Iceland, so he sent his wizard on a reconnaissance mission. The wizard did not sail to Iceland, but shape-shifted himself into the form of a whale. When he reached Iceland, the whale-wizard was warned off by four guardian beings. At Vopnafjord, on the northeastern (signifying the north) coast of the island, he encountered a dragon. At Breidhifjord in the southeast (signifying the east), an enormous bull guarded the shore. In the south, at Reykjanes Peninsula, a rock-giant with an iron staff drove him away. In the west, at Eyjafjord, a massive eagle attacked him. The wizard returned to Norway and told the king, who promptly called off the invasion.

THE TIME-HOUSES OF THE RUNES

✦ ✦ ✦ ✦ ✦ ✦ ✦ ✦ ✦ ✦ ✦ ✦ ✦ ✦ ✦ ✦

Runic Hours

BELOW The 24 runes of the Elder Futhark each correspond to one of the hours of the day. Each also thereby relates to the sun at a particular position in its daily cycle. Eight traditional Central European symbols are at the center of this circle.

EACH OF THE 24 hours of the day corresponds to one of the 24 runes of the Elder Futhark. The whole circle of runes can be visualized as if you were standing inside a circular building with stained-glass windows all around, with each rune in its appropriate position, occupying one twenty-fourth of the circle. At any instant, the sun is in one of the runic directions that corresponds with the time of day or night using local solar time. When the sun stands due east, the time is 6:00. When it is due south, it is noon, and when it is in the west, the time is 18:00. At midnight, the sun's direction is due north. Each of these stations of the sun have corresponding runes. The rune of completion and fulfillment, Jera, stands in the north, while Dagaz in the south. The rune of the east is Berkana, and that of the west, Kenaz.

The other runes fit in the correct order into their corresponding "slots" in the circle. Using the 24-hour clock, the runic hour of Jera runs from 23:30 hours, until 00:30 hours. The next runic hour, Eihwaz, runs from 00:30 until 1:30. Then Perdhro runs from 1:30 until 2:30, and so on around the clock. The next half-circle begins with the first rune, Fehu, at 12:30, running until 13:30, when the rune for the next hour is Uruz. The power of a rune is most powerful at the center point of its section. Times close to the cusps between runic sections are influenced by both the preceding and following runes.

The time-quality of each part of each day can be described by two runes. For example, 11 a.m. on February 9 is ruled by the hour-rune Othala and the half-month rune Elhaz (*see opposite*). The time of birth is also ruled by two runes, and these are the basis of the birth chart of runic astrology.

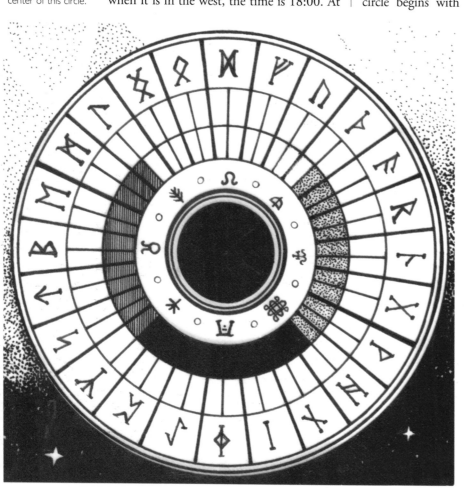

Runic Half-months

Just as the circle of the day is divided into 24, so is the circle of the year, which is divided into 24 "half-months." In runic astrology, the quality of each rune rules over its corresponding half-month. In runic divination, the dates of these half-months are also used to choose the "Significator," the person who is the subject of the reading. (For the sake of simplicity, each half-month is shown as beginning on the same day as the previous one ended, although, in fact, the actual changeover time varies and is too complex to go into here.)

The runic year begins on June 29. According to the lore of East Anglia in eastern England, this is the day of the herb harvest, when herbs are at their maximum strength. The first half-month is ruled by the wealth-rune, Fehu. It runs from June 29 until July 14, when the half-month of Uruz starts. Uruz rules until July 29. Next comes Thurisaz, from July 29 to August 13. The half month of Ansuz begins on August 13 and is current until August 29.

The power of Raidho rules from August 29 until September 13, when Kenaz takes over. Kenaz rules until September 28. It is followed by Gebo's half-month, September 28 to Winter's Day, October 13. This is the beginning of the winter in the old Scandinavian calendar. Wunjo rules from Winter's Day until October 28. Now come the runes of ice and cold. First, the hail rune Hagalaz, October 28 until November 13. Next, the need rune, Naudhiz, November 13 to November 28, and then the ice rune, Isa, from November 28 until December 13.

The festive season of Yuletide is ruled by the rune of harvest plenty, Jera (December 13 to December 28). It is followed by Eihwaz, which rules from December 28 until Midwinter's Day, January 13, traditionally the center of the winter. Next comes Perdhro, ruling until January 28, then Elhaz (January 28 until February 12). As the days get longer, the next rune is the sun rune, Sowulo (February 12–February 27). Teiwaz follows from 27 February to 14 March.

The spring equinox falls within the rune of new birth, Berkana, March 14 to March 30. Now follow runes of movement, growth, and flow. The horse rune, Ehwaz rules from March 30 until Summer's Day, April 14. This is the traditional beginning of the summer half of the year. Mannaz rules from April 14 until April 29. Then comes the half-month of strong flow and growth that includes May Day. It is ruled by Laguz (April 29–May 14). Next is Inguz (May 14–May 29), then Othala, May 29 to June 14. The year cycle is completed by Dagaz, which rules the half-month around the longest day, the Summer Solstice. Dagaz's half-month is from June 14 until June 29, when the endless cycle begins again.

BELOW Midsummer dancing in Sweden in 1901. Even today, Midsummer Day is celebrated with a festival in the country.

THE TWELVE HALLS OF HEAVEN

* * * * * * * * * * * * * * * *

ABOVE Sowulo, associated with Valaheim (Aquarius).

ABOVE Dagaz, associated with Himinbjorg (Cancer).

ANCIENT RUNEUSERS DID not use the Greco-Roman zodiac. Instead, they appear to have used the Twelve Halls of Heaven of the Norse gods. They are listed in the Norse text called *Grimnismál*. In it we are told how Odin was taken prisoner by King Geirrod and tortured by being hung up between two fires. But a boy named Agnar gave Odin a drink that helped him to come through the ordeal. In exchange, Odin described to him Asgard, the heavenly abode of the gods, and the 12 magical palaces there. In her book *Leaves of Yggdrasil*, Freya Aswynn correlates these 12 halls or palaces with the signs of the traditional Greco-Roman zodiac. Each hall is the residence of a Norse goddess or god, and symbolizes some or all of the deity's characteristics. Each also corresponds to a time of year that covers the same period as the corresponding zodiac sign, and each has a corresponding rune that rules the main part of its time period.

Himinbjorg, the "Cliffs of Heaven," the hall of the watcher-god Heimdall, is equivalent to the zodiac sign Cancer. It runs from June 21 to July 20, and includes the runes Dagaz, Fehu, and Uruz. The cattle runes Fehu and Uruz recall Gjallarhorn, Heimdall's great warning-horn. Dagaz and Uruz overlap the beginning and end of the sign, but Fehu (June 29 to July 14) falls completely within Himinbjorg.

Next comes Breidablikk, or "Broad Gleaming," covering the period from July 21 to August 21, ruled by Leo. This is the hall of the solar god Baldr the Beautiful, a place without evil. Runes covering this sector are Uruz, Thurisaz, and Ansuz.

Thurisaz (July 29 to August 13) is the rune completely within Breidablikk.

Breidablikk is followed by Sokkvabekk, equivalent to the zodiac sign Virgo, August 22 to September 22. This is the hall of Sága, the goddess of time and events. Raidho (August 29 to September 13) is the main rune of Sokkvabekk, between the runes Ansuz and Kenaz.

Glitnir parallels the sign of the Scales, Libra, September 23 to October 22. It is the gold and silver "Hall of Splendor" of Forseti, god of justice, settler of quarrels. Its runes are Kenaz, Gebo (September 28 to October 13), and Wunjo.

The zodiac sign of Scorpio, October 23 to November 22, is represented by the gods' "Joyous Home," Gladsheim – the hall where the gods and goddesses of the Aesir and Asyniur had their high seats. The principal seat, Valaskjálf, belonged to Odin. Its main rune is Hagalaz (October 28 to November 13), between Wunjo and Naudhiz.

After Gladsheim comes Ydalir, "The Valley of Yew Trees," paralleling Sagittarius, November 23 to December 20. Isa is its main rune (November 28 to December 13). Ydalir is the dwelling-place of Ullr, winter-time god of archery and skiing. Traditionally, both bows and skis were made of yew wood. The Naudhiz rune occupies the first part of Ydalir, and Jera the last.

Landvidi, "The White Land," is home to the silent god, Vidar. It corresponds to Capricorn, December 21 to January 19. The runes of Landvidi are Jera, Eihwaz, and Perdhro. Eihwaz (December 28 to January 13) is the main rune of this hall.

ABOVE Teiwaz, associated with Noatun (Pisces).

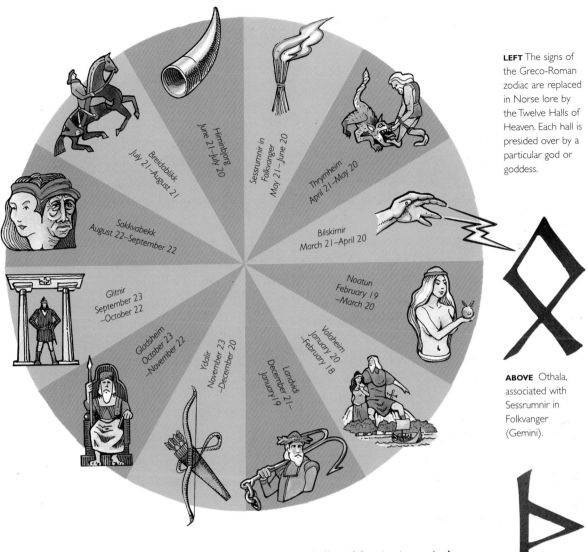

LEFT The signs of the Greco-Roman zodiac are replaced in Norse lore by the Twelve Halls of Heaven. Each hall is presided over by a particular god or goddess.

The signs shown on the wheel:

- Himinbjorg, June 21–July 20
- Sessrumnir in Folkvanger, May 21–June 20
- Thrymheim, April 21–May 20
- Breidablikk, July 21–August 21
- Bilskirnir, March 21–April 20
- Sokkvabekk, August 22–September 22
- Noatun, February 19–March 20
- Glitnir, September 23–October 22
- Valaheim, January 20–February 18
- Gladsheim, October 23–November 22
- Landvidi, December 21–January 19
- Ydalir, November 23–December 20

ABOVE Othala, associated with Sessrumnir in Folkvanger (Gemini).

ABOVE Thurisaz, associated with Breidablikk (Leo).

ABOVE Gebo, associated with Glitnir (Libra).

"The Halls of Silver," Valaheim, correspond with Aquarius, January 20 to February 18, a period that is the old Norse month called Lios-Beri, "The Light-Bringer." It is the time of the god Vali, who became the Christian saint, Valentine. In the myth of *Ragnarök*, the destruction of the world, Vali survives to bring in the new age after the other gods are slain. Elhaz (January 28 to February 12) is the main rune of Valaheim, between Perdhro and Sowulo.

Next comes Noatun, "Ship Haven," hall of the maritime god Njord. It parallels the sign of the fishes, Pisces, February 19 to March 20. Sowulo, Teiwaz (February 27 to March 14), and Berkana are Noatun's runes.

Thor's hall, Bilskirnir, is equivalent to Aries, March 21 to April 20. Its name means "Lightning." Its runes are Berkana, Ehwaz (March 30 to April 14), and Mannaz.

Thrymheim, the hall of the giant Thiazzi and his daughter, Skadi, corresponds with Taurus, April 21 to May 20. Its name means "The Noisy Place." Its runes are Mannaz, Laguz (April 29 to May 14), and Inguz.

Finally, the runic wheel of the zodiac is completed with the hall of the goddess Freyja, Sessrumnir in Folkvanger, the "Field of Folk." Here, paralleling the sign Gemini, May 21 to June 20, are nine halls. Their runes are Inguz, Othala (May 29 to June 14), and Dagaz.

Runic Combinations

* * * * * * * * * * * * * * * * * *

To enhance and increase the power of the runes, individual characters combine with others to make bindrunes. Unless otherwise specified, all the runes below are used in their upright form (facing in other directions alters their meaning).

Runic Diads

Diads are formed by combining two runes together. The following diads come from the three aettir of the Elder Futhark.

First aett

Fehu with Ansuz signifies success through intellectual activities. With Sowulo, hard work brings wealth. With Uruz, healing is taking place, and with Othala, reward comes through perseverance. With Dagaz, Fehu means increased prosperity.

Uruz with Raidho tells us we are strong enough to make changes. Uruz inverted with Raidho means change is necessary, but we lack the strength to make it at present. When Uruz falls reversed with Ehwaz or Laguz, we should let an opportunity pass us by. Reversed with Gebo or Wunjo, Uruz shows domination by a stronger personality.

Thurisaz with Ansuz, Jera, or Mannaz warns us not to try anything new alone. With Hagalaz, Isa, or Naudhiz, it warns against carrying on with a project. With Eihwaz and Elhaz, it brings good luck and protection. With Kenaz reversed, we have been outdone by a colleague or pupil. Reversed with Raidho, it denotes personal control.

Ansuz with Wunjo signifies creative mental effort. Paired with Gebo, it produces the bindrune Gibu-Auja, for good luck. With Jera, Ansuz advises us to consult a lawyer. Ansuz and Perdhro promise discovery of hidden knowledge. But reversed with Perdhro also inverted, it signifies forgetfulness and lost knowledge. Ansuz with Ehwaz indicates a journey, and with Berkana refers to the parent/child relationship. With Mannaz and Laguz, Ansuz denotes wisdom and academic success.

Raidho and Kenaz are the runes of creative work. Raidho with Ehwaz indicates a journey. With Teiwaz, litigation will have a successful outcome if the questioner is in the right. With Perdhro reversed, Raidho tells of a broken promise. With Elhaz reversed, Raidho suggests we have been fooled.

Kenaz with Berkana or Inguz signifies a birth. Kenaz with Ansuz, Raidho, Wunjo, Hagalaz, or Elhaz, denotes creative work, and with Sowulo, seeing clearly. Kenaz with Naudhiz or Isa tell of delays and disempowerment. With Othala reversed, Kenaz warns that our attempts to do things will be blocked.

Gebo with reversed Berkana denotes concern over your partner's health. With Ansuz, it makes the Gibo-Auja bindrune.

Wunjo reversed with binding runes such as Isa and Naudhiz warns us of unpleasant times in the future.

SECOND AETT

Hagalaz with Raidho sends back others' ill-wishes. With Naudhiz, it promises an unexpected and unpleasant event. With Isa or reversed Othala, we must expect delays. Hagalaz with Jera warns us against following an unsuitable career or lifestyle. Perdhro and Hagalaz mean money obtained by means other than work. Teiwaz and Hagalaz is a creative combination. Hagalaz and Dagaz warn us that we have negative expectations. With inverted runes, Hagalaz emphasizes their negative qualities.

Naudhiz generally binds or limits the powers of runes it is paired with. With the success-oriented runes Fehu, Ansuz, and Sowulo, Naudhiz warns us not to change things. With Hagalaz, Naudhiz warns that a sudden delay is imminent, but this may save us from something harmful. When paired with Jera, Naudhiz tells us that we have to pay for a mistake made in the past.

Isa in general binds, inhibits, and disempowers the runes it is paired with. Combined with Dagaz, Isa makes the symbol of the double-ax or Labrys, the symbol of inflexible authority. With Thurisaz reversed, Isa tells of frustration and delay.

Jera with Ansuz tells us to take legal advice. Jera paired with Perdhro represents an inheritance, while with Sowulo, it promises recovery from illness. With Mannaz reversed there may be a legal wrangle on the way.

Eihwaz combined with Thurisaz promises protection against harm and, when found with Sowulo and Elhaz, indicates that magical protection against a whole variety of ills is available.

Perdhro falling with Uruz, Kenaz, Gebo, Teiwaz, Berkana, or Laguz indicates sexual compatibility. When any but the noninvertible Gebo or Perdhro itself are reversed, then there may be compatibility problems. With Fehu or Hagalaz, Perdhro promises a sudden gain of money, unearned, as in a lottery win. When paired with Jera or Othala, Perdhro suggests the questioner will be about to inherit some money.

Elhaz and Thurisaz protect us from all harm. Elhaz and Sowulo together shield us from problems. When Elhaz is reversed, it is not a good omen. It warns us of likely defeat and failure. When found reversed with Raidho, it tells us we have been the victim of a confidence trick.

Sowulo's solar power improves any runes paired with it. Sowulo with Raidho or Wunjo means obsession with work. Power comes when Sowulo combines with Kenaz and Teiwaz. Combined with Elhaz, Sowulo shields us from harm, and with Gebo, Inguz, and Dagaz, it restores balance. With Jera and Mannaz, Sowulo denotes a rapid recovery from illness. When paired with runes of delay and binding, it does not completely counteract their negative effect but it is able to minimize it.

THIRD AETT

Teiwaz generally reinforces the beneficial aspects of runes paired with it. With Eihwaz, Teiwaz denotes inner power; with Perdhro, sexual attraction, and with Sowulo, power and success. With Mannaz reversed, it indicates a fight. When the questioner is a woman, Teiwaz and Laguz signifies that she must assert her rights. When Teiwaz is reversed with Othala, beware of accidents. If Mannaz and Teiwaz are both reversed, we are likely to lose a current dispute.

Berkana reversed with Ansuz upright warns us to look out for a child's welfare. When Berkana is coupled with Mannaz, they are telling us not to make a decision at present.

Ehwaz with Raidho denotes a journey. With Mannaz, Ehwaz states "I am," as an assertion of one's being. Ehwaz and Laguz warn of breakdown and confusion. With Inguz, Ehwaz denotes a long life. When reversed with Uruz, Ehwaz denotes an unexpected happening, bringing a change of plan. Reversed with Raidho or Laguz, it indicates a long, one-way journey, perhaps to a new dwelling, or even something as radical as emigration.

Mannaz and Ansuz bring knowledge and wisdom. Mannaz with Thurisaz, Naudhiz, Isa, and Berkana upright and with Othala reversed warns us to postpone any important decisions. Mannaz with Laguz denotes intellectual strength. Mannaz reversed cancels or counteracts other runes.

Laguz generally signifies flow and movement. Laguz with Ansuz denotes academic success, but with Ehwaz or Dagaz, confusion and breakdown. With Ehwaz reversed, it tells of a long journey without return. Laguz reversed with Jera indicates that the questioner's secrets may be revealed to the world.

Inguz with another rune emphasizes its qualities of becoming – it accelerates alterations already under way and brings things to completion. Paired with Ehwaz, Inguz denotes longevity.

Dagaz is the rune of opening and closing. It enhances the growing, expansive qualities of Berkana and Laguz, while with Othala it denotes increased status and prestige. When Dagaz falls with Naudhiz or Isa, it reduces their negative effects. With Thurisaz, Dagaz indicates difficulties, and with Laguz, confusion. Dagaz with Wunjo or Mannaz reversed tells us that we should not turn down possible solutions to our problems.

Othala with Ansuz or Mannaz tells of visionary ideals. With Fehu, Jera, or Berkana, Othala warns us against materialism. With Uruz and Perdhro, Othala tells us success comes from persistence. With Teiwaz reversed, Othala warns us to beware of accidents. Reversed Othala paired with Hagalaz promises delay and interruption. With Mannaz, it warns us not to make immediate decisions. Finally, with Dagaz, it warns us that we are being unnecessarily pessimistic.

Runic Triads

Bindrunes are also formed from more than two runes. Some of the most effective three-rune combinations are key words or names in the runic tradition. In some cases, the name is considered more important than the meaning of the three runes together. More often, however, the runes and word are in harmony. For example, Uruz, Laguz, and Fehu together form the triad ULF, meaning wolf, and carry the animal's aggressive power. Similarly, Berkana, Ansuz and Raidho make BAR, bear.

Bindrunes of divine names are most powerful. The triple bindrune of Wunjo, Odal, and Dag makes the word WOD, as in Woden/Odin, meaning "divine inspiration," and transforms a bad situation into a good one. The three runes Inguz, Naudhiz, and Gebo spell the word ING, the name of the god of generation and increase, a fertility talisman. Together, Sowulo, Othala, and Laguz make the name of the sun-goddess SOL. This is a more developed version of the rune Sól, giving the inner strength and stability to cope with changes.

Other triads symbolize qualities. Ansuz, Laguz, and Uruz spell the word of power, ALU. Literally, this means "ale," but it symbolizes the mystic "water of life," the primal power of the gods. ALU promises a change for the better. Ansuz, Sowulo (or Ziu), and Ken make the runic word ASC, the sacred ash tree of the gods, Yggdrasil, containing the strength to survive all kinds of troubles.

Othala, Naudhiz, and Dag combine to make the bindrune ÖND. Önd is the vital breath, the universal soul of all things, whose power we can use to defeat major problems. By coming into harmony with our circumstances, we overcome difficulties.

Jera, Raidho, and Thurisaz bound together make the runic power-word JRTh (Jörth), the earth. JRTh brings about favorable conditions for a project, but it will work only in harmony with the way of the world, for it cannot alter the course of events.

Some runic triads are important even though they do not make words or names. Elhaz, Othala, and Thurisaz are runes of powerful protection. They defend us against bad consequences of our actions. The bindrune of Perdhro, Ansuz, and Raidho gives us access to hidden or forgotten knowledge. It helps us to see important points that we may have overlooked. Jera, Fehu, and Wunjo help us to bring together the things we need to create an abundant, joyful life. Jera, Uruz, and Sowulo can help in problem-solving.

LEFT Runic triads are three-rune combinations that form words or names with powerful meanings.

LEFT The runes Inguz, Naudhiz, and Gebo together spell ING, the god of fertility, creating a fertility talisman.

PART FIVE

REVEALING THE UNSEEN

★ ★ ★ ★ ★

Life is uncertain, even under the best conditions, and people have always looked for ways of finding out what the future holds. Over time, many methods of prediction have been developed, which have included the visionary techniques of shamans, soothsayers, and clairvoyants. Their visions, however, are intensely personal. We have no independent check on what they say. Everything depends on their personal credibility. We only have their word for their personal "revelations," and we cannot know how honest they are — they may only be telling us what we want to hear.

ABOVE Throwing runic dice is one of the many ways in which runes can be used for divination.

Divination is different, because it gives actual results that anyone can achieve and see. We do not need special psychic abilities to interpret what is there in front of us. The runes are there, and we can read them. Only our interpretation is personal. Runic divination tells us the present state of things, revealing unseen factors and trends, giving us a wider view of where we are. Because the results are symbolic, runic divination gives us a new perspective. They enable us to develop strategies for dealing with possible coming events.

DIVINING THE FUTURE

★ ★ ★ ★ ★ ★ ★ ★ ★ ★ ★ ★ ★ ★ ★ ★ ★

IT IS IMPORTANT to define the runic approach to the future. There are radically different views as to what the word "future" actually means. Some philosophies teach that our existence is predestined. Believers claim that everything that happens now has already been worked out in advance by superior beings. Nothing can be changed, for the present is merely an operation of unchanging destiny, and we are merely helpless pawns in a cosmic game. This grim view sees divination as totally predictive, like turning over a page to see what is already printed there. Believers claim that all time – past, present, and future – is already present in the "Book of Existence." If we employ the right methods, we can read it in advance, but not change it. This is the doctrine of fatalism. In the fatalist's eyes, we can do nothing creative. The future already exists, and we are passive victims. According to this picture of existence, we are literally "fated," and our lives are no more than those of characters in a novel.

This worldview is paradoxical, for fatalism makes divination itself a pointless exercise. If we have no freewill in our actions, then the divination itself must have been prearranged, along with everything else. Such a paranoid view of the world makes life nothing but a meaningless, mechanical performance.

The opposite worldview is that the future, which has no reality, is completely random and therefore totally unknowable. People who hold this viewpoint often see divination as a sort of game, particularly

RIGHT The Tarot is widely consulted as a way of seeking advice on the future and appropriate action to take.

FAR RIGHT In the Tarot, the Wheel of Fortune card symbolizes the concept of destiny.

RIGHT A painting of a casino in 1899 by Edward Cucuel. The roulette wheel is the gambler's own "wheel of fortune" on which outcomes depend on random chance instead of predetermined destiny.

used in gambling, such as the "prediction" of lottery numbers or the winners of horse races. However, except under exceptional conditions, divination does not concern itself with that sort of prediction.

Users of runic divination hold neither a fatalistic nor random view of the future. Underlying rune use is the Northern-Tradition concept of Örlog, the "primal laws" and "primal layers" of existence. Our Örlog is the way things are for us. The "now" we experience has come about both through these natural laws and the accumulated layers of events that have happened in the past. The past is important because it has shaped the present. Past events have made the present what it is now, and have determined the relatively limited range of possibilities regarding what might develop from these conditions in the future.

LA·ROUE·DE·FORTUNE

All points on the continuum that we call space-time are unique. But they are not separate: they are interconnected with everything else that also exists at that moment. Each event on the space-time continuum therefore contains the quality of the moment. This means that the unique quality of each individual point in space-time can be discovered, and we can do this by investigating its relationship to every other point on that continuum. This phenomenon can only be expressed in the symbolic language that is present in both nature and human consciousness. The runes are the vocabulary of this symbolic language.

The techniques of runic divination give us a "report" on the current state of Örlog. Because it accesses immediate existence, divination delivers an overview of current trends and processes and their probable outcome. The outcome is not fixed in advance but is only what is liable to occur if nothing alters the process now under way. We have the ability, with our freewill, to turn aside from the current course. This makes divination a valuable tool in decision-making, by showing us what actions are possible in a given situation. A runecast can give us new insights into the causes of problems, thereby creating new solutions to them. Far from just telling us of our impending doom in a fixed future, divination gives us the means to foresee and avoid problems, and so to live a better, more conscious life.

ABOVE The principle of runic divination is similar to chess: the future is not set, but has been shaped by the past.

BELOW A runecast can help us to understand our present state and to gain an idea of future events.

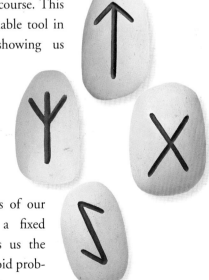

PRINCIPLES OF DIVINATION

★ ★ ★ ★ ★ ★ ★ ★ ★ ★ ★ ★ ★ ★ ★ ★

ALTHOUGH THE PRACTICE of divination is often no more than a fairground sideshow or a televised spectacle, in its true form it is nevertheless a serious business. However, divination is frequently practiced under the wrong conditions, by the wrong person, and at the wrong time. When this happens, it is extremely unlikely that there will be useful results. The reason why divinations are often made under the wrong conditions is because the diviner is not aware of them, and is therefore not able to take them into account.

Ancient wisdom recognized that not all locations are the same. Methods that work in one place will not necessarily work in another location. Divination operates by coming into harmony with the prevailing conditions, not fighting against them. Traditional diviners have always stressed the importance of performing divinations under the right conditions. The medieval writer Gerardus Cremonensis (1114–87) and the Renaissance wizard Heinrich Cornelius Agrippa (1468–1535), both warned against performing divinations in the wrong frame of mind or in unfavorable conditions. "You must always take heed," wrote Gerardus, "that you do not ask a question in very rainy, cloudy, or very windy weather, or when you are angry, or when the mind is busied with many affairs; nor with tempters or deriders, neither should you recast and reiterate the same question once again under the same figure or form. For this is error."

The first thing you must do before conducting a divination is to get into a suitable frame of mind. If you are disturbed by anger, worries, or other preoccupations, then you cannot function efficiently. To try under these conditions will certainly lead to failure. Second, you must take the weather into account, because thunder, rain, hail, snow, or other adverse weather conditions will also affect performance. Third, the presence of people that Gerardus called "tempters or deriders" – skeptics, cynics, and critics – will certainly bring failure. For example, esoteric researchers have often noted that certain people have negative influences that block the effective functioning of water-diviners. We experience the same effect on runic divinations. Physical conditions can also disrupt divination. A house or room close to high-voltage power lines is inappropriate. Continuous traffic noise or other interruptions will also distract us from paying full attention to our readings.

Timing is important, too. It was traditional in many lands to conduct divination only on certain holy days. In former times in Britain, it was customary to make divinations only on Halloween, New Year's Day, and on a few other days whose saints ruled matters of love. When using the runes, we can employ runic astrology to find the best days for divination.

If we try to make a runic reading without a serious reason, or in an uninterested way, then we run the risk of blunting our intuitive powers. Casting the runes repeatedly at the wrong time or under the wrong conditions can permanently reduce our ability to get meaningful results. It is also important not to perform divinations for each and every trivial incident that occurs in everyday life. The runes, or any form of divination, should be an aid to personal liberation, telling us of our possible actions in circumstances where the way ahead is not clear. The runes should never become a substitute for the exercise of freewill.

ANCIENT DIVINATION TECHNIQUES

★★★★★★★★★★★★★★★★★

HISTORICALLY, DIVINATION appears to have developed out of shamanism, the magical religion of many ancient peoples. Shamanism works well in nomadic cultures, where its spontaneous nature fits in well with everyday life. But more developed societies need more reliable methods. The direct experience of the otherworld gained by the shamans and trance-oracles, who have their revelations while in a state of trance, was replaced eventually by more precise readings taken from a variety of sources.

RIGHT Animals have commonly been used in divination: Roman soothsayers would examine the entrails of a bull.

In very ancient times, people used various techniques of divination whose results could be "read" in particular shapes, images, or symbols. These methods were more definite than the more ethereal seership that relied upon the often vague psychic impressions of an individual. The methods included reading portents from objects and phenomena in the natural world, as well as in human-made artifacts. The most fundamental method of this type involves reading meaning into natural forces. Each of the traditional four elements have their corresponding divinatory art. Fire-divination is known as pyromancy; aeromancy reads the winds and clouds; hydromancy examines the patterns of flow and movement of water in its many forms; while geomancy reads oracles from the Earth.

ABOVE Animal bones, especially the knuckle-bones of sheep, have featured widely in the divination techniques of ancient cultures.

Another, and one of the earliest-known, divinatory techniques is the use of animal bones, most especially *astragali*. These are the knuckle-bones of sheep, which, because of their shape, can fall in four distinct ways. Astragali were used by diviners in ancient Babylon and Greece, where they read oracular meanings from the various ways in which the bones fell. Astragali were the forerunner of dice, which appeared as tools of divination – said in Iceland to have been invented by Odin – before they became the gambler's doom. It is possible that the idea of alphabetic characters in divination came from the four differing faces of astragali and their combinations.

The entrails of sacrificed animals, rather than their bones, provided the basis of a highly specialized technique known as hepatoscopy, which was used by ancient Babylonian, Greek, and Etruscan diviners in attempts to predict the future. Gradually, interpretations were standardized, giving some degree of uniformity in readings. This made the task of the diviner easier, and less a matter of personal interpretation. Rules were developed that ascribed precise predictive meanings to certain abnormalities. For the purposes of teaching new initiates, the entrails of sacrificed animals were modeled in clay and bronze, and eventually replaced the real thing. besides being cheaper than sacrificing an animal every time a divination took place, this formal system was faster, more convenient, and easier to interpret. A

variety of kinds of divination subsequently developed from this foundation and took over from the simplified remains of hepatoscopy.

Among other forms of divination, practitioners have interpreted dreams by oneiromancy. They have used divining rods in rhabdomancy, and sieves in coscinoscopy, in which the turning of a suspended sieve is used to identify a thief. Kleidoscopy interprets the movements of a key suspended on string or cord, a specialized form of the more frequently used pendulum.

Interpreting shapes, however, is the most popular divination of all. In crystalomancy, for example, the seer peers into a crystal ball to see the shapes of things to come. In Ireland, the wise women called *banfathi* would gaze at running water to interpret the patterns there. More definite techniques use methods to create shapes that can be looked at for as long as interpretation takes. One way is to fix liquid patterns. Ceroscopists pour molten wax into cold water and interpret the shapes. Lead is another material used in this way in the present day in Austria for New Year divinations, in a technique called plumbomancy. Geomancy is a highly developed form of divination that uses stones, beans, or cowrie shells to make certain formal patterns. There are 16 named geomantic figures, each with its own meaning. Other varieties of pattern-recognition divination include crithomancy, which uses the patterns formed in the baking of bread or cakes to answer questions.

The most popular divination systems today are the most formalized one, which use easily recognized symbols. They include Tarot cards and the runes. They have an advantage over other methods because users can get immediate results that need only direct interpretation.

ABOVE LEFT Because of their powerful imagery, Tarot cards are a popular way of foretelling the future.

LEFT Gazing into a crystal ball to read the future has become almost symbolic of the practice of divination, but it is just one of many techniques.

RUNE-ROW DIFFERENCES

★ ★ ★ ★ ★ ★ ★ ★ ★ ★ ★ ★ ★ ★ ★ ★

BECAUSE EACH RUNE-ROW came into being in a certain country at a specific time, it has its own special character. The same rune in England, Norway, and Iceland was sometimes perceived differently. Because of this, each rune-row is unique. This means that the readings that we do will vary according to which rune-row we use.

The Elder Futhark, having 24 runes, is the most balanced. This is why it is the most popular rune-row among present-day rune users. The Younger Futhark of 16 runes is more limited than the 24-rune row. The longer rune-rows, the Anglo-Saxon, with 29, and the Northumbrian, with 33, have additional runes that cover a wider area. They explore natural and cosmic powers, including the World Tree, and the forces inherent in ocean, stone, fire and death. The longer rows give readings that reveal the cosmic will. They may be too grand in scope for solving everyday problems, but they are useful when we ask very serious questions of them. The Gothic alphabet, which is largely derived from the runes, is also used in divination. The same techniques are used with the Gothic letters. Because of its connection with Greek culture, especially the solar tradition connected with the god Apollo, the Gothic alphabet gives readings that tend to be "light" and optimistic in nature.

Few rune users use the Swedish Dotted Runes, because historically they were used mainly for writing. There is no rune poem or other text that describes their meanings. So when we use them we take the meanings from other rune-rows. If we use the 18-rune Armanen system, devised by Guido List as a means to propagate his pan-Germanic historical and political theories, we need to take their origins into account. List's interpretations express his beliefs and are biased toward the qualities of power, struggle, and heaviness. Readings with the Armanen Runes will reflect this tendency. Another modern rune-row, popularized in the 1980s by Michael Howard, editor of the Pagan journal *The Cauldron*, has 17 runes. These runes are based on the ideas of Wicca (modern witchcraft), so any readings using them will be colored by this belief system.

RUNIC PATTERNS

Runic patterns occur everywhere in nature. They can be seen in the branches of trees, in cracks in the dry earth, in rocks, in the patterns that are made by flowing water, and in the shapes made by the clouds. The natural

RIGHT Runic patterns can be seen all around us, even in the earth at our feet.

BELOW Stick-casting involves using nine twigs cut from a tree and throwing them onto a casting sheet or cloth.

world is the link between older forms of divination and the runes. Because patterns occur spontaneously in nature, they can also be made by random actions. Casting sticks to make runic characters is one means of doing this and of learning to see runic readings in apparently random patterns.

RUNE STICKS

The technique of stick-casting uses nine sticks. First, cut nine sticks from a tree (birch or rowan is best). Then dedicate them to their use with a small ceremony in which you state that these sticks are to be used to find the truth. To cast the sticks, hold them loosely, with both hands together, then think of the question to which you seek an answer. Throw the sticks forward onto the casting sheet or cloth (*see page 160 for description*). Take away any sticks that have not fallen completely on the sheet, and look for rune shapes in the overlapping patterns of the remaining sticks. Sometimes a strong runic pattern will be seen immediately. In that case, the reading is plain. On other occasions, you will have to look carefully and consider what the sticks are telling you.

Casting slivers of wood marked with runes is a development of stick-casting. It is likely that this is the ancient German technique recorded by the Roman writer Tacitus. Its advantage is that it always gives an unambiguous reading. Its disadvantage is that only one of any rune can appear, unlike the stick-casting, where more than one of the same rune reinforces its message.

RUNESTONES

Natural pebbles with quartz veins often have runic patterns. You can make a runic divination by walking along a beach or riverside looking at pebbles. When you see one that looks runic, pick it up and examine it for runes. When you see a rune, that is the result of the divination. Alternatively, you can collect pebbles with runes until you have every rune in a natural stone. It may take a long time to collect a complete set, but when you have them, you can use them in divination wherever you are. Another way of making runestones is to collect plain pebbles and paint runes on them. Runestones like this are made for sale, along with ceramic and plastic versions. But since you will be using the stones for personal divination, it is better that they should have a personal connection.

MECHANICAL RUNE DIVINATION

Almost any kind of random tool can be used in runic divination. Dice with runes inscribed upon them or rune balls can be thrown or pulled from a bag. Spinners with runes (like the small tops used in gambling games) or a roulette wheel with runes upon it instead of numbers are also used occasionally. Where the ball stops, that rune is chosen.

LEFT Collecting your own set of runestones can be satisfying, especially if you only pick the same kind of stone.

BELOW Dice can easily be adapted for use in divination by painting runes on their faces.

RUNECARDS

★ ★ ★ ★ ★ ★ ★ ★ ★ ★ ★ ★ ★ ★ ★ ★

CARDS OFFER A simple means of doing runic divinations, and there are many runecard decks available today. Some are inspired by Tarot or other fortunetelling decks, having a symbolic illustration for each rune. In the Tarot, there are four suits called the Minor Arcana and 22 other cards called the Major Arcana. Each Tarot card has traditional image, a specific name and meaning. Although there are some similarities between the runes and the Tarot, the runes do not work in the same way. Although they are divided into three aettir, they do not function like the Tarot suits. Also, although they may be likened to the Major Arcana in that they represent individual qualities and principles, there are no traditional images associated with the runes as there are for the Tarot. This means that different runecard decks are more likely to express the artist's or designer's personal interpretation of the runes. Unlike the standard Tarot deck of 78 cards, runecards have been made for most of the different runic rows, and so they range from 16 to 33 cards. There is also a deck in the Gothic alphabet.

Since the 1980s, artists have risen to the creative challenge of depicting the runes on cards. The most basic runecard decks have only a rune on each card, without any other image. In 1985, a set of such runecards to cut out appeared in Michael Howard's book *The Wisdom of the Runes*. Klaus Holizka's Elder Futhark *Nordische Weisheit* ("Norse Wisdom") of 1994, illustrating Ralph Tegtmeier's book *Runen – Alphabet der Erkenntnis* ("Runes – the Alphabet of Knowledge") is another such deck. Kaledon Naddair's 1987 *Runic Cards* depict the basic runes below which are diagrams that express his personal theory of what he calls "Pictish Shamanism." Other

ABOVE Runecards can be made from any of the runic systems.

BELOW Runes designed by the German painter Hermann Haindl in 1990.

15. WARRIOR

17. MOVEMENT

25. THE UNKNOWABLE

1. THE SELF

ABOVE Ralph Blum's cards for *The Book of Rune Cards*.

decks in which the runes themselves are dominant but have simple pictures include Donald Tyson's and Robin Wood's *Runic Magic Cards* of 1989 and Witta Jensen's *Danish Magiske Runer* ("Danish Magical

Runes") of 1992. Cards published by *Astrella* magazine in Italy in 1989 show the runes as birch twigs tied together, with small illustrations to emphasize the meanings.

Following the style of the Tarot, runecard designers have taken to producing artwork that symbolically expresses the runes' meanings. This idea began in the 1980s. *The Phoenix Runes* by Tricia Bramwell (1983), have human figures that represent the runes. The author's own *Hugin and Munin Rune Cards* of 1985 have large runes accompanied by symbolic drawings, as does Anthony Clark's *Aquarian Rune Pack* of 1987. *La Tavole Runiche* ("The Runic Table"), published in Trieste, Italy, in 1989, has runes, together with drawings and texts that explain each card's meaning.

The cards that accompany Ralph Blum's *The Book of Rune Cards* (1989) have pictures that symbolize each rune's quality. Later decks, such as Alois Hanslian's Armanen runecards of 1990, and Nigel Jackson's 1997 runecards, depict the runes through symbolic images. The so-called blank rune that originated in California runestones has also found its way into runecards. It appears in Ralph Blum's runecards as a picture of the moon and stars peeping through clouds. In the Anglo-Saxon runecards by Tony Linsell and Brian Partridge (1992), where it is called "Wyrd," it is shown as a white sheet whose threads come from a line of skulls at the foot.

Most runecard decks use the 24-rune Elder Futhark, but some designs are compromises that contain elements from different systems. The Haindl runecards (1990), designed by the German painter Hermann Haindl with whom I worked in collaboration, uses elements of the Elder Futhark and the Armanen system. We avoided the blank rune, replacing it with a twenty-fifth card representing the World Tree, Yggdrasil. The first Gothic-alphabet divination card deck, *Gotlandia*, also designed by the author, was published in 1991.

With such a variety of runecards to choose from, it is little wonder that readings with them tend to be colored by whatever cards we use. Runecards in general are less neutral than techniques using runestones or other methods. Because they are derived from other fortunetelling cards, runecard readings follow closely the spreads used by Tarot readers. Several Tarot techniques are standard for use with runecards. But because the runes are the operating system of the divination, empowering techniques of traditional runecasting are often used.

RIDING THE WAGON

★ ★ ★ ★ ★ ★ ★ ★ ★ ★ ★ ★ ★ ★ ★ ★ ★

ONE OF THE most important ancient ceremonial techniques of rune reading is called *Raed Waen*, which means "riding the wagon." The runecaster is envisaged as a rider in the heavenly wagon of the gods from which all things can be seen. "Riding the wagon" is the ceremony of runecasting; the runecast, or spread, itself is called the *shoat*.

When we cast the wooden or stone runes ceremonially, we must take account of our environment. When casting indoors, the main axis of the room is our guide. This is called the *rig* or "right line." It is an imaginary straight line along the floor, and is simple to find. Symbolically, the rig is the alignment best in harmony with the energies of the earth in the room. In a building where the walls are oriented according to ancient European tradition, facing the four cardinal directions, the axis of the rig should run from east to west. According to Northern Tradition teachings, this is the direction of equality. (North-south is the direction of legal judgement. The judge

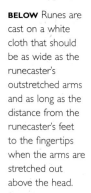

RIGHT Thor in a heavenly wagon pulled by goats in a painting from 1983 by Gordon Wain. Thor's chariot is an image of the wagon we ride when casting the runes.

BELOW Runes are cast on a white cloth that should be as wide as the runecaster's outstretched arms and as long as the distance from the runecaster's feet to the fingertips when the arms are stretched out above the head.

Width of outstretched arms

Length with arms outstretched above head

sits at the north end, called the presence, facing south.) If you cannot orient the line in this way, you should make it parallel to the longer wall, dividing the floor space into two parts.

The shoat is lined up along the rig. The runes are cast on a white cloth, whose size should be the same as the bodily measurements of the runecaster. This is the runecaster's own length from his or her feet to the fingertips, held at full stretch above the head. The cloth's width is taken from the distance between the runecaster's outstretched arms from fingertip to fingertip. This is the traditional measure called the fathom. Put the casting cloth on the floor so that its central point is located one-third of the way along the rig. Your view along it is toward the longer part of the room. The wall you face is said to be positive, and the wall behind you is negative. Correct orientation means that east is positive, west negative, with the presence in the north to the left, and south to the right. As you view it, the direction along the rig toward the positive wall is said to be "up," and that nearer to the runecaster, "down." "Left" and "right" refer to your own left and right.

It is better to cast the runes out-of-doors. Here, the rig should face toward the sun at the time that the divination is taking place. Northern Tradition teachings tell that the direction of human energy flow is toward the sun, in return for the sun's energy flowing toward the world of humans. Naturally, this direction depends on the time of day. At true midday, the sun stands due south, and at midnight (though invisible "beneath the Earth"), it is due north. Other times of day and night have their own orientation, the sun appearing to complete a whole cycle in 24 hours. It is not recommended that you make runic divinations during the hours of darkness. According to ancient tradition, they should take place "in the face of the sun, and the eye of the light." But under special circumstances, runecasts may have to be performed at night.

Whatever the location and circumstances of the divination, it is useful to have a pillow to sit upon at the negative end of the shoat. Some runic diviners used a special ceremonial pillow embroidered with appropriate runic signs, known as the stol. When making a runecast, many runecasters set another cloth on the white cloth at the positive end of the shoat. On this, the runecaster puts his or her personal talisman, known as a "mearomot." The mearomot may be a pouch made of leather or silk, a special stone, a crystal, a raven's feather, or any other object with which you have a personal relationship. Whatever it is, it should embody something of your essence, or the person for whom you are doing the reading. A mearomot can help you to concentrate better.

A piece of paper with the question written on it should accompany the mearomot. Symbolic objects are also located at the four corners of the shoat. When the arrangement is complete, you should perform your mental cleansings and ceremonies – banishing all distracting thoughts, getting into the right frame of mind and so on, as for runic meditation, *see pages 126–27* – and then the question should be asked.

ABOVE Runic divination should be carried out facing the sun.

BELOW A mearomot, or personal talisman, can be a silk or leather pouch, a raven's feather, or any object that has a special connection with you.

Raven's feather

Pouch

Framed picture of a child's face

TECHNIQUES OF RUNIC DIVINATION

* * * * * * * * * * * * * * * * *

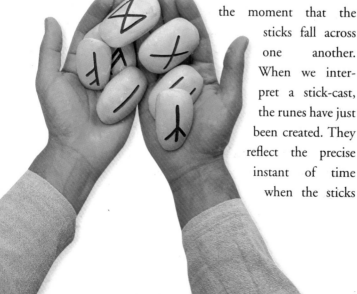

WHETHER WE USE sticks, stones or cards, we can employ many different techniques of runic divination. Each different method has its own qualities, giving a unique style of reading. Every rune user has his or her own favorites, but none is actually better than any other in answering a question. We may have a personal preference for one style or another, but every method can give useful results. In the final analysis, it is only the skill and competence of the runecaster that really matters.

RIGHT Runecasting with sticks has a particular freshness, because the runes do not exist until the sticks have landed.

RUNECASTS

The earliest writers tell how diviners cast "lots" onto a cloth. We still do this today by throwing all kinds of objects onto a surface to see what patterns they form. Because runes can be seen in sticks crossing over one another, we can throw them in divination. For this, it is customary to use birch sticks. When they fall together, we can read the runes that they make. This technique has an advantage over all others, because the runes do not exist until the moment that the sticks fall across one another. When we interpret a stick-cast, the runes have just been created. They reflect the precise instant of time when the sticks

BELOW Whatever objects are used, runecasting begins by passing them from hand to hand at least three times.

came to rest. In this way, we are able to create new runes each time we make the cast, accessing the hidden inner realities of the moment.

Using sticks has an advantage over all the others because two or more of the same rune, from the same or different futharks, can appear in a cast. This is known as "doubling." When doubling occurs, the runes have given us a powerful message. Doubling is impossible in casts that use sets of rune "stones," wooden slivers ("tines"), or cards that already have runes upon them. These materials contain just one of each rune in any futhark, so only that one rune will be available in a reading. Stick-casting is also more flexible because runes from the whole range may appear, including the medieval runes outside the conventional futharks. Casting sticks gives us the greatest range of possibilities. Not only do they offer the possibility of doubling, but – unlike the "prepared" runes on stones or cards – they are literally created by the fall of the sticks, and thus contain the essence of the moment.

Whichever medium we choose, the technique is basically the same. Before you make the cast, randomly mix the runestones or tines by passing them from hand to hand at least three times. This empowers them with your own personal energy. Then, seated on the *stol* or ceremonial pillow, cast all of the sticks, slivers, or stones along the rig, the line of orientation, in a single throw. The position that they fall in determines the meaning

LEFT The number of runes you choose to read in divination is a matter of personal preference.

of the runecast. When we use stones or slivers, some will fall face up. Others will be face down. We count only those that fall face up. The others are not valid in the divination, so remove them from the cloth.

Now, pick up the remaining stones or tines, one by one. The number of runes you choose and how you make your choice may vary, depending on your personal preference. Some runecasters choose only three runes, some prefer nine, while others examine all of the runes that have fallen the right way up. Most commonly, runecasters pick up the number they wish from those that fall nearest to them. Others mark a

that works best for you. In runecasting, there is no inflexible rule telling us how to pick up the runes from the shoat. The most important factor in rune reading is the relationship between the runes and the reader.

RUNE SPREADS

Rune spreads are more formal than runes that are thrown because they involve placing runestones or cards carefully in meaningful patterns. In both runecasts and

point or line at some distance from their sitting-place and take the nine runes nearest to it. Yet others choose the nine runes lying nearest to the rig along the center. If we are choosing nine runes, we use the Grid of Nine (*see pages 170–71*) spread to interpret them. When fewer runes present themselves, we must choose a spread that is appropriate to the number we have.

If none of these methods appeals to you, then it is possible to use another method, one

rune spreads, the runes are considered to be "upright" when they face toward you and are read in the normal way. They are "reversed" or "inverted" when they appear upside down. Some runes, known as the "non invertible runes," are the same either way up and have the same meaning whichever way up they fall. The only exception is in some specialized runecard decks that have designs as well as runes, and all their cards can be upright or reversed.

ABOVE To cast runes, sit on a ceremonial pillow and throw the runes onto the mat in front of you in a single action.

RUNIC READINGS

* * * * * * * * * * * * * * * * *

THERE ARE A number of useful runic readings using stones or cards that are derived from popular Tarot rune spreads, as well as those rune readings that come directly from the Northern Tradition. They cover the most simple to the most complex possibilities, and use different numbers of runes accordingly. In ascending order of complexity, they are the Single Rune (1 rune); Pros and Cons (2 runes); the Three Norns (3 runes); the Five Directions (5 runes); the Runic Cross (6 runes); the Vé (7); Teiwaz's Shoat (7); the Runic Wheel (8 runes); the Nine Runes (9 runes); the Grid of Nine (also 9); the Celtic Cross (10 runes); and the Cosmic Axis (11 runes). There are even more complex spreads, based on the Twelve Halls of Heaven and other mythical traditions. These require much time and effort to interpret.

The most popular rune spreads are sometimes called by other names. The names used here for these systems are those that the author uses in his own rune work, but it is a matter of personal preference which names you choose to use. An example of a spread with different names is the Five Directions, which Michael Howard refers to as the "Cross of Thor," even though the thunder-god's symbol is not a cross, but his hammer, Mjöllnir. In *The Book of Runes* (1984), Ralph Blum describes a version of this layout that he calls "Three

BELOW Before making readings with runestones they should be shuffled together, either in their bag, or face down on a cloth.

Lifetimes." He recommends it as a means to access the investigator's supposed "previous lives." However, it is not necessary to believe in reincarnation to use the runes effectively because the names we give to the spreads are not as important as their principles, which have been well established by runic readers and may prove useful to the reader.

Although there are obvious connections between the basic spreads and the more complex spreads, each of them is an independent technique, and can be used and read without reference to the others. Before doing a reading, it is best to orientate yourself as for Riding the Wagon (*pages 160–61*), if possible. Although not absolutely necessary, a casting cloth is useful, as is a special bag in which to keep your runestones.

Certain of the following techniques involve "randomizing" the runes before choosing those that you will use in the reading. In the case of cards, you can do this simply by shuffling and cutting them. If you are using runestones, you can either scramble them in their bag, or pile them up, face down, and then take any (as for dominoes). Alternatively, you can "wash" the stones or cards by spreading them around with your hand before making your selection.

Instructions for the various spreads follow, beginning with the most basic and simple of them all, the Single Rune.

THE SINGLE RUNE

This is the simplest form of rune reading. When using cards, this is called the Single Card Draw. It is also known as the Odin Card. If using runestones, the technique is

Kaun

simple. After getting into the proper meditative frame of mind, and deciding on the question, the reader pulls a single stone from the runebag. If using cards, the deck is shuffled, and the questioner draws a single card from it, face down. Then it is turned over from right to left. This ensures that the orientation of the card (upright or reversed) is kept. If selecting a stone, take it as it comes; if it is lying sideways, give it one turn *deosil* (sunwise) to orientate it. Whether on stone or on card, the meaning of the single rune in relation to the question is then evaluated. The Single Rune technique is a simple way of getting a result.

PROS AND CONS

The Pros and Cons reading is carried out in the same manner as the previous one, but instead of one, two stones or cards are drawn at random. The combination of the two cards gives a more detailed reading than a single one, for their meanings can either reinforce or counter one another. (*See runic diads, page 144.*)

Teiwaz

Mannaz

THE THREE NORNS

This is a basic three-rune reading that is quick and easy to do. This reading is named after the Three Fates or Three Norns, the goddesslike weaving sisters of Norse mythology who represent the past, the present, and the future. In this interpretation, each of the three runes signifies one of these three states of being. First, mix the runestones or shuffle the deck of cards. Then, take the first three runes and lay them face down on the casting cloth, in a line across the rig (*see pages 160–61*). The rune on the left corresponds with the Norn Urd, signifying past actions that affect the matter in

Urd   *Verdandi*   *Skuld*

question. The second, middle, rune, is that of the Norn Verdandi and signifies the present. It represents processes in the present that relate directly to the question. The third rune, on the right, is the rune of Skuld, "that which is to become." It represents the result of the reading, showing the main trend or direction of present influences that will come into being if things continue unchanged.

Some rune readers prefer to use an alternative reading of the runes in this runecast that does not follow the traditional triad of "past – present – future." Instead, it reads the runes as "first state – action – resultant state." In this interpretation, the first rune represents the present state of affairs, the middle rune signifies the action that may be taken, and the third rune denotes the best possible outcome.

The Five Directions, the Runic Cross, and the Vé

* * * * * * * * * * * * * * * * * * *

THE FIVE DIRECTIONS

The pattern of the runes in the Five Directions spread represents the four basic directions of space around a center. For the Five Directions reading, randomize the runestones or cards and draw them as usual. Then lay them face down, onto the casting cloth, to make a cross of four with a fifth rune at the center, in the following order. Place the first rune at the bottom of the cross; put the second to the left of it; lay the third above the first, at the top of the cross; place the fourth to the right; finally, put the fifth at the center between the other four. This completes the pattern. The general direction of the rune-cast is an inward-moving *deosil* (sunwise/clockwise) spiral. This is the direction of creative introspection.

Next, turn over the runes, one by one, in the order in which they were laid. The lowest stone or card stands for the basic influences that underlie the question. The second rune denotes the problems and obstacles affecting the inquirer. The third rune, at the top, represents beneficial processes and influences, while to the right, the fourth rune shows the immediate outcome of the reading. Finally, at the center, the fifth rune indicates future influences. This central rune also denotes the overall influence acting on the reader.

THE RUNIC CROSS

The Runic Cross reading uses six runes. They are laid out in a cross, with four runes in an upright column flanked by one more rune on each side. The runes are laid in the following order. The first rune lies to the left of the column, representing the past. The second rune lies second from the bottom of the column, denoting the present. The third rune, to the right of the column, describes the possible future. The fourth rune, below the second and at the base of the column, describes the basic principles that underlie the matter in question. The fifth rune, above the second, denotes those events that may hinder or obstruct the inquirer's progress toward the outcome. The sixth rune, at the top of the column, denotes the likely outcome of the matter into which the petitioner is inquiring.

THE VÉ

This reading, using seven runes, is named for the Scandinavian sacred V-shaped enclosure of standing stones, used for worship and runecasting. A royal Vé exists to this day at Jellinge in Denmark. In the Vé rune-reading, the stones are taken or cards are shuffled in the usual manner. Lay the first seven on the cloth in a V shape, starting with

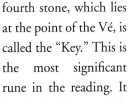

the top left-hand rune. Lay the other six in order until the seventh one lies at the top right. Then turn over the cards or runestones one by one in the same order in which you laid them. The place of each rune in the Vé has a special meaning. At the top left, the first rune indicates influences that were operative in the past. The second rune tells of the influences operating at the present time. The third stands for the reader's prospects for the future. The fourth stone, which lies at the point of the Vé, is called the "Key." This is the most significant rune in the reading. It shows the inquirer's best-possible course of action. On the right-hand side of the Vé, the fifth rune tells of the feelings and attitudes of people close to the questioner. The sixth rune indicates the blockages and delays that might prevent a good outcome. Finally, the seventh stone denotes the likely outcome of the matter.

LEFT The shape of the Runic Cross is very simple, but it is important that the runes are laid out in the correct order.

LEFT In the Vé, the runes are laid out in a V-shape. This was the shape used in Scandinavia for standing stones that enclosed religious places.

Teiwaz's Shoat and the Runic Wheel
★ ★ ★ ★ ★ ★ ★ ★ ★ ★ ★ ★ ★ ★ ★ ★ ★

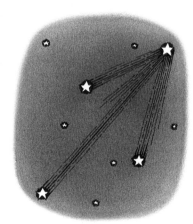

TEIWAZ'S SHOAT

This reading is named after the Teiwaz rune, in whose shape it is laid out. This is the only spread that reproduces the shape of a rune. One of the meanings of the Teiwaz rune is the "special sign" that "keeps faithful, always on course through the dark night, never failing." Because of the rune's straightforward meaning, Teiwaz's Shoat promises an accurate reading every time we use it. The spread uses seven runes that represent the Seven Stars of the constellation named Tir in the traditional Northern European astronomy called the "Skylore of the North." This was used for navigation by the Scandinavian seamen who regularly sailed across the Atlantic Ocean over a thousand years ago.

First, randomize the runes, then take the first four runes that come, or the first four cards from the top of the deck. Lay them face down on the casting cloth, beginning with one on the left, in a "widdershins" (counter-clockwise) arrangement (left, below, right, above). Now the runes are laid out in the form of a cross. Randomize the remaining runes, then take three more. Put them inside the first cross of four cards in the shape of a triangle. This time, lay them in a *deosil* (clockwise) arrangement, going from left to right, then place the last rune so that the apex of the triangle is at the bottom, pointing toward yourself.

Now you have laid out seven runes and have made the shape of the Teiwaz rune.

The first rune, at the outer left, represents the origin of the question, those basic feelings and influences that underlie the question. The second, lowest, rune, which is nearest the reader, signifies the level of highest attainment. This is the best possible outcome. The third rune, lying at the outer right, indicates those hindrances and obstacles that may prevent the result from coming into reality. At the top of the spread, the fourth rune denotes those factors that may bring failure. The fifth rune, lying inside on the left, signifies influences from the past, while the sixth, lying inside on the right, denotes the influences of the present. Lastly, the seventh rune, known as the Seventh Star, at the lowest point inside, provides insights into future influences.

RIGHT The Seven Stars of the constellation Tir in Norse astronomy were used in navigation.

ABOVE One of the meanings of Teiwaz is faithful perseverance. Because of this, Teiwaz's Shoat is believed always to give accurate readings.

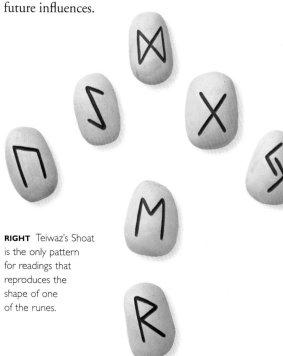

RIGHT Teiwaz's Shoat is the only pattern for readings that reproduces the shape of one of the runes.

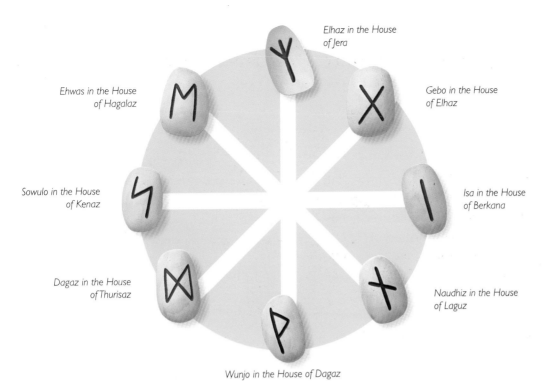

Elhaz in the House of Jera

Ehwas in the House of Hagalaz

Gebo in the House of Elhaz

Sowulo in the House of Kenaz

Isa in the House of Berkana

Dagaz in the House of Thurisaz

Naudhiz in the House of Laguz

Wunjo in the House of Dagaz

LEFT The Runic Wheel repeats the Nordic division of space into eight directions. Each direction is governed by a rune, and the meaning is determined by the relation of that rune to the one that is cast there.

THE RUNIC WHEEL

The Runic Wheel pattern reflects the traditional eightfold division of space. It works by casting the runes in a circle whose eight directions have specific meanings taken from the wheel of the year and the wheel of the day. To do the reading, first decide on your question. Then randomize the runes in the usual way. Take the first eight, and lay them *deosil* on the casting cloth one by one, beginning in the east. Lay one rune in each of the directions. Each of these eight directions or "houses" is ruled by a particular rune. The qualities of these runes provide the basis for interpreting this reading.

The eastern house is ruled by Berkana. It deals with matters concerning the Great Mother Goddess – motherhood in general, fecundity, birth, beginnings, and purification. To the southeast, the house of Laguz signifies vigorous growth, flow, and increase in life-energy. In the south, the house of Dagaz signifies daytime, the bright light of noon, matters of entry, and also possible sudden changes. Southwest is the house of Thurisaz, which signifies protection from attack. In the west is Kenaz. It is the house of learning and illumination. The north-western house is ruled by Hagalaz. It is the house of transformation. To the north, the house of Jera represents completion and success. Finally, in the northeast, the house of Elhaz signifies the powers of defense against all harm, inner strength, and deterrence.

To interpret the reading, begin at the house corresponding with your question. For example, if your question concerns growth, begin at the southeastern house ruled by Laguz. Because each house is ruled by a particular rune, the eight runes that fall in each of the eight houses will interact with the quality of the ruling rune. If a rune falls in a house ruled by itself, its meaning is reinforced. If a rune falls in a house whose ruling rune has the opposite meaning, then it is neutralized. Two runes in any one house have a combined meaning, which must be interpreted according to the question asked. Consult the section on bindrunes for important combinations (*see pages 144–146*).

The Grid of Nine

★ ★ ★ ★ ★ ★ ★ ★ ★ ★ ★ ★ ★ ★ ★ ★ ★

A SQUARE GRID MADE UP of nine smaller squares is one of the most powerful ancient European magical symbols. This, the Grid of Nine, has been used for over 3,000 years, and is known from artifacts dating from as far back as the Bronze Age.

As a geometric shape, the Grid of Nine consists of a central square surrounded on its four sides by rows of three squares each, which together form a larger square. In this way, the central square is "protected" on all sides by the rows of other squares, and the Grid of Nine was therefore an appropriate form to be used traditionally for protection against bad luck and evil. It is still used today in Central European folk magic to ward off evil spirits.

ABOVE Bannocks, pancakes baked the day before May Day in Scotland, reflect the Grid of Nine.

The Grid of Nine is associated with the "weird" times of year, when the veil between the worlds is thin and people can access otherworldly consciousness. A Scottish May Eve, or Beltane, custom digs the Grid of Nine in the ground, taking out eight squares of turf. The spiritually cleansing fire of Beltane is then lit on the middle square where the turf is left intact. Scottish ceremonial oatcakes called bannocks, cooked on the Beltane fire, are made in the shape of the Grid of Nine. In Irish tradition, the Grid of Nine is called the "Eight Ifins," the sacred vineyard of inspiration. In the heart of this formation of eight is the ninth part, the wellspring of divine wisdom.

Norse spirituality similarly recognizes this pattern of nine squares in one as the sacred enclosure. Wise women contacted the

RIGHT The Grid of Nine is one of the oldest-known magical symbols. Its three rows represent past, present, and future.

The outcome to the question	Hidden influences on outcome	Best outcome	Attitude to outcome

The present	Hidden influences on present	Present state	Attitude to present
The past	Hidden influences on past	Effect of past	Attitude to past

otherworld through *Utiseta*, literally "sitting out," a form of trance-divination, on wooden platforms divided into nine squares. These were set up on top of burial mounds, earth lodges, holy hills, and sacred mountains. Sometimes the platform was covered with an ox-hide on which nine squares were painted. The wise woman "sat out" on the grid's middle square until she went into a trance. She faced north, the direction of the gods. During this time, she communed with the spirits of nature and received knowledge from them. Because of this historical use, the Grid of Nine makes a most appropriate runic divination spread.

The Grid of Nine is also what is known as a "magic square" – a grid made up of numbered compartments. The numbers are sequential, but are placed within the compartments so that the sum of any one row of three is the same as that of any other row. Astrologically, each of the known magic squares is ruled by a planet. The Grid of Nine, which is the simplest magic square, is ruled by the planet Saturn, and is therefore known as the Magic Square of Saturn. It contains the numbers 1 to 9. They are arranged so that each line adds up to 15, and the total of all of the squares adds up to 45. The numbers of the Magic Square of Saturn are arranged as follows:

4	9	2
3	5	7
8	1	6

To do the Grid of Nine runic reading, the runes must be arranged as they turn up one by one in the numerical sequence of the Magic Square of Saturn. First, lay them face down, then take them one by one as they come, and place them on the grid according to the order in which you have drawn them – the first rune you draw should go on square 1, the second on square 2, and so on, until all nine runes are laid on their respective squares. Keep thinking of your question as you lay them out. Now interpret them in groups of three. First read the lowest horizontal line, nearest to you. It represents the past, those factors and processes that have acted upon the matter in hand before now. The rune to the left (8) reveals the hidden influences that acted in the past. The middle rune (1) tells of the basic past influences. The right-hand rune (6) denotes the questioner's present attitude to these past events.

Next, look at the central line, which represents those forces operating at present. The left-hand rune (3) shows the hidden influences acting now. The middle rune (5) indicates the present state of events. The right-hand one (7) shows the questioner's attitude toward them.

Finally, read the upper three runes. This line represents the outcome of the question. The rune on the left (4) represents hidden influences – delays, hindrances, and obstacles that may prevent the best possible outcome. The central rune (9) is the key rune, indicating the best possible outcome of the matter in question. The final rune (2), shows the inquirer's response to the result.

ABOVE Fragments of a tapestry found in the Oseberg ship burial are believed to represent a Grid of Nine.

The Celtic Cross and The Nine Runes

★ ★ ★ ★ ★ ★ ★ ★ ★ ★ ★ ★ ★ ★ ★ ★

THE CELTIC CROSS is best known as a Tarot spread, but it works equally well with the runes. It is named after the cross of cards or stones that makes up the first part of the reading. However, this cross is not really a Celtic one, which has a wheel around the crossing-point. Despite this discrepancy, the spread has no other name. Fortunately, its inaccurate name does not diminish its usefulness in any way. Many Tarot readers believe that it is the most satisfying method of divination of all. The Celtic Cross spread gives a number of simultaneous viewpoints of the matter in question, and is very useful for making decisions in crucial situations. These include changes in relationships, career, or living place. The Celtic Cross is also a useful spread to use at New Year or on your birthday.

The first stage of the runecast makes the cross. First, select a card or runestone to represent the inquirer, or the subject of the reading. This card or stone is the Significator, and there are several ways in which to choose it. It could be a rune which corresponds with the subject's birth date in runic astrology (*see The Time-houses of the Runes, on pages 140–41*), or with his or her own personal self-image. Most frequently, the rune chosen as the Significator is one that expresses the matter in question. For example, if the question concerns money, the Significator would be Fehu. One concerning happiness would use Wunjo, or a journey, Raidho, and so on. Of course, once chosen, this rune cannot now appear anywhere else in the reading, which may be considered the disadvantage of this spread.

Lay the Significator down, face upward. Then randomize the remaining runes. If you are using runecards, shuffle and cut them, then take cards from the top of the deck. If using stones, mix them in the bag or pile. The first rune you turn up is placed over the Significator, "covering" the question's symbol. (If using stones, place this first runestone next to the Significator, remembering which is which.) This rune denotes the general influences acting upon the question, and also the general prevailing conditions. The second rune or card "crosses" the Significator. Place it crossways over the first one (or, if using a stone, next to it). This rune is read as upright, whether or not it is actually upright or reversed. It shows the forces or powers that might hinder or oppose the questioner.

Next, lay the third rune "beneath" the Significator, in other words below it, to form the "tail" of the cross. This indicates the basic underlying influences and the questioner's own personal experience of the matter. Lay the next rune to the left of, or "behind," the Significator. It indicates

ABOVE A true Celtic cross, like this tenth-century example from Monasterboice in Ireland, has a ring around its center.

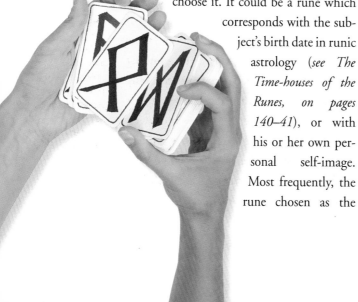

BELOW Laying out the Celtic Cross starts with a deliberate choice of the rune that relates most closely to the subject the inquirer is exploring.

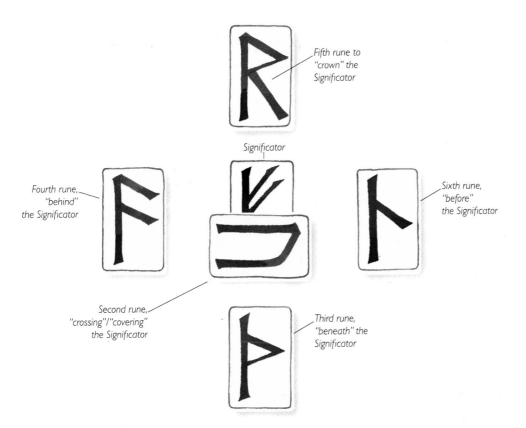

Fifth rune to "crown" the Significator

Significator

Fourth rune, "behind" the Significator

Sixth rune, "before" the Significator

Second rune, "crossing"/"covering" the Significator

Third rune, "beneath" the Significator

Tenth rune, representing the final result

Ninth rune, representing beliefs and hopes

Eighth rune, representing the immediate environment

Seventh rune, representing negative feelings

influences that are passing away, or have just ended. The next rune, the fifth, should "crown" the Significator. Put it directly above the Significator. It denotes influences likely to become important in the medium to long term. Next, lay a sixth rune to the right of the Significator, "before" it. This reveals the influence acting upon the questioner in the near future. Now the first part of the spread, the cross, is complete.

For the second part of the runecast, return to your cards or stones, and lay the next four runes that you turn up in a column to the right of the cross. Start with the seventh rune, placing it at the bottom of the column, and work upward until the tenth rune is in place.

The seventh rune, at the bottom of the column, represents any negative feelings and fears that the inquirer may have. The eighth rune, in the second position, indicates the questioner's immediate environment. This includes influences brought to the matter in question by friends and relatives. The next rune, the ninth, stands for the beliefs and hopes of the questioner. Lastly, at the top of the column, the tenth rune denotes the final result of the matter in question. It is the summation of all of the influences indicated by the other nine runes.

The Nine Runes reading is almost identical to the Celtic Cross method. The only difference is that it leaves out the second rune of the Celtic Cross, the one that is placed over the Significator and shows the immediate influences acting upon the questioner. Apart from this, the other runes of the Nine Runes method have the same meanings as those in the corresponding positions in the Celtic Cross, so the only time we use this method is when we do not want to know the immediate influences. Because of this, the Nine Runes is, in fact, only rarely used. The much more popular Grid of Nine is far better if we need a nine-rune spread for symbolic reasons.

ABOVE The Nine Runes and the Celtic Cross are almost identical, the only difference being that the Nine Runes omits the second rune, which is laid to cover the Significator.

The Cosmic Axis

★ ★ ★ ★ ★ ★ ★ ★ ★ ★ ★ ★ ★ ★ ★ ★

The Cosmic Axis layout is a three-dimensional develop-ment of the Grid of Nine layout. However, unlike the Grid of Nine, there are other runes between the three levels. They are the cosmic axis itself, the passage between the three worlds. The lower link rune denotes the tendencies and influ-ences leading from the past to the present. The upper link rune represents influences leading to the future.

RIGHT The cosmic axis is symbolized on Earth by the sacred ash tree.

Mix the runestones or shuffle the cards in the usual manner. Then take cards from the top of the deck, or stones from the bag or pile, and lay them out. If you want to, use a Significator, as in the Celtic Cross spread. This should be placed at the central point of the spread, exactly in the middle of the shoat. Whether or not you use a Significator, lay the first rune or card at the foot of the central column. Then follow it with one rune to the left, and another to the right of it. Together, these three runes or cards make the lower level of the Cosmic Axis spread.

Take the next rune and put it directly above the first one laid. This is the lower link rune. Next, lay the fifth rune or card directly above this one. This will lie on top of the Significator if one is used (or next to it if using stones). Lay the next runes to the left and right of this one. This makes the central level of the axis. Next, lay another rune or card above the middle card. This is the upper

ABOVE A ninth-century pendant showing a priest of the cult of Odin. Gods and shamans travel the cosmic axis between the worlds.

link rune, joining the middle tier with the upper one. As before, follow this with one more above it. Finally, place one to the left and another to the right of the one at the center. This finishes the spread, using in all 11 runestones or cards.

There are two ways of interpreting the Cosmic Axis spread. The sim-plest interpretation makes the lowest level signify the past. The central rune here denotes the major past influence on the questioner. To the left is the subconscious response, and to the right is the conscious response. Above them, the lowest link rune signifies the outcome of these influences which have led to present conditions. The present is signified by the rune directly above the link rune. This lies above the Significator, when one is used. The left-hand rune on this level symbolizes current subconscious influences. The right-hand rune tells us of conscious influences. Above the central rune, the upper link rune tells us the results that present influences will bring if we do nothing to alter the situation. Above this, the upper level of the Cosmic Axis spread denotes the probable outcome. The rune at the center shows the major out-come of the process. As with the other levels, its subconscious effect is to its left and its conscious effect to its right.

The other interpretation takes the Cosmic Axis spread more literally, as it appears in Northern Tradition spirituality. The lower tier represents Utgard, the

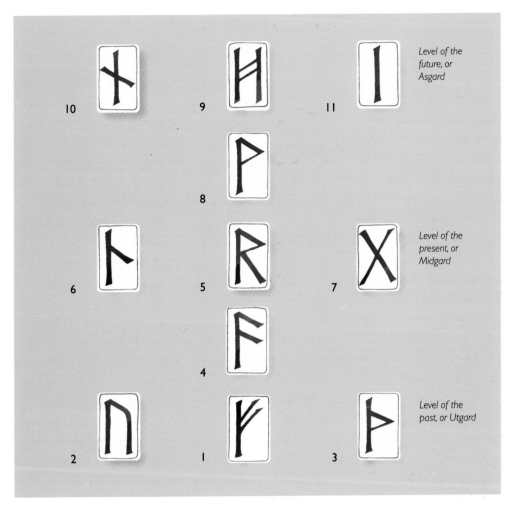

10

9

11   *Level of the future, or Asgard*

8

6   5   7   *Level of the present, or Midgard*

4

2   1   3   *Level of the past, or Utgard*

LEFT The Cosmic Axis can be read as showing past, present, and future, or the three levels of creation, with a link rune between each. If you use a Significator, it is placed in the middle, and the fifth card is laid on top of it.

underworldly realm of unformed spirits and unevolved matter. Again, each level has three aspects. The unconscious is shown by the left-hand rune, the present reality by the central rune, and the conscious condition by the right-hand rune. Linking the level of Utgard with the stage above it is the lower link rune. This shows spiritual evolution from a lower state of existence onto the material plane. The central row of runes represents the present, material world, Midgard or Middle Earth. We exist now in this realm. We interpret the runes here in the same way as the other rows of three.

Connecting this plane with higher things is the upper link rune, which signifies processes tending either to accelerate or block our spiritual progress. Above this is the upper level, the higher plane of existence. This is the upper world, Asgard, the realm of divine power and those souls that have evolved beyond the Earthly plane. We interpret the three runes of the upper level in the same way as those on the other two levels. However, the central rune represents spiritual, rather than material, existence. This second method of interpreting the Cosmic Axis spread can, however, be difficult for beginners.

This runecast is useful for investigating our spiritual pathways. But because it has a sensitive nature, we should only make this reading if we are in immediate need of this information. If we do need it, then we must conduct the divination only with reverence and under appropriate conditions.

A SAMPLE READING

★ ★ ★ ★ ★ ★ ★ ★ ★ ★ ★ ★ ★ ★ ★ ★ ★

PERHAPS THE MOST important thing in a runic divination is the question. In legend and folktale, those who do not ask the right question at the right time fail in their quest. A key episode in the legend of the Holy Grail, for example, hinges upon the hero's failure to ask. It is the same in real life. So, before starting our divination, we must think hard about what it is that we want to ask. Then we must frame the question in straightforward words. This is an important task, because the same runes appearing in the same order in two readings can have quite different meanings. The answer we get depends entirely on the question we asked.

ABOVE In giving a reading for someone else, you may be faced with an important question. The runecards will help guide the inquirer toward making a decision or reaching a solution to a particular problem.

A GRID OF NINE DIVINATION

In this sample spread, you are doing a reading for a woman faced with a life-changing decision. She has been stuck in the same situation for a long time, and now she asks whether she has the strength to go through with the changes she needs to make in order to live a better life. Her question is "Is now the right time for me to make a complete change in my circumstances?" Although the precise circumstances are not defined, this is a basic question that can be answered "yes" or "no," still giving the runes scope to comment upon the answer.

First, mix the stones or shuffle the cards, then pass them from hand to hand at least three times to empower them with your own personal energy. If you are using stones, you can perform *Raed Waen* (*see Riding the Wagon, pages 160–61*). Sitting on the stol, take all the runes in your two hands and throw them together along the rig. Take away those falling face down. Pick up the nine runes nearest to you. Then arrange them, one at a time, as the Grid of Nine, in the number-order of the Magic Square of Saturn:

4	9	2
3	5	7
8	1	6

If you are using runecards, cut the deck three times before dealing out the first nine cards from the top. Now you have three rows of three runes. Lay them face down first, then turn them over one by one in the sequence in which they will be read. Examine each row in order, from left to right. First, look at the horizontal line lying nearest to you (runes 8, 1, and 6). This line represents factors and processes that affected the questioner in the past. The runes Mannaz, Isa, and Teiwaz have turned up.

The left-hand rune (8), Mannaz, shows her hidden past influences. The center rune (1), Isa, shows the basis of the past influences. The right-hand rune (6), Teiwaz, indicates her present attitude to past events.

Mannaz, the rune of the human being, tells that human circumstances and relationships are the hidden influences of the past. Isa, the ice rune, shows that the root of the past situation was her inability to alter things. Teiwaz is the rune of the god Tyr (Tîwaz), who had to overcome problems of his own making by self-sacrifice. Teiwaz shows that

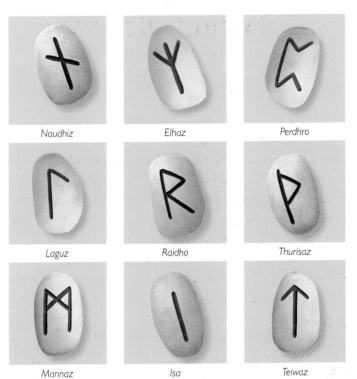

Naudhiz   Elhaz   Perdhro

Laguz   Raidho   Thurisaz

Mannaz   Isa   Teiwaz

LEFT The sample runes as they appear in the Magic Square of Saturn.

she now recognizes that the problem has gone on for too long. She must give up her present behavior to overcome her problem, even though this entails painful sacrifices.

Next, study the center line, runes 3, 5, and 7. It signifies the forces operating now. Laguz, Raidho, and Thurisaz have turned up here. The left-hand rune (3), Laguz, indicates hidden influences on the questioner at present. The center rune (5), Raidho, shows the present state of things. The right-hand one (7), Thurisaz, reveals her present attitude toward them.

Laguz, the rune of flow, shows that powerful forces of growth are operating within the questioner now. Raidho, the traveling rune, shows that there is movement in her situation. These two runes show that rapid changes are taking place in the present. Thurisaz shows that she feels defensive about these changes.

Finally, examine the upper line, runes 4, 9, and 2. These three runes denote the question's outcome. Here, they are Naudhiz, Elhaz, and Perdhro. The left-hand rune (4), Naudhiz, tells of the hidden influences, especially the obstacles, that may block the best possible outcome. The middle rune (9), Elhaz, is the key rune. It explains the best possible result. The ninth rune (2), Perdhro, indicates her response to the result.

Naudhiz, the need rune, tells her that the process has already begun. It will not be easy, but she must go through whatever happens now. Elhaz tells her that she now has the ability to defend herself against her problems – at last she is empowered to deal with the situation. Perdhro, the rune of fate, here is clearly the "play of life." At last, she can live her life creatively.

This sample reading only describes the "bare bones" of how a full runic divination can be carried out, for the human element is missing in such a description. In a real reading, personal contact between rune-caster and client is crucial. The runes facilitate, but do not replace, the important interaction between reader and subject.

AFTERWORD

* * * * * * * * * * * * * * * * *

THE RUNES HAVE existed for around 2,200 years. During that time they have gone through many changes. They have always been flexible and have, in one way or another, always lain at the heart of Northern European culture. At one time they were the only form of writing used by whole nations. At other times they were known by only a few, who used them as a secret code in war and peace. Pagan priestesses and wizards wrote runes to invoke the gods and heal the sick. English and Scandinavian churchmen carved them on stone crosses and wrote Christian poetry in Runic. In Iceland, they were condemned as witchcraft and driven underground. There, rune-users were persecuted and killed. For a thousand years, the runes marked the passage of time on farmers' calendars. In the twentieth century, extremists used them for political ends, and later they became part of the New Age repertoire. Today, they serve personal development.

In every period of their history, they have adapted to prevailing conditions and survived. Every human activity that lasts for generations must evolve continually or die. Today, the runes are more widespread than ever before. More people know about them, and in terms of sheer numbers more people use them now than the population of whole tribes in the early Middle Ages. Today, with global communication, we can draw from more

ABOVE In this woodcarving, Regin reforges the sword of the Viking hero Sigurd's father. Runes have been a part of Northern European culture for over 2,200 years.

cultural sources than anyone in the past could have imagined. The runes have taken their rightful place in the repertoire of world spiritual traditions.

Every ancient culture that survives today contains a potential conflict between tradition and innovation, and the culture behind runes is no exception. To maintain the runes as a living force in contemporary culture, a delicate balance must be struck. Tradition defines the runes' basic meanings, while innovation brings new ways of using them and new interpretations. Both are important, but we need great sensitivity to maintain this balance today, since behind us lie 2,200 years of runecraft tradition.

Runecraft has always been flexible within limits. It has never ruled out new insights. The great strength of the runes is that they have always allowed progress to take place, and it has always been possible to interpret them widely without destroying their inner essence. Such creativity and freedom from dogma is a characteristic of the Northern Tradition. In the laws of ancient Wales, for example, this principle was stated openly with regard to the diviners called Vates. They were not initiates, like the Druids and bards, who had studied for years before being admitted to the mysteries. The Vates were different. They were recognized as spiritual teachers because they had been born with special powers, or had gained them later through life experience. Once empowered and recognized by others, their task was to bring new insights to the tradition, as long as they were positively useful and did not conflict with its eternal essence.

In divination, progress has been made by exploring the correspondences between different divinatory systems, while still respecting their integrity. For example, nineteenth-century mystics drew up useful connections between the Hebrew alphabet and the Tarot trumps. However, sometimes such comparisons do not succeed. Unless we are able to understand both of them very well, our attempts to mix together two separate cultural traditions are more than likely going to involve losing the essence of both of them. If we ignore or completely alter the basic meanings of the runes, then there is a real chance that we will bring confusion rather than clarity. Novel interpretations are not always better than traditional ones. But as long as rune-users attempt to break new ground, applying the eternal spiritual essence of the runes to new forms, then they will continue to be of value in contemporary living.

For the runes to have any value today, we must use them in a contemporary way. Using the runes should not be seen as an attempt to return to the past. This is impossible anyway, even if it were desirable. The vast majority of rune users are not romantic escapists trying to reenact Viking lifestyles. Since they came into being 2,200 years ago, the runes have always been concerned with the present. Throughout history, their users have continually redefined their role, adapting them to the circumstances current in their own lifetimes. Now, as then, the runes express a positive attitude toward life. Through them, we can explore the possibilities open to us and gain new insights into the here and now.

BELOW Modern users redefine the role of the runes to suit their own needs and lifestyles.

GLOSSARY

★ ★ ★ ★ ★ ★ ★ ★ ★ ★ ★ ★ ★ ★ ★ ★ ★

Aegishjalmur "Helm of Awe," a talismanic insigil (q.v.) gained by the hero Sigurd from the dragon Fafner. It is the symbol of invincibility and was used by warriors in preparation for combat.

Aesir Deities of the later Norse pantheon, governing agriculture, trade, battle, and law. Specifically, the Aesir were the gods, and the Asyniur (q.v.) the goddesses (*see also* "Vanir").

aett (plural aettir) Group of eight runes or compass direction.

ann Pattern of iron rods in pattern-welded sword, resembling swathes of mown grain.

Armanen runes System of runes devised by Austrian mystic Guido List (1848–1919).

Asgard Homeland of the Aesir gods and goddesses.

Asyniur Goddesses of the later Norse pantheon (*see also* "Aesir" and "Vanir").

Audhumla Primal cow of the Norse creation myth.

biargrune Rune used in childbirth.

bindrune Two or more joined runes, often with a common stem.

blodidha Pattern of iron rods in pattern-welded sword resembling "eddies of blood."

blodvarp Term meaning "blood warp" that refers to a pattern of iron rods in pattern-welded sword.

bracteate Medallion pendant, usually gold, bearing a stamped image of a god and often an inscription in runes.

brunrunes Runes used to ensure safe journeys by sea.

bumerker Norwegian runic property marks used mainly by farmers and merchants.

burin Tool for carving runes (it is also called a "ristir").

clog almanac Ancient English wooden runic calendar.

cusp Boundary between two runic "halls" or houses in runic astrology.

daemonium A reversed rune (in the German tradition).

deosil The sunwise (clockwise) direction.

Dotted Runes Rune-row with 25 runes, developed in Sweden around 1200. Also called "Pointed Runes."

Elder Futhark The original rune-row (c. 200 B.C.E.), having 24 characters divided into three aettir (q.v.).

Erilaz A runemaster, from the name of the ancient Heruli tribe (q.v.).

Escarbuncle Medieval heraldic sign, a version of the Aegishjalmur (q.v.).

Fachwerk Style of German timber-framed building.

Feisifín Magical insigils in the form of the shield of the Irish hero Fionn MacCumhaill (Fionn's Shield).

Fylgja A partly separate aspect of the human being, also known as the *Fetch*, sometimes appearing in animal form.

galdr Runic sound-calling, a magical song, incantation.

Gall Ogham A form of runes used in medieval Ireland.

Gandno Ancient Germanic magic.

180

glódhker Ceremonial fire-brazier, used in consecrations.

God's Nail Sigil of an Inguz rune with an eight-petaled flower at the center representing the midnight sun, used in English house-protection.

guising The wearing of disguise, such as masks, for performing rites and ceremonies.

hahalrúna "Hook-runes," runic encryption by hook-shaped runes.

half-month The runic time-period lasting one twenty-fourth of a year.

haliarunos Wise women of the Gothic nation.

hällrinstningar Ancient Scandinavian rock-carvings with pictures and symbols including runelike signs.

Hamingja A person's "luck" or his or her "guardian angel."

Hamr Personal shape, body-image.

Heruli Gothic tribe which carried the runes through Europe, giving their name to the runemasters – Erilaz (q.v.).

hex sign Runic-derived protective sigil used in Pennsylvania Dutch house-building.

house-mark Family sigil, often derived from runes, used to mark property.

Hugr The human power of cognition and perception.

hugrune Rune connected with the intellect.

idvarp Pattern of iron rods in pattern-welded sword resembling "intestine-warp."

Iis runes Cryptic system using Isa runes to denote the number of a rune in its aett (q.v.).

insigil Talisman created by drawing a number of runes on radial lines, set in a circle.

Julian calendar The "Old Style" calendar set up by Julius Caesar (46 B.C.E.), but superseded by the Gregorian Calendar, introduced 1582.

kenning Poetic metaphor or allusion to a mythological or historical theme.

kloprúna Coded runes transmitted aurally by clapping or knocking, forerunners of the Morse Code.

kotruvers Icelandic magical scripts used for winning at backgammon.

kvistrúna "Branch Runes," a cryptic system using the number of branches to denote the number of the aett (q.v.) on one side and the number of the rune in the aett on the other.

Lagu runes Like Iis runes (q.v.), but using Laguz runes.

Lík The human body (also known as *Lich*).

liuthrindi Magical patterns used on shields in ancient Ireland to dazzle opponents.

limrunes Runes used to heal the sick.

Lockland Ogham A form of runes used in medieval Ireland.

malrunes Runes used to bring advantage in speaking.

Man-Jaer Runes Runes from the Isle of Man.

mearomot A personal charm, used for concentration in runecasting.

merkelapper Norwegian runic tags for marking property.

Midgard "Middle Earth," the dwelling-place of human beings.

Minni The mind.

mudra Hand-position in yoga. In runic yoga (q.v.), the mudras are in the form of runic hand signs.

mumming The performance of traditional Northern European folk plays, including "death and resurrection" plays, usually performed in disguise.

nidhstong "Niding pole," runic staff with horse's skull, used in Viking times to curse enemies.

Norns The three "weird sisters" of Norse mythology, Urd, Verdandi, and Skuld, symbolizing the past, present, and future.

Northern Tradition The spiritual tradition of Northern Europe, including the customs, traditions and beliefs of the Germanic, Celtic, and Scandinavian peoples.

Od Magnetic force said to be channeled in runic yoga.

Odhr Human faculty of inspiration.

Ogham The Celtic tree alphabet, used mainly in Ireland and western Britain, where each character represented a tree.

Önd The "cosmic breath" that empowers existence.

Örlog Literally "primal layers/laws," the combination of past forces and events that make the present what it is.

otherworld The area of consciousness beyond the everyday world. The parallel world of the supernatural.

Phoenikeia "Phoenician Things," the ancient Greek name for the alphabet.

Pointed Runes *see* "Dotted Runes."

primestave Wooden almanac with day, month, lunar, and solar notation in runes.

Raed Waen Literally meaning, "riding the wagon," runic divination that is carried out with full ceremony.

ramrune A rune that is used magically.

rig Straight line along which runes are cast in divination. Also a strip of land that is allocated by runes in traditional Scottish folk law.

rimstock Danish wooden rune almanac.

ristir Tool for carving runes (also called a "burin" q.v.).

rune Literally a secret, mystery, or hidden thing. Also a sign or character in any of the runic futharks.

Runenhäuser Houses whose timber-framing pattern resembles runes.

runester A person skilled in using the runes.

runic yoga Runic posture exercises.

Runrig Traditional Scottish land-allocation using runic lots to choose rigs (q.v.) of land.

sál After-death image, shade, or ghost.

scramasax Single-edged, pointed short sword used by Saxon warriors.

seidhr The practice of magical arts including shamanic trance, Utiseta (q.v.) and "seer's journeys."

sett stick Stick with colored threads encoding the pattern for Scottish tartan weaving.

shoat A runecast.

sigil A written spiritual sign, denoting a specific principle.

Significator In a divination, the rune that symbolizes the questioner.

sigrune Rune for victory.

Sleepthorn (Svefnthorn) Icelandic bind-rune (q.v.) for inducing inactivity or sleep.

S.S. (Schutz-Staffel) German Nazi élite military corps ("protective squadron"), originally Hitler's bodyguard.

stadhagaldr Runic postures with sound-calling.

stol Pillow used by the caster in runecasts.

Svefnthorn *see* "Sleepthorn"

tent runes Cryptic system using branches on an X-shaped base to denote the number of an aett (q.v.) and the number of runes in the aett.

tine Small wooden runic talisman.

Utgard The underworld.

Utiseta "Sitting out," a technique of trance-meditation used in pagan Scandinavia.

vaegir "Wave-sword" (waegsweard) with pattern of iron rods resembling waves.

Vanir The Norse goddesses and gods of the organic world.

vardlokkur Norse magical art of warding off harm and binding evil spirits.

vargamors Swedish wild women of the woods, who communed with the wolves.

vólva Norse wise woman.

waegsweard *see* "vaegir."

wall-anchor Metal end-plate connecting the beams of a building to a brick wall, often in the form of a rune or house-mark.

walus Old German magical staff.

wardstaff A staff of office.

warlock A male magician skilled in the arts of vardlokkur (q.v.).

wendrune Rune written backward from right to left.

widdershins Anticlockwise, the opposite motion to deosil (q.v.).

witta wijven Wise women of Drenthe province, Holland, who practiced trance magic until they were eradicated in the witch hunt of the 1600s.

wyrd Fate, but not in the sense of predestiny.

Yggdrasil The "World Tree" of Norse cosmology.

Younger Futhark Shorter rune-row with 16 runes, developed in Scandinavia. The true "Viking Runes."

yries The "Pagan Trackway," spirit-paths marked by rags, shoes, and other offerings.

zimmermann Member of the German timber-frame builders' guild.

FURTHER READING

★★★★★★★★★★★★★★★★★

ARNTZ, Helmut, HANDBUCH DER RUNENKUNDE. Haale, 1944.

ASWYNN, Freya, LEAVES OF YGGDRASIL. London, 1988.

BIENERT, Josef, RAUNENDE RUNES. Winnenden, 1964.

BLACHETTA, Walther, DAS BUCH DER DEUTSCHER SINNZEICHEN. Berlin, 1941.

BLUM, Ralph, THE BOOK OF RUNES. London, 1984.

BRANSTON, Brian, THE GODS OF THE NORTH. London, 1955.

BUCKNELL, Peter A., ENTERTAINMENT AND RITUAL, 600–1600. London, 1979.

COOPER, D. Jason, RUNE STONES: A COMPREHENSIVE INTRODUCTION TO THE ART OF RUNECRAFT. Wellingborough, 1991.

DICKENS, B., RUNIC AND HEROIC POEMS. Cambridge, 1915.

DIWEL, Klaus, RUNENKUNDE. Stuttgart, 1968.

ELIOT, Ralph W. V., RUNES: AN INTRODUCTION. Manchester, 1959.

ELLIS, Hilda R., THE ROAD TO HEL. Cambridge, 1943.

FLOWERS, Stephen E., RUNES AND MAGIC: MAGICAL FORMULAIC ELEMENTS IN THE OLDER RUNIC TRADITION. Bern, 1986. THE GALDRABÓK: AN ICELANDIC GRIMOIRE. York Beach, 1989.

GELLING, Peter, and ELLIS-DAVIDSON, Hilda, THE CHARIOT OF THE SUN AND OTHER RITES AND SYMBOLS OF THE NORTHERN BRONZE AGE. London, 1969.

GORSLEBEN, Rudolf John, DIE HOCHZEIT DER MENSCHHEIT. Leipzig, 1930.

GUNDARSSON, Kvedúlfr Hagan, OUR TROTH. Seattle, 1993.

HAMMOND, Wayne G., and SCULL, Christina, J.R.R. TOLKIEN: ARTIST AND ILLUSTRATOR. London, 1995.

HEINZ, Ulrich Jürgen, DIE RUNEN. Freiburg-im-Breisgau, 1987.

HOWARD, Michael, THE MAGIC OF THE RUNES. London, 1980. THE WISDOM OF THE RUNES. London, 1985.

JANSSEN, Sven, RUNES OF SWEDEN. Bedminster, 1962.

JENSEN, K. Frank, MAGISKE RUNER. Copenhagen, 1991.

JONES, Prudence, SUNDIAL AND COMPASS ROSE: EIGHT-FOLD TIME DIVISION IN NORTHERN EUROPE. Bar Hill, 1982.

JONES, Prudence, and PENNICK, Nigel, A HISTORY OF PAGAN EUROPE. London, 1995.

KEMBLE, J. M., ANGLO-SAXON RUNES. London, 1976.

KOSBAB, Werner, DAS RUNEN-ORAKEL. Freiburg-im-Breisgau, 1982.

KRAUSE, Wolfgang, RUNEN. Berlin, 1970.

KUMMER, Siegfried Adolf, HEILIGE RUNENMACHT. Hamburg, 1932.

LEBECH, Mogens, FRA RUNESTAV TIL ALMANAK. Copenhagen, 1969.

LINE, David, and LINE, Julia, FORTUNE-TELLING BY RUNES. Wellingborough, 1984.

LIST, Guido von, DAS GEHEIMNIS DER RUNEN. Vienna, 1908.

MARBY, Friedrich Bernhard, RUNENSCHRIFT, RUNENWORT, RUNENGYMNASTIK. Stuttgart, 1931.
MARBY RUNEN-GYMNASTIK. Stuttgart, 1932.
DER WEG ZU DEN MÜTTERN. Stuttgart, 1955.
DIE DREI SCHWÄNE. Stuttgart, 1957.

MILLER, Katlyn, RUNES FROM THE WORLD TREE. Berkeley, 1987.

MOTA, Jordi, and INFIESTA, Maria, DAS WERK RICHARD WAGNERS IM SPIEGEL DER KUNST. Tübingen, 1995.

OSBORN, Marijane, and LONGLAND, Stella, RUNE GAMES. London, 1982.

PAGE, R. I., AN INTRODUCTION TO ENGLISH RUNES. London, 1973.

PENNICK, Nigel, OGHAM AND RUNIC: MAGICAL WRITING OF OLD BRITAIN AND NORTHERN EUROPE. Bar Hill, 1978.
RUNIC ASTROLOGY. Wellingborough, 1990.

DAS RUNEN ORAKEL. Munich, 1990.
THE SECRET LORE OF RUNES AND OTHER ANCIENT ALPHABETS. London, 1991.
RUNE MAGIC. London, 1992.
THE BASIC RUNES. Bar Hill, 1993.
THE INNER MYSTERIES OF THE GOTHS. Chieveley, 1995.
SECRET SIGNS, SYMBOLS AND SIGILS. Chieveley, 1996.
CROSSING THE BORDERLINES. Chieveley, 1998.

PUSHONG, Carlyle, RUNE MAGIC. London, 1978.

SCHUTTE, Gudmund, DÄNISCHES HEIDENTUM. Heidelberg, 1923.

SHIPPEY, T. A., POEMS OF WISDOM AND LEARNING IN OLD ENGLISH. Cambridge, 1976.

SPIESBERGER, Karl, RUNENMAGIE. Berlin, 1955.
RUNENEXERZITEN FÜR JEDERMANN. Freiburg-im-Breisgau, 1976.

TEGTMEIER, Ralph, RUNEN. ALPHABET DER ERKENNTNIS. Munich, 1988.

THORSSON, Edred, THE RUNIC MAGIC OF THE ARMANEN. Austin, 1980.

FUTHARK: A HANDBOOK OF RUNE MAGIC. York Beach, 1987.
AT THE WELL OF WYRD: A HANDBOOK OF RUNIC DIVINATION. York Beach, 1988.
GREEN RUNA. Austin, 1993.
RUNE MIGHT. SECRET PRACTICES OF THE GERMAN RUNE MAGICIANS. St. Paul, 1994.

TURLUSON, Snorri, THE PROSE EDDA, trans. Jean I. Young. Berkeley, 1966.

WARDLE, Thorolf, RUNELORE. Brunswick, 1983.
THE RUNENAMES. Brunswick, 1984.

WEBER, Edmund, RUNENKUNDE. Berlin, 1941.

WILLIS, Tony, THE RUNIC WORKBOOK. Wellingborough, 1986.

WIRTH, Hermann, DIE HEILIGE URSCHRIFT DER MENSCHHEIT. Leipzig, 1931–36.

ZABORSKY, Oskar von, URVÄTER-ERBE IN DEUTSCHER VOLKSKUNST. Leipzig, 1936.

ZELLER, Otto, DER URSPRUNG DER BUCHSTABENSCHRIFT UND DAS RUNENALPHABET. Osnabrück, 1977.

INDEX